HORTON FOOTE

HORTON FOOTE has had plays produced on Broadway, Off–Broadway, Off–Off–Broadway and many regional theatres. They include: THE CHASE, THE TRAVELING LADY, THE TRIP TO BOUNTIFUL, THE HABITATION OF DRAGONS, NIGHT SEASONS, IN A COFFIN IN EGYPT, TOMORROW, COURTSHIP, VALENTINE'S DAY, 1918, LILY DALE, THE WIDOW CLAIRE, COUSINS, THE DEATH OF PAPA, DIVIDING THE ESTATE, TALKING PICTURES, GETTING FRANKIE MARRIED–AND AFTERWARDS, and THE YOUNG MAN FROM ATLANTA. His films include: TO KILL A MOCKINGBIRD, BABY THE RAIN MUST FALL, TOMORROW, COURTSHIP, ON VALENTINE'S DAY, 1918, CONVICTS, TENDER MERCIES, THE TRIP TO BOUNTIFUL and OF MICE AND MEN.

"When you act in a Horton Foote piece most of your work is already done. You have only to try to go inside and find an innocence and believe in love again. Horton is pure Love – the purest voice we have today in the American Theatre."

Elizabeth Franz

"Horton Foote's rock solid artistic integrity shines through every word he has ever put down on paper. He writes from his innermost instincts, has total empathy with the world of which he writes, and has never trimmed his sails for current fashion.

And what roles he has given to actors! His people are supremely rewarding to explore and act; *human* beings with all their fears, strengths, foibles, cowardice, courage. Those of us who love theatre, love him."

Nan Martin

HORTON FOOTE *4 New Plays*

Contemporary Playwrights Series

SK
A Smith and Kraus Book

A Smith and Kraus Book
Published by Smith and Kraus, Inc.

COVER AND TEXT DESIGN BY JULIA HILL
Manufactured in the United States of America

First Edition: September 1993
10 9 8 7 6 5 4 3 2

Library of Congress Cataloging-in-Publication Data

Foote, Horton.
[Plays. Selections]
4 new plays / Horton Foote. —1st ed.
p. cm. — (Plays for Actors)
ISBN 1-880399-41-5 : $14.95 paper
ISBN 1-880399-53-9 : $23.95 cloth
I. Title. II. Title: Four new plays. III. Series.
PS3511.0344A6 1993 93-33306
812'.54—dc20 CIP

For Lillian.

CONTENTS

Introduction by Jerry Tallmer
page ix

Preface by Horton Foote
page xv

The Habitation of Dragons
page 1

Night Seasons
page 63

Dividing The Estate
page 115

Talking Pictures
page 175

INTRODUCTION

SOME people get up in the morning and go to Wall Street. Or to their job in a department store. Or a supermarket. Or a newspaper office. Or to fly an airplane.

Horton Foote gets up in the morning and writes plays.

I first heard of Horton Foote not as a playwright but as a name that popped out from a television screen back in the 1950's and early 60's. Whenever something of quality put in a rare appearance on that damned little box — *The Trip to Bountiful, The Traveling Lady, The Midnight Caller* — somehow the name Horton Foote would be attached to it. A good plain American name, like the good plain American people he wrote about — writes about.

But there are no good plain American people. There are no good plain people. There are people — and each of them ever born contains the entire drama of the history of the world, not to mention that little atom of the world that is the parched, worked–out cotton and oil country of Texas, USA, in and around the City of Galveston on the Gulf of Mexico. Horton Foote knows this and something else too. "The thing that is relevant for all time," he told an interviewer a few years ago, "is the subject of grief."

No matter how placid the exterior, how "plain" the talk of all the plays in this volume, grief and loss — great loss — lie just beneath the low-key surface. In the one with in fact the least placid exterior, the almost wilfully melodramatic *The Habitation of Dragons*, a man named Leonard bursts out toward the end: "I sat there watching the lawyers fighting . . . and I thought, ' My God, how a man's life can change in a day, a week, an hour, a second.' I wanted to stand up and scream out to everybody, have compassion, have humility. Your lives, the fabric, the pattern, the bone, the essence, can be destroyed overnight. Can be torn so to pieces that they can never be out together again . . . Lonny, would you go out in the kitchen and make a fresh pot of coffee for me?"

What has changed in a second in this man's life is the drowning, all at once, of his two small sons. You might think that, like much else in *The Habitation of Dragons*, such an incident is a slight exaggeration. But as I read it I suddenly had a flash of something my own two children, now in their 30's, do not know. When they were 3 years old I heard a neighbor woman gasp, glanced up from my newspaper, saw no heads, plunged in, somehow found my two drowning kids and hauled them up from beneath the surface of a pond on Long Island. Another second and they were gone. Horton Foote puts it in Harrison, Texas, that's all. And has God look the other way.

Harrison, which is really Wharton, Texas, where Albert Horton Foote Jr. was born on March 14, 1916, the town where he sets all these plays and much of everything else he has ever written. A town where the old hymns, the old music, the old memories — *Rock of Ages, Nearer, My God, to Thee, Beulah Land, Go Tell Aunt Rhodie, Sweet Alice, Ben Bolt* — mingle with and are overcome by the fast-food smell of Whataburgers, the culture of plastics factories, VCRs, *Cosmopolitan* and *People* magazines, the collapse of real estate and an entire statewide economy, the chatter of bored and desperate women at their bridge games, those once comfortably-off wives, widows, and grass widows (how long has it been since you heard *that* phrase?) who keep needling one another: "You've never worked a day in your life."

Life and love, grief and loss. Purify, simplify: less is more. "I lost you and you lost me. How many years ago?" says the man to the woman — Barsoty to Laura Lee — in *Night Seasons*. This is a play, with all the stasis of *The Three Sisters*, about a woman who not only can't get to Moscow — that is to say, 90 miles away to Galveston — but spends an entire lifetime, 60 years, trying and failing to get away from the mother and the house that she detests. In that lifetime the lovely girl who was Laura Lee has had two chances at happiness twisted away from her, one by the snobbism of her family — tyrannical old mother, manipulative banker brother — toward her baker fiancé, nice Mr. Chestnut, the other through Laura Lee's own inability to make up her mind about Mr. Barsoty, the suitor with a golden voice in the old days *(Sweet Alice, Ben Bolt)* but no real occupation.

Dividing the Estate is just what the title says it is, a play about division of the spoils — but the spoils are spoiled, as it turns out, by that land-poor Texas depression. Here it is the son, oddly called Son, that's his name, Son Gordon — something Foote shares with Tennessee Williams is a touch with names — who, as the manager of his mama's estate, will remind you of several characters in Chekhov. The estate itself was founded in the undead past by a carpetbagging Yankee great-grandfather, one of the many understated ironies all through the work and voice of Horton Foote everywhere. The voice that can speak the following exchange, for instance — one tiny instance — between Mama and another son, the ne'er-do-well Lewis, in this play, *Dividing the Estate*: "I smell liquor on your breath. Have you been drinking?" "Yes, Mama." "So early in the morning?" "Yes, Mama." "I don't allow liquor in this house." "I know that, Mama. I don't drink in this house."

Or if you want to see how that same dry irony can sketch character in a line, an entire marriage in two lines – the raging war between the manipulative banker brother and his bitch of a wife — here's this from *Night Seasons*: "They'll kill each other one day." "No, they won't. They'll kill everybody else first." Or this, from *Talking Pictures*:

KATIE BELL: "Willis says you're not going to Hell if you go to the Picture shows."

MYRA: "I wasn't worried. Thank you anyway, Willis, for telling me."

Horton Foote writes the way people talk, or *the way you think they talk*, or the way you wish you thought they talk, or once did talk, in your mind's eye (and ear). The way they talk in that perfect/imperfect

American of "Yes, Ma'am" and "Yes, Sir" which you may or may not have been born into, since it probably precedes your own birth, but in any event you long for with the sweet exciting ache of what I once termed *nostalgia manqué*, nostalgia for something before your time that you never knew, not directly — just as, in some of the plays and movies not in this book (*1918*, *Valentine's Day*, the whole *Robedaux cycle*), Horton Foote longs for the World War I and pre-World War I life and times of his own parents and grandparents. Or just as I have always thought that I was born into the world and the America of Grovers Corners, New Hampshire, the town right next door to Harrison, Texas which I wasn't.

It was, as a matter of fact, to New Hampshire that Horton Foote, fed up with the working and non-working theater, had retreated from the mid-60's into the 1980s —the "15-year intermission" that he speaks of as "while I was away in the country." (To actress daughter Hallie it was "as if he'd dropped off the face of the earth.") He'd come of age as a playwright in the great days of Julie Harris, Kim Stanley, Geraldine Page. Now the Broadway that he'd known was disappearing in front of his eyes. "And still is," he said, after emerging in triumph in 1983 with *Tender Mercies* — his second Oscar-winning script, the first having come 20 years earlier for *To Kill a Mockingbird*.

What is also disappearing, except when people like Horton Foote write them, are the kind of movies that I care about, movies about human beings, not robots, not automobiles, not ghosts, not body builders, not super warriors, not dinosaurs, not twerps and nerds. (Well, there are twerps in Foote too, but interesting ones.) *Talking Pictures*, my personal favorite in this collection, has as its central character a woman, Myra Tolliver, who is about to lose her job playing piano in movie theater that — in 1929 — is converting from silent films to sound. She rooms in a house whose owner, a railroad engineer, faces similar obsolescence, "One day we could wake up and find there are no trains at all, he tells his wife. "That's foolishness, of course," the wife says. "There will always be trains." Little does she know.

Talking Pictures is rich with the names and images of what would be *manqué* except that we still have the movies to look at, some of them: *Ben Hur* and *Romona* and Bessie Love and Clara Bow and Lupe Velez and

Corinne Griffith and Al Jolson in *The Singing Fool* and "Why does he put on blackface when he sings?" the people in the play keep asking one another, though not the black people who so casually and idiosyncratically inhabit most of these works. *Talking Pictures* is a play, a short play, that mixes light and heavy and light again, just as the shadows of a movie do. In it, a 14-year-old boy, Myra's son Pete, has occasion to say, of his relationship with his father: "Well. I knew it wouldn't work out. Nothing ever does." He's right, the kid is, but he's also wrong.

That too is one of the truths that Horton Foote knows about this world. What he further knows, and this is what distinguishes him and some of his more rapacious Little Foxian characters from those of Lillian Hellman, is what a crazy old man named Virgil dreams in *The Habitation of Dragons*: himself, crying, as a boy of 8 or 9, while a Preacher says: "Forgiveness." Heartbreak and forgiveness. That's all she wrote. Or he, Horton Foote.

JERRY TALLMER is a critic/reporter/feature writer for the New York Post. He was one of the founders of the Village Voice, *where in 1955/1956 he started the Off–Broadway Obie awards. Mr. Tallmer is a winner of the George Jean Nathan award in drama criticism.*

PREFACE

I learned early on in my training as an actor from my teachers: Tamara Daykarhonova, Andrius Jilinsky and Vera Soloviova, all former members of the Moscow Art Theater, that the theater is, or should be, a collaborative medium. The actor, the director, the writer, the producer all have essential contributions to make to a production, and a theater dominated by any of the four is finally a lopsided theater. What is the ego that makes one want to have a Playwrights Theater, or an Actors Theater, or a Directors Theater?

When the American Theater was mostly confined to New York City, one soon got to know what other theater workers shared in your sense of collaboration.

But now that our new plays are being produced all over America, it's not so easy to always make a judgement about this.

Fortunately, on the productions I've had of these four plays, some, of course, better than others, there has always been a sense of collaboration not only from the directors, the actors and the producers, but from scene designers, costume designers, light designers, composers and sound designers. It has allowed me to see my plays free from any dominating egos.

The plays finally printed here have each gone through changes because of those productions; never done under pressure or in hysteria, as it was so often the case in the old Broadway tryout systems, but in an unpressured way, sometimes in rehearsal, sometimes weeks or months after the production had closed.

I've seen two productions of *Talking Pictures*, two of *Habitation of Dragons*, (one on the stage, which I directed, one for Cable's "Writers Cinema"), three of *Dividing the Estate*, (the last two in different theaters, by the same director, Gerald Freedman, and the same actors except one who died soon after her appearance in Freedman's first production), one of *Night Seasons*, which I also directed and a second scheduled early in December. It's always interesting to me as a writer how talented people can, without deconstruction, bring new emphasis to a play and its characters. Who would want a rigidity of interpretation or performance?

So, I'm most grateful to all the actors, the directors, the producers and the designers that were so understanding in their support, and so generous with their talents. And to Smith and Kraus for establishing a publishing house for plays, scenes from plays and other theater works.

THE HABITATION OF DRAGONS

THE HABITATION OF DRAGONS premiered at Pittsburgh Public Theatre on September 20, 1988. It was directed by Horton Foote with the following cast:

GEORGE TOLLIVER: Horton Foote, Jr.
LONNY: Peter Francis James
MISS HELEN: Eugenia Rawls
LEONARD TOLLIVER: Marco St. John
MR. CHARLIE: Emmett O'Sullivan-Moore
LENORA TOLLIVER: Isa Thomas
MARGARET TOLLIVER: Hallie Foote
LEONARD TOLLIVER, JR.: Mac Fleischmann
HORACE TOLLIVER: Stephen Robert Hanna
WALLY SMITH: Matt Mulhern
BILLY DALTON: Harley Venton
VIRGIL TOLLIVER: Conrad McLaren
LESTER WHYTE: Ben Tatar
BERNICE DAYTON: Ann Kittredge
SHERIFF: David Butler
EVELYN SPARKS: Denise du Maurier

Characters

GEORGE TOLLIVER
LONNY JOHNSON
LENORA TOLLIVER
HELEN TAYLOR
LEONARD TOLLIVER
CHARLIE TAYLOR
MARGARET TOLLIVER
LEONARD TOLLIVER, JR.
HORACE TOLLIVER
WALLY SMITH
BILLY DALTON
VIRGIL TOLLIVER
LESTER WHYTE
BERNICE DAYTON
SHERIFF
EVELYN SPARKS

"In the habitation of dragons, where each lay, shall be grass with reeds and rushes."

Isaiah 35:7

Setting

Place: Harrison, Texas. Time: 1935–1936.

THE HABITATION OF DRAGONS

ACT I

SCENE 1

The early morning of a cold, grey January's day. We see the sidewalk, the very small front lawn, front hall and living room of the Lenora Tolliver house. Off left is a heavily travelled highway. It is still too early for the highway to have much traffic, so it is relatively quiet now. Just once in a while the noise of a big cotton truck or the radio of a car going to or from the Coast can be heard. The house itself is a large, rambling one story Victorian structure. It actually houses two families: LENORA TOLLIVER, her son GEORGE, and her roomer, MISS HELEN, live in the original house facing us. In the back a wing has been built, making an apartment for Lenora's older son, LEONARD, his wife and two children. GEORGE TOLLIVER comes in from left followed by LONNY JOHNSON. GEORGE is 33; his face seems sad, marked almost by some hidden, secret hurt. LONNY is a light African-American in his early forties. MRS. TOLLIVER, GEORGE's mother, comes into the living room and looks anxiously out the window. MISS HELEN TAYLOR, 65, comes out of the house.

MISS HELEN: Good morning, George. Good morning, Lonny.
GEORGE: Good morning, Cousin Helen.
LONNY: Good morning, Miss Helen.
GEORGE: Come in and have a cup of coffee.
LONNY: Thanks. (*He and LONNY go into the house. LEONARD, GEORGE's older brother, comes around the side of the house. He is handsome, 39, his face tired and driven looking.*)
MISS HELEN: Hello, Leonard.
LEONARD: Hello, Cousin Helen. (*CHARLIE, 70, MISS HELEN's brother, comes along the sidewalk into the yard.*)
CHARLIE: Ready for breakfast, Sister?
MISS HELEN: Yes, I am. (*She joins her brother, and they start out.*)

CHARLIE: (*Calling back to LEONARD.*) How are you this morning?

LEONARD: Fine, thank you. How are you, Mr. Charlie? (*They go as MRS. TOLLIVER comes out of the house.*)

MRS. TOLLIVER: George is back, Leonard.

LEONARD: I know. I saw him.

MRS. TOLLIVER: I woke up at three this morning, and I felt frightened, and I came into his room and he was gone. One of his law books was lying on the bed, his pajamas on the floor. When I came out to the living room, I found another law book in that chair.

LEONARD: Did you tell him about Billy?

MRS. TOLLIVER: No, I tried to tell him last night, but he seemed too nervous and upset to talk to then.

LEONARD: I'll tell him myself. (*GEORGE comes into the yard.*) George, Billy has decided to come back here to practice law. I'm taking him into my law firm.

GEORGE: Oh.

LEONARD: As my associate, not as my partner.

GEORGE: I thought he was going to a Houston law firm. (*LONNY enters.*)

LEONARD: I talked him out of it. Those Houston law firms can be very cold blooded, you know. He could spend 15 or 20 years in those big offices and not get anywhere.

GEORGE: He told me once he'd never come back here.

LEONARD: I know. That's because he was hurt by his father's behavior with that woman, but everybody has forgotten that, and he has too.

GEORGE: When is he coming?

LEONARD: Today. He should be along any time now. He'll start at the office tomorrow. (*MRS. TOLLIVER, LEONARD, and GEORGE start for the front room of the house.*) Today your day off?

GEORGE: Yes.

LEONARD: Are you enjoying your work at the store?

GEORGE: Pretty well.

LEONARD: (*As he enters the house.*) Good morning, Lonny.

LONNY: Good morning.

GEORGE: You know, a funny thing happened yesterday, Leonard. I was out at the farm when C.O. Becker drove up and asked which part of the farm belonged to you, and I told him we'd never divided. He said if we ever divided, he'd be interested in buying my part.

LEONARD: I hope you told him it wasn't for sale. (A *pause. They go into the room. GEORGE seems very nervous.*)

GEORGE: Lewis Hart is not running for County Attorney again.

LEONARD: I know.

GEORGE: I'm thinking about trying for it. I was discussing it last night with Lonny.

LEONARD: I thought you planned to get married.

GEORGE: I do.

LEONARD: How can you marry when you don't have a steady job?

GEORGE: Let Bernice and me worry about that.

LEONARD: Brother, I honestly don't feel it's wise to keep changing your mind about what you want to do. You're going to be married soon. You'll have a wife to support.

GEORGE: Just because I quit practicing law with you doesn't mean that I don't want anything to do with law ever again. I realize that it's difficult just to open a law office and expect to make any kind of living, so I thought getting elected County Attorney would be a way for me to begin on my own.

LEONARD: It will, if you can get elected.

GEORGE: I won't know that unless I try.

LEONARD: Do you realize, Brother, that there are at least three other young lawyers here thinking of running for County Attorney? It's very expensive. You'll certainly have to give up your job at the store. I know Billy is planning to run, and if you do, it will make it very embarrassing for me. Billy asked me for my support last week if he made the race, and I promised that I would give it to him.

MRS. TOLLIVER: Can't you tell him you didn't know what George's plans were at the time? I'm sure he would understand. Billy is only thirty . . .

LEONARD: (*Interrupting sharply.*) I won't do that, Mother. That's not fair to Billy. He discussed his plans with me before resigning his job. Brother doesn't discuss his plans with me any more.

GEORGE: I don't discuss my plans with you because it occurs to me that everything I want to do on my own you immediately oppose. I know in advance what your reaction will be. It has been precisely the same to anything I wanted to do that didn't sacrifice my life to building up your career, your law practice, your ego, and I might add, your bank account. (*A pause.*) Anyway, I'm going to run for County Attorney, and if I lose, I'll continue to practice law. Mama says I can use my room for my office, because it has its own entrance, and I can sleep in here at night on the couch.

LEONARD: Well, that's up to you and Mama, Brother. But where will you get the money needed for your County Attorney race?

GEORGE: I want to divide the farm so I can sell my half.

MRS. TOLLIVER: Oh, George. Do you know what you're doing? I won't let you do this.

GEORGE: It belongs to me, Mama.

MRS. TOLLIVER: But once that's gone, honey, you'll have nothing.

GEORGE: I'm going to do it, Mama.

LEONARD: If you're going to sell, I want to buy your part.

GEORGE: What will you offer me?

LEONARD: A hundred and fifty dollars an acre.

GEORGE: I'd like more than that.

LEONARD: I guess you would, but I don't think I should be penalized because I have to keep these two hundred and twenty eight acres together, and I have to keep them together. Do you realize what Wally Smith and I invested when we brought in our cattle? Do you think I would have done that, or brought him here, if I'd known you were going to ask that the land be divided? My God, man, when are you going to settle on one thing? I asked six months ago for your permission to develop the farm, and you said go ahead. Now, after I invest ten thousand dollars that will be a complete loss unless I can use the entire acreage, you tell me, without any warning, you tell me you want to divide and sell your share. (*A pause. Now LEONARD is very excited.*) Mama, you know this is unreasonable of him. He had no right to let me go ahead and invest all this money if this is what he was going to do.

GEORGE: I didn't know it then.

LEONARD: Well, then I'm sorry. You have to sell to me now, at a price I can afford.

GEORGE: C. O. Becker will pay me . . .

LEONARD: (*He screams at him.*) I don't care what C. O. Becker will pay you. C. O. Becker hasn't made an investment because of your promises. Anyway this land wasn't bought by you or me; it was our father's, and no matter how we've needed money, we've never touched it. If you insist on an exorbitant price, I'll borrow the money some way.

GEORGE: I don't want you to do that.

MRS. TOLLIVER: Why don't you try borrowing the money, George, and not selling your land?

GEORGE: I went to the bank, Mother, and they turned me down.

LEONARD: I'll loan you some money.

GEORGE: I don't want to borrow from you. I don't want to be indebted to you for anything ever again.

MRS. TOLLIVER: Leonard. George. Please stop this quarreling.

LEONARD: Mama.

MRS. TOLLIVER: Listen to me, Leonard. Please. I'm not saying he's right, but George feels he's been deprived of many of your advantages. You do have so much more than he does.

LEONARD: I worked for it. No one has given me anything.

MRS. TOLLIVER: I know. I know. But George feels so much of his time and energy and mine, went into helping you get established.

LEONARD: Oh, Mama. He got just as much help as I did. Dollar for dollar. He just wasn't able to take advantage of the help that was given him. I've done a lot for my brother. Just as much as he ever did for me.

MRS. TOLLIVER: I know that. I know that George has forgotten many wonderful things you did for him, but I think if he can only win this office . . .

LEONARD: (*Interrupting.*) Mother, I told you a long time ago I will not indulge these feelings of Brother's. The truth is that he has not been deprived of anything that he really needed or wanted . . .

MRS. TOLLIVER: I'm just trying to explain to you what he feels. He feels we've broken our word to him many times.

LEONARD: How? Name me one instance.

GEORGE: Your promise that if I waited two years before starting college, you would then see me through college before getting married, and then . . .

LEONARD: (*Interrupting.*) I married with your permission, at your insistence. You heard him at the time, Mama. "Brother, don't be a fool, go ahead and get married. If you don't I'll never forgive you. I'll get myself through law school." You told me the important thing was for me to have a law practice established that you could go into when you graduated.

GEORGE: Leonard . . .

LEONARD: (*Interrupting again.*) I had that practice, and I made a place for you in the firm, but you resent authority.

GEORGE: Didn't you tell me when you dissolved our partnership that you realized that you couldn't work with anyone in your office, and now you're taking in Billy.

LEONARD: I said I would never have a partner. Billy is not going to be my partner. He is my associate.

GEORGE: That's not what you said. You said . . .

LEONARD: (*Interrupting.*) God knows what I said. I would have said anything to get you out. There was such constant bickering and fighting between us. And I don't want to hear any more about your sacrifice. You thought if I had a law practice going, you could go to any kind of law school, make any kind of grades and come back and make a living. Well, it didn't work. When people came to my office, they didn't want to use you. They wanted me. And I don't care who you are, it takes time to build up a practice, and I tried to explain that to you. I tried to counsel you to have patience. And every time I would make a suggestion to you over a way to improve something, you would be furious. Well, why go into all this again. Our partnership didn't work. But instead of being a man and saying, "I planned wrong; I failed," you have to blame me. I don't accept it. Everything you've touched in the last seven years has failed. You're a loser. You're infected with losing. The truth is you envy me on everything I have. You would take it all for yourself if you could. You can't stand it that I'm succeeding. And I'm succeeding not because I've cheated you, but because I'm brighter than you are, because I have more talent for law than you have. Billy will succeed for the same reasons. Because he's brighter and smarter than you are. (*A pause.*) And you're being just sentimental, Mama, when you encourage him in these attitudes, and in these rationalizations. George wants something that can never be. He wants us to go back five years, ten years, twenty years. He wants us sharing everything. He wants me unmarried. He wants us all together constantly. (*A pause. They have all had their say; their anger has spent itself. There is quiet in the room and they all seem uncomfortable with each other. GEORGE looks at LONNY and then over at LEONARD and his mother.*)

GEORGE: I'm sorry. I'm very sorry. I apologize to you, Mama. I apologize to you, Leonard. I've been very nervous lately. Lonny can tell you. Anyway, I took a vow last night in this very room that I wouldn't blow up again, no matter what happened and then the first thing this morning, I go and break my vow. And I'm sorry. (*A pause.*) I'll sell you the land for what you want.

LEONARD: Thank you. I'll draw up an agreement and have it for you to look at this afternoon. I suppose you'd like the money as soon as possible.

GEORGE: Yes, I would.

LEONARD: All right, I'll go to the bank this afternoon and get you the money. (*A pause. He goes to the window and looks out.*)

GEORGE: Mama, Lonny is going to California to live.

MRS. TOLLIVER: Are you? When, Lonny?

LONNY: After the election. Eloise has been trying to get me to go for a long time.

MRS. TOLLIVER: All her family are there now, aren't they?

LONNY: Yes.

GEORGE: Mama, Lonny told me that when one of Henry Jackson's boys was working in Goliad, he met Papa's brother. He said when he found out he was from here, he asked him all about Leonard and me.

MRS. TOLLIVER: Did he? I haven't heard from him in so many years. They were never close as a family. (*A pause.*)

LEONARD: I'm going to get a cup of coffee. Do you want some, Mama?

MRS. TOLLIVER: No, thank you.

LEONARD: George? Lonny?

GEORGE: I'll get it.

LEONARD: No, I'll bring it to you.

GEORGE: Thank you.

LONNY: I'll help you. (*LEONARD and LONNY leave.*)

MRS. TOLLIVER: I know you criticize Leonard often and feel bitterly towards him, but when you were growing up, he was like a father to you. He worked and schemed and planned every day of his life that things might be easier for all of us.

GEORGE: I know that. (*A pause.*) I don't want to feel bitterly towards Leonard or anyone. (*A pause.*) I thought last night of all the men I've known shuffling around this town, shackled by resentment because they felt a father, a sister, a cousin, or a friend had deprived them of land, or money, or power. (*A pause.*) You tell me Leonard was my father, and I know he was in many ways. But Lonny was, too. Last night I couldn't sleep, and I went by Lonny's house, and I got him to ride with me. We rode out into the country, and we talked about when he used to live here with us, why my partnership with Leonard didn't work, what I did wrong, what Leonard did wrong. (*LEONARD and LONNY come in with their coffee and George's. LONNY hands a cup to GEORGE.*)

GEORGE: Thanks.

MRS. TOLLIVER: Have you had your breakfast, Leonard?

LEONARD: No, ma'am. I'm not very hungry.

MRS. TOLLIVER: What about you, George, Lonny?

LONNY: Coffee is all I want.

GEORGE: Will Billy live here with you and Margaret?

LEONARD: Yes. At least until after the election. (*MARGARET TOLLIVER, Leonard's wife, comes into the living room. Her two boys, LEONARD, JR., 6, and HORACE, 4, come into the front yard.*)

MARGARET: Good morning.

MRS. TOLLIVER: Good morning, Margaret.

LEONARD: Are the boys with you?

MARGARET: They're outside. (*LEONARD goes to the window. GEORGE and LONNY leave.*)

LEONARD: (*Calling.*) Hey, boys. Come say good morning to your grandmother. (*They go inside. They run to her and embrace her.*)

MRS. TOLLIVER: Good morning, darlings.

MARGARET: I'm taking the boys out to the farm with Wally, Leonard.

LEONARD: All right. (*MARGARET exits. He draws his boys close to him.*) I'm going to build up a ranch out there for you boys. And some day when you're grown I'm going to turn it all over to you. (*He pats them and they run off back out in the yard.*)

LEONARD: Mama, when George gets married, I wish you'd let Cousin Helen get a room some place else, and then you can be free to do as you like. I can afford to take care of you now.

MRS. TOLLIVER: Thank you, but I think not. I'm free enough as it is. When George marries and moves, I intend renting his room out, too.

LEONARD: But that is so foolish, Mama. I have plenty. I can take care of you.

MRS. TOLLIVER: I know, but I don't want you to.

LEONARD: You don't make anything off Cousin Helen anyway. You feed her half the time. She pays the same rent she did fifteen years ago.

MRS. TOLLIVER: She can't afford any more. Anyway, I don't know what I'd do without Cousin Helen around. I've outlived my brothers and my sisters and all my friends except Cousin Helen. (*A pause. MARGARET enters with coffee.*)

MARGARET: I've cleaned out all the drawers and the closet in the room Billy is to have. (*She yawns.*) I'm so tired. I was up playing bridge until all hours last night. Didn't have a bit of luck either. Wally tells me you're thinking of renting a thousand acres and buying more cattle.

LEONARD: Yes, I am. And Margaret, I'm to own our farm completely now. Brother is selling me his share.

MARGARET: Now, I'll never see you. I don't know what your son wants a wife for, Mrs. Tolliver. We never see each other. He's always working.

LEONARD: I don't know what you'd do if I didn't make money, as extravagant as you are.

MRS. TOLLIVER: I agree with Margaret. I think you work too hard, Leonard.

LEONARD: Well, that's why I have Wally helping me and why I'm bringing her brother here.

MRS. TOLLIVER: But then why take on this extra land—you're never home as it is now.

LEONARD: I want to provide for my family, thank you. I don't want my children and Margaret ever left like we were, Mama. I don't want my children to ever have to worry about money until they're grown and it's right for them to worry about it. (*WALLY SMITH, 32, his face and arms tanned from working out of doors, comes into the yard. LEONARD, JR., and HORACE run up to greet him, and WALLY* *swings HORACE up on his shoulders. LEONARD, JR. goes running into the living room.*)

LEONARD JR.: Hi, Mama. Wally is here.

MARGARET: Tell him to come in and say hello. (*LEONARD, JR. runs back out.*)

MRS. TOLLIVER: Excuse me. I want to straighten up a little bit. I wasn't expecting company. I look terrible. (*She goes out. WALLY comes in.*)

WALLY: Good morning.

MARGARET AND LEONARD: Good morning. (*WALLY looks around.*)

WALLY: This is the first time I've been in your mother's part of the house. Was this the original part?

MARGARET: Yes, it was. When Leonard and I were first married, we had Miss Helen's room and then we built the extension in the back for our apartment.

LEONARD: I'm going to get some more coffee. You all want some?

WALLY: No, thank you.

MARGARET: No, thank you. (*LEONARD goes.*)

WALLY: (*WALLY looks at a picture on the wall.*) Is that Leonard as a boy?

MARGARET: No, that's George. This is Leonard.

WALLY: He was handsome. (*He peers at another picture.*) This your wedding picture?

MARGARET: Yes, and this one is my mother and my brother, Billy.

WALLY: How long have you and Leonard been married?

MARGARET: Fifteen years. We were engaged for four years before that. You see, Leonard was very poor as a boy, and he didn't want to get married until he'd saved some money, and finally, I said I wouldn't wait any longer, and I had my way. (*A pause.*) I never went with any boy but Leonard. I was fifteen when I had my first date with him. I think that's a mistake. I think a girl should date a lot of boys.

WALLY: (*Pointing.*) Who's this?

MARGARET: Leonard's father. He died when Leonard was fifteen. It was very tragic . . . a hunting accident. He was climbing through a barbed wire fence, and his gun accidentally went off. (*MRS. TOLLIVER comes back in.*)

WALLY: Hello, Mrs. Tolliver.

MRS. TOLLIVER: Hello, Mr. Smith. On your way out to the farm?

WALLY: Yes'm. I'm taking Margaret and the boys with me. I'm making cowboys out of your grandsons.

MARGARET: The boys idolize Wally. He loves to ride and fish and hunt and he takes them with him.

MRS. TOLLIVER: Leonard loved to hunt and fish with his father when he wasn't much older than they are. He and his father were inseparable. The day my husband was killed he wanted to take Leonard with him, but it was cold and damp, and I didn't want him to go. The doctor told Leonard if he'd gone he might have gotten help to save his father's life. When Leonard heard that, he grieved so he took sick, and Lonny and I had to take turns staying up nights nursing him. When the fever left him, and he was up again, Leonard put his gun away and has never gone hunting or fishing again. (*LEONARD, SR. comes back in with his coffee. HORACE and LEONARD, JR. come running back in to go to WALLY.*)

LEONARD, JR.: Wally, let's go out to the country now.

WALLY: First show your grandmother your muscles, boys. (*They double up their arms and go to her.*)

MRS. TOLLIVER: My goodness.

WALLY: We're toughening them up. (*BILLY DALTON, 30, MARGARET's brother, comes in, carrying a suitcase. LEONARD sees him.*)

LEONARD: There's Billy? (*Calling.*) Welcome, Billy. (*He goes out of the house to greet him. MARGARET and the children follow after him. The children embrace and climb over their uncle. MARGARET kisses him.*)

MARGARET: Welcome, Brother.

BILLY: Thank you, Sister.

MARGARET: Doesn't he look well, Leonard.

LEONARD: Yes, he does.

BILLY: I'm feeling fine. I'm excited about being back with you again.

LEONARD: Well, I can't tell you how glad I am to have you. I'm worked to death.

MARGARET: Let's do something tonight to celebrate. Let's have a party.

BILLY: Sure.

LEONARD: Oh, we can't tonight, Margaret. I have many things to go over with Billy at the office, and we have to make some plans for the County Attorney race.

MARGARET: All right.

BILLY: Have you all eaten breakfast? I haven't and I'm starved.

LEONARD: Come on in the house, and I'll get Mama to fix some for you.

MRS. TOLLIVER: (*Mrs. Tolliver joins them.*) Hello, Billy.

BILLY: Hello, Miss Lenora.

LEONARD: Wally, this is Margaret's brother, Billy Dalton. (*They shake hands.*)

WALLY: Hello, Billy.

LEONARD: Mama, Billy hasn't had any breakfast.

MRS. TOLLIVER: Why don't I scramble eggs for all of you?

WALLY: Thank you, but I'm going to have to go. Margaret, you and the boys stay and I'll take you another day.

LEONARD, JR.: No, I want to go now, Mama.

MARGARET: All right. All right. We'll go. I know Billy and Daddy want to talk business anyway. I'll see you at dinner.

MRS. TOLLIVER: Why don't you all have dinner with me, Margaret?

MARGARET: Oh, there's so many of us.

MRS. TOLLIVER: I enjoy having you.

MARGARET: All right. I always like to get out of cooking. (*They go out.*)

BILLY: Where did Wally Smith come from, Leonard?

LEONARD: Calhoun County. He's worked around ranches and farms all his life. He was working as foreman over at the Jackson ranch in this county, and I got to talking to him uptown and asking him some questions about cattle and telling how hard it was trying to have cattle and a law practice at the same time, and he asked me if I ever thought of taking in a partner, and I said I hadn't but I'd be interested. (*GEORGE and LONNY come around the side of the house. GEORGE carries a sign reading: "GEORGE TOLLIVER—Attorney at Law," a hammer and a nail. BILLY sees them and walks over to them.*)

GEORGE: Welcome home, Billy.

BILLY: Thank you, George. Hello, Lonny.

LONNY: Welcome home.

LEONARD: Brother is going to give us a little competition in the County Attorney's race, Billy. He told me this morning he was going to try for it.

GEORGE: I didn't know about you even coming here, Billy.

BILLY: That's all right. A little competition never hurt anybody, (*Laughing.*) and if you win I'll support you, if I win, you'll support me.

GEORGE: O.K. That's a deal. (*BILLY and LEONARD go into the house. GEORGE takes the sign and puts it up against the house.*)

GEORGE: How does it look?

LONNY: Fine. (*Reading.*) George Tolliver, Attorney at Law. My goodness.

GEORGE: All I need now are some clients.

LONNY: You'll get them.

GEORGE: You think I can do anything.

LONNY: Just about.

GEORGE: Do you think I can get elected County Attorney?

LONNY: If you put your mind to it, I think you could get elected governor. If you put your mind to it.

GEORGE: (*Laughing.*) What about President?

LONNY: That too.

GEORGE: When I get my money from Leonard today, I want to give you what you need to pay down on your house in California.

LONNY: I can't let you do that. You're gonna need your money.

GEORGE: I want you to have it.

LONNY: Well, all right. It sure will help me. But only as a loan. I'm gonna pay you back one day.

GEORGE: We'll see about that.

LONNY: Thank you. Before you go in, I want to tell you something I never told anyone before.

GEORGE: What is it, Lonny?

LONNY: (*A pause.*) You asked me last night if I'd ever known any bitterness, and I told you no, and that was a lie. There was a time I felt great bitterness towards my father.

GEORGE: Did you Lonny?

LONNY: Yes. Not because he was white, but because he never really did anything for me. Oh, I had his name, and while he lived he always recognized me as his son, and yet he didn't really care enough about me to feed me or clothe me. I think during the time he lived he gave me maybe three nickels. When Mama was dying, she had to ask your mother, the woman she worked for, to take care of me, to give me food and let me sleep in your kitchen until I was grown and I could do for myself. Mind you, she did that and more than that. I slept in the room with you and Mr. Leonard. I had warm clothes and good food. You were like brothers to me. (*A small shrivelled man comes into the yard. He is VIRGIL TOLLIVER.*)

VIRGIL: How do you do. Is this where George Tolliver and his Mama live?

GEORGE: Yes?

VIRGIL: Are you George Tolliver?

GEORGE: Yes, sir.

VIRGIL: I'm your Uncle Virgil.

GEORGE: Oh, how do you do?

VIRGIL: I'm on my way to Mississippi, but I figured I'd drive a few miles out of the way and stop off and say hello.

GEORGE: Well, I'm glad you did, Uncle Virgil. (*LEONARD comes into the yard.*) Uncle Virgil, this is my brother, Leonard and this is Lonny. (*VIRGIL and LEONARD shake hands.*)

VIRGIL: Hello, Lonny.

LONNY: Hello, Mr. Virgil. I've got to be getting back to work. Nice to have seen you, Mr. Virgil. (*VIRGIL nods to him, and LONNY leaves.*)

LEONARD: Can you have breakfast with us, Uncle Virgil?

VIRGIL: I've eaten.

LEONARD: Can you stay for dinner?

VIRGIL: No, I can't do that. I have to make it to Beaumont before dark. I never travel on highways at night. I have to be in Mississippi by day after tomorrow, noon.

GEORGE: Excuse me, I'll tell Mama you're here. (*GEORGE goes into the house. VIRGIL points to George's sign.*)

VIRGIL: Is he a lawyer?

LEONARD: Yes, sir.

VIRGIL: I thought that colored boy I met from here told me he was a merchant and worked in a department store?

LEONARD: He was. He was. You see, it's all a little confusing. He was practicing law with me, but that didn't work out, and he temporarily got himself a job working in a department store, and now he's going to run for County Attorney and have his own law office.

VIRGIL: Where is he getting the money for all this?

LEONARD: Well . . .

VIRGIL: I hope he's not going into debt. There's a rule I've used all my life. Never do anything that you have to go into debt for. How much do you remember about your father?

LEONARD: Well . . .

VIRGIL: Your daddy was a very impatient, stubborn, hard-headed and impractical man. I was never very close to him after we were grown. He didn't seem to want to fool with Sister and me then. "What kind of a trade are you following," he used to say to me, "being a bookkeeper in a plantation store. Plantations and their stores are things of the past. Wake up. Come to Texas. Get rich." "Let him go," Sister said to me. "Stop worrying about him, Virgil. He has to learn same as the rest of us." "But, Sister, he's the baby," I said. "No baby now," she said. "Let him go." And we did. Had to let him walk right out of our lives. We visited him twice here. It almost broke my heart to see him. Here he was no more than a boy himself, straddled with you children and a wife. Course when we heard about the hunting accident, we weren't surprised. I said to Sister, "It came as no surprise. I was expecting it."

LEONARD: What do you mean?

VIRGIL: Son, I don't think your daddy was in no hunting accident. I think he fixed it to look that way. I think he was burdened with debt and responsibilities and he deliberately pulled that trigger.

LEONARD: What's the matter with you, old man? Are you crazy? Why did you come here after all these years to tell me this? What difference does it make now, how my Papa died? That was twenty five years ago. Why don't you let him rest in peace? Get out of here if you can't. Get out of here and don't come back. (*LEONARD goes into the house as GEORGE comes into the hall.*) I think he's crazy. He was trying to tell me Daddy committed suicide, that he was in debt. (*GEORGE looks back out the door.*)

GEORGE: He's crying out there. (*Goes out on the porch steps.*) What are you crying for, old man?

VIRGIL: My sister's dead, and my brother's dead, and I want to die because I'm all alone, but I can't because I'm too mean to die. (*GEORGE goes to him.*) I don't know what gets into me, boy, to say the things I do. I get excited and say the first thing that comes into my head. I'm old and I've got to be in Mississippi, noon the day after tomorrow, and I hate driving the highways at night. I'm going to Mississippi to put a tombstone on the grave of my sister. I promised not to bury her in a watery grave and put up a glorious tombstone, and that she is to have, because she was very devoted to me all her life. I was her father, her husband, her children. I was her brother and she was my sister. (*He goes on, a step or two, then sways gently back and forth, almost as if he were slightly drunk. GEORGE goes to him, giving him assistance.*) I'm rich. That was the thing that fooled them all. I finally got to Texas, too, but I was rich when I got there. That even surprised Sister. Once I let her look at my bank book. "How in the name of God, Virgil, did you get all that money?" she asked. "Because all my life I did the practical thing. All my life I lived that way. Conservatively. Cautiously. Here a little. There a little. Precept upon precept. Line upon line. And suddenly, I looked and I was rich. My sister said, "How did it happen? How did it happen?" "By taking my time, Sister. By biding my time." (*MRS. TOLLIVER comes out. She sees VIRGIL and goes to him.*)

MRS. TOLLIVER: Hello, Virgil.

VIRGIL: Lenora?

MRS. TOLLIVER: Yes.

VIRGIL: You're an old woman now.

MRS. TOLLIVER: Yes, I guess I am. An you're an old man.

VIRGIL: Where is Horace buried?

MRS. TOLLIVER: Here.

VIRGIL: Is there a tombstone on the grave?

MRS. TOLLIVER: Yes.

VIRGIL: Who put it there?

MRS. TOLLIVER: I did.

VIRGIL: When I come back I'll have to stop and take some flowers to my brother's grave. (*Again he tries to start on but pauses, breathless.*) Lenora. (*She comes toward him.*) Where's your family? Where are the sisters and the brothers?

MRS. TOLLIVER: They're all dead, Virgil. I'm the last.

VIRGIL: And I'm the last. I'm a very wealthy man, and I've come to make up to you and the children.

MRS. TOLLIVER: (*Interrupting.*) Well, I'm happy for you, but Leonard and George are not children now, and they don't need you, and I don't need you, so I thank you to leave.

VIRGIL: I'm your dead husband's brother, Lenora.

MRS. TOLLIVER: I know who you are, but you are a stranger to me and my children, so please go.

VIRGIL: Lenora . . .

MRS. TOLLIVER: I want you to go. I have nothing to say to you. My boys have no feeling for you, and I don't have any for you. You didn't come near us when we needed you, and we want nothing from you now, so just please leave.

VIRGIL: All right. All right. I meant no harm . . . (*He turns to GEORGE.*) Goodbye. (*A pause. He tries to remember his name.*) Leonard?

GEORGE: No, no. I'm George.

VIRGIL: (*To GEORGE.*) Oh. Yes. You're the one prospering with a law firm?

GEORGE: No. That's Leonard. I'm the one running for County Attorney.

VIRGIL: Oh, yes. And you're the oldest . . .

GEORGE: No. I'm the youngest. (*BILLY comes into the yard from around the house. VIRGIL stumbles; GEORGE catches him.*)

VIRGIL: (*Softly.*) Leonard . . .

GEORGE: No, George.

VIRGIL: George, take me in the house, boy, so I can get some rest. I've come a long way and God A'mighty, I'm tired. (*He gasps and slumps toward George.*)

GEORGE: Billy. Billy. Help me. (*BILLY takes the other side of the old man. They help him into the house. LEONARD stands at the window watching as the lights fade.*)

ACT I

SCENE 2

Mid-May. The afternoon of the election. LESTER WHYTE stands on the corner. He is in his late fifties but looks much older. He is emaciated, unshaven, dissipated and shabbily dressed. VIRGIL TOLLIVER is seated on a small wicker chair in the yard, dozing. He looks frail and weak. It is very late afternoon in spring.

WALLY SMITH comes into the yard with the two boys, LEONARD, JR. and HORACE. They all go over to VIRGIL.

WALLY: Excuse me, Mr. Virgil. (*VIRGIL opens his eyes and looks up at him.*) Have you seen Margaret?

VIRGIL: No.

WALLY: I can't find her anywhere. She was supposed to meet me and the boys at the polls.

VIRGIL: Were there many people voting?

WALLY: Yes, sir.

VIRGIL: Who do you think will win? (*WALLY looks around to see if anyone is listening.*)

WALLY: Billy.

VIRGIL: How are you, boys? (*The boys look at him and grin but don't answer.*)

WALLY: Tell your Uncle Virgil how you are, boys.

LEONARD JR.: We're fine. (*LEONARD comes around the side of the house. The boys run to him.*)

BOYS: Hey, daddy!

WALLY: Do you know where Margaret is?

LEONARD: No.

WALLY: Well, I guess we'll find her around town. Come on, boys.

LEONARD: You don't have to be responsible for them. Leave them here with Mama.

WALLY: All right. (*LEONARD goes to the boys. WALLY exits.*)

LEONARD: Boys, I want you all to stay here with your grandmother and mind her.

LEONARD, JR.: Let us go with you, Daddy.

HORACE: Please.

LEONARD, JR.: We never see you or Mama.

LEONARD: I know, son. But tonight is the election. We can't be with you boys tonight. Now mind your grandmother. (*The boys go into the house as LEONARD exits. VIRGIL sees LESTER WHYTE standing at the corner and goes over to him.*)

VIRGIL: Evening. I've seen you so often standing out here from my window in there. I'm Virgil Tolliver. This is only my second day out of bed. I don't know if you've heard of my illness or not, but I was seized with a heart attack right here in the yard, not four months ago. (*LESTER WHYTE pays no attention to him and makes no sign of even having heard him. He goes on out. VIRGIL watches him go, then returns to his chair. CHARLIE comes in.*) What's the matter with that man that stands out here all the time? I tried to get him into a conversation, but he just walked away.

CHARLIE: Oh, that's old Lester Whyte. He doesn't speak to me either, and he's known me all his life. He doesn't speak to anyone any more except his daughter when she comes to visit him for a day or two, once a year. (*They start toward the house. LESTER WHYTE comes back to the corner.*)

CHARLIE: (*Whispering.*) He killed a man named Jim Sparks about sixteen years ago. I saw it. I was standing on the corner by the picture show when I saw them coming towards each other. Lester had a Winchester in his hand, and when Jim saw him coming towards him with that gun, he turned and started running the other way, and Lester shot him in the back as he ran. Then he got in his car and drove away and left Jim bleeding on the street.

VIRGIL: Why did he kill him?

CHARLIE: He was his wife's lover.

VIRGIL: Was he tried for murder?

CHARLIE: Yes, and convicted, but he only got a suspended sentence. His trial almost tore this town apart. Anyone who testified even as a character witness for Lester Whyte, Jim Sparks' mama Evelyn would scream and curse at when she met them, or call them up on the phone and threaten to kill them. She still lives here. She runs the boarding house Wally Smith lives in. She still swears that it wasn't a fair trial, that Lester Whyte bought his way free.

VIRGIL: What happened to his wife?

CHARLIE: She's living in a Houston boarding house crippled with arthritis. (*A pause.*)

VIRGIL: Do you work?

CHARLIE: No more, I used to. I'm retired. In August, I'll get the old age pension.

VIRGIL: Does Helen work?

CHARLIE: No, she gets a little money every week from our brother.

VIRGIL: Who is your brother?

CHARLIE: I don't speak his name.

VIRGIL: Why?

CHARLIE: He stole my birthright and my blessing. He convinced Papa I wasn't capable of managing money. And Papa left everything in his charge, and he saw I got nothing and Helen a pittance.

VIRGIL: Is he older or younger than you?

CHARLIE: Younger. Older than Satan in his ways, but younger than me in his years. (*BERNICE DAYTON, 28, comes into the yard. She is a school teacher. She carries books and papers. She and GEORGE* *have been engaged to be married for a year. She is an attractive girl, but quiet and reserved.*)

BERNICE: Hello, is George in the house?

CHARLIE: Yes, he is, Bernice. He's with his mother and Lonny.

VIRGIL: Did you vote?

BERNICE: Yes, I voted during my lunch hour.

VIRGIL: Well, I know that's one vote George got.

BERNICE: Yes, sir. (*MISS HELEN comes into the yard. She goes over to them.*)

MISS HELEN: (*Whispering.*) Oh, Bernice. New Gulf has come in almost two to one in favor of Billy. It upset me so, I couldn't stay downtown and watch any longer.

BERNICE: How are the other returns?

MISS HELEN: Billy has taken everything so far. He has Iago, Hungerford, New Gulf; East Bernard, Cotton and Harrison are still to come in. They said Harrison was just ready. I couldn't stand the suspense. (*GEORGE comes out on the porch.*)

MISS HELEN: (*Whispering to Bernice.*) Are you going to tell George?

BERNICE: Yes, I think I'll find a way to tell him. (A *pause. GEORGE goes inside the house, and she follows after him. Far away in the distance can be heard the sound of dynamiting.*)

MISS HELEN: It sounds like they're blasting down at the river. Maybe someone is drowned. They ought to keep people out of that river. It's so treacherous; just a pit of death. When I was a girl, a friend of mine, Wilva Russell, got drowned down there while we were all swimming one beautiful moonlit night. One minute we were all swimming and laughing, and the next we heard Wilva's screams as the undertow pulled her down. (*MRS. TOLLIVER comes to the door.*)

MRS. TOLLIVER: Virgil, come to supper.

VIRGIL: Thank you. (*He gets up, and he and the boys go into the house.*)

MRS. TOLLIVER: Have you eaten, Cousin Helen and Cousin Charlie?

MISS HELEN: No.

MRS. TOLLIVER: Come eat with us.

CHARLIE: No, we want to eat downtown and watch the returns.

MISS HELEN: Thank you anyway. (*They start out, as MARGARET and WALLY enter.*)

MARGARET: Good afternoon.

MISS HELEN: Good afternoon, Margaret. Good afternoon, Wally.

MARGARET: Do I have two boys in there?

MRS. TOLLIVER: They're just sitting down to supper. I hope you don't mind.

MARGARET: No.

MRS. TOLLIVER: Won't you all have supper with us?

MARGARET: We've eaten, thank you. We'll just wait in here for them. (*MARGARET, WALLY and MRS. TOLLIVER go into the house. MRS. TOLLIVER goes into the kitchen. MARGARET and WALLY go into the living room. WALLY sits on the sofa.*) You tired?

WALLY: Yes, I am. I was up at five this morning. After I took you home last night I sat up and talked awhile with Evelyn Sparks. She was half drunk. She was telling me all about Lester Whyte killing her boy.

MARGARET: I wish you didn't have to stay in that common old thing's boarding house. She's very immoral, you know.

WALLY: (*Laughing.*) What's the matter—are you jealous?

MARGARET: Don't tease me, Wally. I don't like it.

WALLY: Well, are you?

MARGARET: Why should I be jealous of an old woman like that? (*She takes his hand.*) What happened to your hand? Have you been fighting again?

WALLY: Oh, some joker rammed into my car, and he started cussing me. I must have cut my hand when I hit him. (*She kisses his hand. He takes it away and sits up.*) Don't honey. Someone might see you.

MARGARET: Such a brave man and you're afraid of someone seeing me kiss your hand. (*She goes to the door and looks out.*) There's no one around. They're all out in the kitchen. I can hear them. Are you still afraid to kiss me? (*He goes to her. He kisses her.*)

WALLY: Everybody tells me Billy is going to win. Are you pleased?

MARGARET: Oh, I don't know. I'm sorry now he ever came back here. I never get to see him. All he does is work. He's mad at me . . . We got into a terrible fight the other night, and he barely speaks.

WALLY: What did you fight about?

MARGARET: About our father and how rotten, and I mean really rotten, my mother and Billy treated him while he was sick and dying. You see the year I graduated from college my father began having an affair with a girl living here.

WALLY: Agnes Thomas.

MARGARET: Yes. How did you know that?

WALLY: Evelyn Sparks told me all about it last night.

MARGARET: Were you discussing my father with Evelyn Sparks?

WALLY: I wasn't discussing him with her. She just told me that he was having an affair with this young girl and he was giving her a lot of money until your mother found out about it. Don't look so upset. Your father having an affair isn't the end of the world.

MARGARET: It was to my mother and my brother. My mother told my father he disgusted her and that she would like to send him away, but she wouldn't do anything to embarrass her children publicly. He lived on in the house with us then, but my mother and brother never spoke to him again, except when we had visitors. (*WALLY goes to MARGARET and touches her.*) Don't Wally.

WALLY: I'm sorry. I didn't mean to make you unhappy.

MARGARET: (*Looking at her watch.*) The election returns must be all in by now. Wally, is that Lester Whyte standing out there watching us?

WALLY: Why should he be doing that?

MARGARET: I don't know. I just got the feeling he was looking in here at us. (*WALLY gets up and goes to the window and looks out.*)

WALLY: He's moving on now. It was just your imagination.

MARGARET: I guess so. (*LEONARD, JR. and HORACE come running in. LEONARD, JR. goes to WALLY to be held and HORACE to his mother.*)

LEONARD JR. AND HORACE: Wally! Hey, Wally! Wally!

WALLY: How about some fishing tomorrow morning, boys?

HORACE: The other day when we went fishing at the river, Wally showed us how he could swim.

MARGARET: You be careful swimming in that river, Wally. Some parts of it can be very dangerous even for the best swimmers.

WALLY: Don't worry about me. I know rivers. I began swimming when I was younger than these boys. One day my old man said it was time to swim, and he picked me up and threw me in the water. He said swim or you'll drown. And I swam. But I'm not going to try that on your boys. They sit right on the bank and watch me while I have my swim, don't you boys? Sometimes I mark a little place for them to wade in on warm days while I'm swimming.

HORACE: Mama, I'm tired.

MARGARET: Are you, baby? We'll get you to bed pretty soon.

HORACE: Will you sing to me while I go to sleep?

MARGARET: All right. Ever since Horace was a little boy, he's like me to sing him to sleep.

LEONARD, JR.: I do, too. (*He crosses to her.*)

MARGARET: Yes, you do. The trouble is they don't like the same songs. Horace likes hymns. What's your favorite hymn, honey?

HORACE: "Will There Be Any Stars In My Crown?"

MARGARET: That's right. And "Jesus Loves Me" and "Blessed Assurance."

WALLY: I didn't know you could sing hymns.

MARGARET: There's a lot you don't know about me, Mr. Wally Smith.

LEONARD, JR.: My favorite songs are "Go Tell Aunt Rhodie" and "Old Dan Tucker."

WALLY: Is that so?

LEONARD, JR.: Did your Mama sing to you when you were a little boy, Wally?

WALLY: No.

MARGARET: My Mama sang to me. My Daddy, too. They had sweet voices. My Mother sang in the church choir. Once when Horace was sick I held him and sang to him the whole night long. Didn't I, honey?

HORACE: Yes, Ma'am.

LEONARD, JR.: When I got sick did you sing to me, too?

MARGARET: I certainly did. I sang to you and I read stories to you and I nursed you day and night until you got well. He had scarlet fever. It scared me so—but you got well, didn't you, honey?

HORACE: What did I have?

MARGARET: The epizootic.

HORACE: What's that?

MARGARET: Something horses get—

HORACE: Did I have that?

MARGARET: No. I'm just teasing. You just had a fever of some kind. They're usually pretty healthy—Thank God. (*LEONARD and BILLY enter.*)

LEONARD: Billy won.

MARGARET: Congratulations.

BILLY: Thanks.

LEONARD: Have you been good boys?

LEONARD, JR.: Yes, sir.

LEONARD: Wally, I want you to look around and find a horse for Horace and one for Leonard, Jr. I want them to have horses of their own. We'll keep them out at the farm. Would you like that, Leonard, Jr.?

LEONARD, JR.: Yes, sir.

LEONARD: What about you, Horace?

HORACE: Yes, sir.

WALLY: Well, I'm going to turn in. Congratulations, Billy. Good night. (*He leaves.*)

MARGARET: I better get these young men in bed. Come on, boys.

LEONARD: We'll be over as soon as we see George. (*She takes their hands, and they go out. LEONARD, JR. whispers to MARGARET.*)

LEONARD: When you were a boy did you have a horse of your own?

BILLY: Yes, I did.

LEONARD: I never did and I always wanted one. (*MARGARET comes back in.*)

MARGARET: Excuse me. Leonard, Jr. says he left a toy in here.

LEONARD: What kind of a toy?
MARGARET: A gun, I believe.
LEONARD: I don't see it.
MARGARET: Well, he can get it in the morning. (*She leaves.*)
LEONARD: What's the matter with Margaret? Honestly, I don't know. Have I done anything? Have I said anything to offend her? She acts like she's sorry you won.
BILLY: I think she's hurt with me. We had a quarrel the other night. We were discussing how bitterly my mother felt towards my father and Margaret said there's two sides to everything, even to what Papa did. I told her I didn't want to hear that, because what my father did was low down and despicable. (*GEORGE and LONNY come in.*)
LEONARD: The returns are all in, Brother. Billy came in first and you came in second. Lester Harris was third, and Wilbur Scott last.
GEORGE: I know. I know. Congratulations, Billy.
BILLY: Thanks.
LONNY: Congratulations.
BILLY: Thanks, Lonny.
LEONARD: I have the final count if you want to see it.
GEORGE: Thank you. (*He looks at it.*)
BILLY: I'm going on to the house, Leonard. I'm tired. Good night. (*He leaves. A pause.*)
LEONARD: Oh, I feel one hundred years old all of a sudden. I'm so tired. Billy and I worked so hard, but I guess you did too, Brother.
GEORGE: Yes, I did.
LEONARD: Well, it's like old times our being together in this room. (*A pause.*) I was thinking today, Lonny, when we used to all sneak down to the river to learn to swim, and George was always trying to follow us, and we used to give him nickels to get him to stay at home and not tell Mama where we were. (*A pause.*) Are you still going to California?
LONNY: No, sir. Eloise's father was taken sick and had to have a serious operation, and we had to let him use the money I'd borrowed from Mr. George for my house.
LEONARD: Oh, I'm sorry. How old a man is he?
LONNY: Seventy-three.
LEONARD: Is his wife still living?
LONNY: Yes, and he has two sons and a daughter out there.
LEONARD: Do you need any extra money, Lonny?
LONNY: Yes, I need everything I can get.
LEONARD: Can I loan you some?
LONNY: No, I can't borrow any more money.

LEONARD: I just rented a thousand acres of land next to my farm. I could give you a job working out there in your spare time if that would be of any help.

LONNY: Thank you. It would.

LEONARD: What are your hours at the feed store?

LONNY: I start at nine and quit at six.

LEONARD: Maybe during the summer you could work in the morning from five to eight for me.

LONNY: I sure could.

LEONARD: When would you like to start?

LONNY: Tomorrow.

LEONARD: All right. I'll tell Wally to expect you in the morning.

LONNY: Thank you.

LEONARD: (*He turns to GEORGE.*) Well, Brother, I hope this is the last time we'll ever have to oppose each other.

GEORGE: I hope so. (*LEONARD leaves. GEORGE goes to the window and looks out.*)

LONNY: You came in second and that counts for something.

GEORGE: Yes, I guess it does. One night when I couldn't sleep, I rode out to Matagorda, to the Gulf, where Mama's people came from, to that desolate place where their plantation house stood, where storms and hurricanes have whipped and torn and driven houses and men away, and all that's left to show that they were ever there are a few brick chimneys and part of a crumbling foundation. No grass; no trees; no flowers. Just the sea and the wind and the sand. The gulf was quiet when I got there. There was a kind of primitive stillness about the place. It could have been a hundred years ago, or two hundred, and I, my ancestor, seeing the Coast for the first time, as it had always been, except for the chimneys and the foundation, and the car, and me. And then I rode until I found the graves a mile from the house. Again, there were no flowers, no trees, but weeds, a jungle of weeds, Johnson grass and buffalo grass as high as my waist. And silence. A terrible silence. No one had been near those graves for years, Lonny. The tombstones had toppled over, broken; the graves themselves lost in their covering of weeds. I thought "Here lies power—here lies ambition." Let Leonard have them. (*A pause.*) Leonard gets his way about everything, doesn't he? He always has. Ever since we were boys. He's taken from us and used us. What do we have? I feel such bitterness, Lonny. Help me. I feel such bitterness. (*He goes to Lonny. LONNY comforts him as the lights fade.*)

ACT I

SCENE 3

Mid-June. VIRGIL is seated in the wicker chair in the yard. CHARLIE comes into the yard.

CHARLIE: How do you feel today, Virgil?
VIRGIL: Well, I tell you, one day I feel better and the next, I feel weak and down again. (*GEORGE comes out of his office and into the house.*)
GEORGE: Good morning, gentlemen.
CHARLIE: Good morning, George. You look full of beans.
GEORGE: Well, I am.
CHARLIE: Enjoying the practice of law?
GEORGE: Oh, yes. I am.
VIRGIL: Getting rich?
GEORGE: Trying to.
VIRGIL: Rich as Leonard?
GEORGE: (*Laughing.*) I doubt that.
VIRGIL: How much money do you make?
GEORGE: (*Laughing again.*) Enough, Uncle Virgil, enough.
CHARLIE: George is surprising everybody. He has the beginning of a nice law practice.
VIRGIL: What happened to that old man that used to come here? I haven't seen him for a while.
CHARLIE: He's in the hospital. He's been there ever since day before yesterday. Somebody beat him up. He was found four days ago on a country road.
VIRGIL: Who did it?
CHARLIE: He won't tell if he knows. They think maybe some tramp saw him wandering around and tried to rob him of the little money he had. He evidently wanders around the roads all times of night. (*A fire siren is heard in the distance.*) I'm going to the corner and see where the fire is. (*He leaves. MISS HELEN comes out of the house.*)
VIRGIL: Miss Helen, I want to ask your advice about something.
MISS HELEN: Yes?
VIRGIL: The doctor has told me I'm well enough to go home now.
MISS HELEN: That's good.
VIRGIL: And Leonard came directly to the point yesterday and asked me when I was going.
MISS HELEN: He can be very abrupt, but I don't think he means it.

VIRGIL: I'd like your advice, please. Should I tell them the truth?

MISS HELEN: About what?

VIRGIL: I've lost all my money. I've nothing left.

MISS HELEN: Yes, tell them that. Why haven't you told them before?

VIRGIL: I was afraid they would turn me out.

MISS HELEN: Why would they do that?

VIRGIL: Should I tell Leonard or George?

MISS HELEN: Leonard. He makes the decisions for this family. (*In the distance dynamiting is heard. LEONARD comes into the yard. He seems tense and distraught. He goes past VIRGIL and MISS HELEN and starts for the house.*)

VIRGIL: Leonard . . . (*He pauses. MISS HELEN goes out. VIRGIL goes over to LEONARD.*) Leonard, could we have a little talk?

LEONARD: Some other time, Uncle Virgil. I'm busy now. (*MARGARET comes around the side of the house from her apartment. LEONARD leaves VIRGIL and goes over to her.*) Margaret, I want to talk to you. Let's go back to the apartment.

MARGARET: I can't now, Leonard. Wally has taken the boys fishing and I promised I'd go for them.

LEONARD: I'll get the boys. I don't want you or the boys near Wally Smith again.

MARGARET: (*Nervously.*) Are you crazy, Leonard? . . . Why? . . . (*He hands her a letter; she glances at it.*) Who could write such lies?

LEONARD: Then you deny this?

MARGARET: Certainly. A coward writes an anonymous letter . . .

LEONARD: (*Interrupting.*) Come with me. (*He takes her arm.*)

MARGARET: (*Resisting him.*) Where are we going?

LEONARD: To find Lester Whyte.

MARGARET: Why?

LEONARD: He wrote this letter. (*He takes the letter from her and puts it in his pocket.*) I received it four days ago. I turned it over to the F.B.I. to investigate. They called me this morning to say Lester Whyte had written it. I went to see him at the hospital, and he admitted what he had done, and I asked him what he had against you or me to do something like this. I said I thought he, of all people, must know how serious it was. And he said everything in the letter was true, and that the reason he was in the hospital was that four nights ago he came upon you and Wally and that it hadn't been the first time, but this time Wally had seen him and accused him of spying and beat him up. (*He starts away again.*) We'll go to him now and tell him you deny it. (*A pause. She looks helplessly at him.*) Come on, Margaret.

MARGARET: No, I can't go. I don't deny it. It's true.

LEONARD: Oh, Margaret, no . . .
MARGARET: I'm in love with Wally. I'd like a divorce.
LEONARD: Margaret, knowing what your father's behavior did to you and Billy, how could you do this to your children?
MARGARET: Leonard . . . (*He walks away from her and goes off stage toward their apartment. She stands helplessly for a moment. VIRGIL comes out and goes toward her.*)
VIRGIL: Margaret, I wonder if you would speak to Leonard about something for me. You see . . .
MARGARET: Forgive me, Uncle Virgil. I can't talk to you now. (*She hurries off stage. MISS HELEN comes out.*)
MISS HELEN: Did you speak to Leonard?
VIRGIL: No, he's very busy.
MISS HELEN: Then speak to Lenora. She'll talk to him.
VIRGIL: All right. (*CHARLIE comes in.*)
MISS HELEN: Where was the fire?
CHARLIE: Wasn't a fire. Someone drowned in the river.
MISS HELEN: Probably some Mexican cotton picker's child. (*VIRGIL starts for the house.*)
CHARLIE: Do you want to go eat dinner now?
MISS HELEN: All right. (*They leave. VIRGIL is in the sitting room now. LENORA is there.*)
VIRGIL: Lenora . . . (*LEONARD comes back into the yard from his apartment. He starts for the house.*)
MRS. TOLLIVER: (*Looking up at VIRGIL.*) Yes, Virgil. What is it?
VIRGIL: I have a confession to make to you. I tried earlier to talk to Leonard about it, but he's so busy, and Helen said I should confer with you, so, you see . . . (*LEONARD comes into the room.*)
LEONARD: Excuse me, Uncle Virgil. I have to talk to Mama.
VIRGIL: Certainly. Certainly. (*He goes out of the room and into the yard. LEONARD hands his mother the letter.*)
MRS. TOLLIVER: What's this all about?
LEONARD: Read it. (*The dynamiting stops. GEORGE comes out of his office and into the yard. He sees his uncle.*)
GEORGE: Hello, Uncle Virgil. Enjoying the sunshine?
VIRGIL: Trying to. (*GEORGE goes into the house, down the hallway to the kitchen. MRS. TOLLIVER has finished reading the letter. GEORGE comes into the room.*)
GEORGE: What are you doing home from work, Brother?
LEONARD: I had to talk to Mama. (*CHARLIE comes into the yard. He seems very concerned. He goes to VIRGIL.*)
CHARLIE: Do you know if George is in his office?

VIRGIL: No. He went into the house.

CHARLIE: (*Going toward the house calling.*) George. George. (*GEORGE comes to the window.*)

GEORGE: Yes, Charlie?

CHARLIE: May I talk to you for a moment?

GEORGE: Yes, sir. (*He goes out of the room to the yard to CHARLIE.*)

CHARLIE: A terrible thing has happened, son. The two little boys . . . (*A pause. His voice almost gives way.*) Horace and Leonard, Jr. They were drowned in the river just now. They're down there now looking for their little bodies.

GEORGE: No, Cousin Charlie. No . . .

CHARLIE: It's true. You'd better go and tell your brother and your mother. (*GEORGE stands for a moment trying to compose himself. He is very shaken by the news. Finally, he makes himself start for the house and his brother. MISS HELEN comes into the yard. The three old people huddle together. MISS HELEN begins to cry and CHARLIE comforts her.*)

VIRGIL: How did it happen?

CHARLIE: We heard Wally Smith took them fishing at the river. He wanted to go for a swim and left them walking on a sand bar while he swam across the river. They must have waded too far because when he was half way across, he looked back and they were in deep water screaming for help. They were pulled under by a suck hole before he could get to them. (*GEORGE goes inside the house and into the living room.*)

GEORGE: Leonard . . .

LEONARD: What is it, George? What is it?

GEORGE: I have to tell you this, Brother. I don't want to be the one to do it, but I have to. (*A pause.*) Horace and Leonard, Jr. They were drowned, Brother, in the river . . .

LEONARD: Oh, Jesus. Sweet Jesus.

MRS. TOLLIVER: Oh, my God. Oh, my God.

LEONARD: I want my boys. I want my boys. I want my boys. Horace, Leonard, Jr. Horace, Leonard, Jr. (*He goes out. GEORGE goes running after him.*)

GEORGE: Leonard. Leonard. (*BILLY brings MARGARET into the yard. He supports her. LEONARD stops when he sees them approach.*)

LEONARD: I don't want her here, Billy. It's for her sins my boys were killed. Their death is her punishment.

BILLY: Leonard . . .

LEONARD: Their death is her punishment.

MARGARET: Don't say that. Please don't say that.

LEONARD: Whore. Whore. Whore.

GEORGE: Come on, Leonard. (*BILLY leaps on LEONARD trying to get at his throat.*)

BILLY: I'll kill you. Don't talk that way to my sister. (*GEORGE grabs BILLY'S hands. He pries them free of LEONARD'S throat.*) Let me go. Let me go. I'll kill him.

MARGARET: (*Screaming.*) Don't Billy, don't. It's my punishment. (*MRS. TOLLIVER goes to MARGARET.*)

MRS. TOLLIVER: Come on with me into the house, Margaret. (*MARGARET struggles to be free of her.*)

MARGARET: (*Still screaming.*) I don't want to go in there. Let me die, please. Let me die. Their death is my punishment. I am responsible for the death of my babies. I want to die. (*She struggles again to be free.*)

MRS. TOLLIVER: Margaret. Margaret.

MARGARET: Let me die, please. Let me die. (*A pause.*) I said to Wally, I'm afraid, aren't you afraid? Of what, he said. That we'll be punished, I said. (*She goes to BILLY.*) Don't hate me, Billy. Tell me you don't hate me. I've never done anything like this before. I've never misbehaved before. I've always been a good wife to Leonard before. (*A pause.*) My little boys. Were you there when they found them? I thought they would never find them. They're in the river, they said, drowned, but we can't find them. Leonard, Billy. Help me find them . . . (*She screams.*) Horace . . . Leonard, Jr., your Mama is sorry. Please, please forgive your Mama. Please . . . (*BILLY turns to one side. He buries his face. LENORA leads MARGARET toward the house. MARGARET pulls away from her.*) Don't take me in there. I won't go in there.

MRS. TOLLIVER: You can't stay out here. (*She and GEORGE take her again. MARGARET is crying.*) Come on, Margaret. (*They take her and lead her toward the house. She doesn't resist as the lights fade.*)

ACT I

SCENE 4

Later that night. CHARLIE is in the yard. MARGARET is lying on the bed in the front room. BERNICE is beside her. MARGARET opens her eyes.

MARGARET: Where am I? (*BERNICE gets up and goes over to her.*) Bernice?

BERNICE: Yes?

MARGARET: Where is Billy?

BERNICE: I don't know. He left here about two hours ago. As soon as he gets here they're going to take you to the hospital. Now go back to sleep. The doctor wants you to sleep.

MARGARET: I told Billy what I'd done. I called him in here and asked him to close the door and I told him all by myself. I told him I'd behaved just like Papa, only Papa was killed for what he did wrong, and Billy and I were spared, and my two little boys were killed for what I did wrong, and I was spared.

BERNICE: Now they weren't killed for that.

MARGARET: Weren't they? God bless you for saying that. Then why were they killed?

BERNICE: I don't know.

MARGARET: I begged Billy to go ask Wally Smith to leave town. Because if he stays here, Leonard might kill him, and he shouldn't die. I should die. I pray to die. (*A pause.*) I asked Billy to forgive me.He just stood there and looked at me and didn't say a word. (*A pause.*) I know he is not going to speak to me ever again—like he never spoke to Papa again. (*A clock strikes in the distance.*) What time is it? Sh. One o'clock. In the morning? I've spent many a sleepless, restless night listening to that clock strike as a girl and a woman. Once Leonard, Jr. had the croup and he said he could sleep if I got the clock to stop striking, and I said . . . Go tell Aunt Rhodie, Go tell Aunt Rhodie, Go tell Aunt Rhodie, the old grey goose . . . Horace. Leonard, Jr. Save them. Save them.

BERNICE: Sh. Sh. (*She gives her some sedation. MARGARET takes it. She lies on the bed. MRS. TOLLIVER comes into the room and stands by the door. BERNICE motions to her to be quiet and goes to her.*)

MRS. TOLLIVER: (*Whispering.*) Billy still hasn't come back. I think it's best for her to rest on here tonight. We'll take her to the hospital first thing in the morning. (*MISS HELEN comes to the front door.*)

MISS HELEN: I've made some coffee and sandwiches. They're in the kitchen if you want them.

CHARLIE: Thank you. (*MISS HELEN and CHARLIE go into house. MRS. TOLLIVER goes out into the yard. GEORGE comes in from the street and goes to his mother.*)

MRS. TOLLIVER: Where is Leonard?

GEORGE: He's still at the funeral home. Lonny is with him. I understand out in the country when a Mexican child dies, they don't mourn his death but celebrate, because the child is taken in innocence, knows no sin, and his soul goes immediately to Heaven. I never understood that before. It seemed pagan and unfeeling to me, but when I look at those two little boys, I understand. (*VIRGIL comes into the yard from the house. GEORGE goes into the house.*)

VIRGIL: Have you been asleep at all, Lenora?

MISS TOLLIVER: No.

VIRGIL: I slept awhile in George's office. (*MRS. TOLLIVER goes into the house.*) It's quiet isn't it? I hate it when it's quiet like this. It was quiet like this after Sister died. (*The SHERIFF comes into the yard. He goes over to VIRGIL.*)

SHERIFF: Have you seen Billy Dalton here?

VIRGIL: No.

SHERIFF: Do you know if George is here?

VIRGIL: Yes, he is.

SHERIFF: Would you be kind enough to go inside and ask him to come out and talk to me?

VIRGIL: Yes, sir. (*He goes into the house. LEONARD and LONNY come into the yard.*)

LEONARD: Lonny. Wait a moment, please. (*LONNY stops. The two of them stand in the shadows in the corner of the yard.*)

LONNY: Are you all right?

LEONARD: Yes. But let's just stand here for a moment before we go into the house. Can you see who's in the yard?

LONNY: Yes, sir. Just the Sheriff.

LEONARD: Riding over here from the funeral parlor, I thought, I'm dreaming all of this. If I go home now, I'll find Margaret in our room just coming home from a late night bridge game, undressing and getting ready for bed, and Horace and Leonard, Jr. will be in their beds asleep. But it's dark back there in a way I've never seen it dark, and I know I could search all the rooms from now until the end of time and find no one there ever again who was mine or belonged to me. (*A pause.*) It's cold all of a sudden. (*He shivers.*) Are you cold?

LONNY: Let's go inside.

LEONARD: I keep saying to myself: Is it true? Is it true? Yesterday morning I got up the same as any other morning, shaved, had my breakfast, went out to the farms, came back to my office. (*A pause.*) I'm tired. I've been going twenty-four hours without a stop. (*He starts for the house. As they pass the SHERIFF, he stops.*) Hello, Steve. (*They shake hands.*)

SHERIFF: I was sorry to hear about your boys, Leonard. I was at the other end of the county or I would have been down at the river myself.

LEONARD: I know that. Thank you. It was kind of you to come and tell me though. (*BILLY comes into the yard. The SHERIFF goes to him.*)

SHERIFF: Billy, I think you'd better come with me. (*GEORGE crosses to the SHERIFF.*)

GEORGE: What is it, Steve? What's he done?

SHERIFF: He killed Wally Smith.

LEONARD: Oh, Billy.

BILLY: I want my sister.

GEORGE: She's inside. She's very sick. (*BILLY moves toward the house. The SHERIFF takes BILLY's arm again.*)

BILLY: I just want to see my sister.

SHERIFF: Come on, Billy. We'll see your sister later. (*BILLY looks at the SHERIFF.*)

BILLY: All right. (*BILLY starts out of the yard, the SHERIFF follows after him. LEONARD, GEORGE, and LONNY stand in silence watching BILLY and the SHERIFF leave. MARGARET opens her eyes.*)

MARGARET: (*Singing to herself.*) Jesus loves me, this I know. For the Bible tells me so.

BERNICE: Margaret, shhh . . . (*There is silence as the lights fade.*)

ACT II

SCENE 1

Three days later. MISS HELEN is alone in the living room. BERNICE comes into the room.

BERNICE: The house is all straightened now.

MISS HELEN: I can't seem to get back to any kind of routine. I keep saying to myself, the little boys are dead; they are buried; the funeral is over; and you have to start back now to your usual duties. But I can't get started. I just sit here. I'm glad the doctor wouldn't let Margaret go to the funeral. I think it would have been much too difficult for her. Lavinia Harris told me yesterday that Evelyn Sparks, who owns the rooming house Wally was staying in, says she was watching from her window when the killing took place. (*LEONARD comes in. He has a package.*)

LEONARD: What were you saying about Billy, Cousin Helen?

MISS HELEN: I told Bernice that Evelyn Sparks says she was watching from her window when Billy shot Wally Smith.

LEONARD: Evelyn Sparks is a dissipated, loose-living, whorish woman. We all know that. I don't think what she claims to have seen can be trusted. (*MISS HELEN and BERNICE go. LEONARD goes outside as GEORGE comes into the yard.*)

LEONARD: Did you talk with Billy?

GEORGE: Yes.

LEONARD: How is he?

GEORGE: He's heartbroken about the boys, of course. He asked how you were bearing up. I told him Margaret was still in the hospital. (*A pause.*) He's resigning as County Attorney.

LEONARD: Did you tell him I didn't want him to do that?

GEORGE: Yes. I said you felt he would go free, and that no one here wants him to quit. He said he had to get out of it. He asked me to write a letter of resignation for him. They set his bail at ten thousand dollars.

LEONARD: I'll take care of that immediately.

GEORGE: I told him you would. Wally's mother and father were at the jail today. They came to get Wally's body. They've been to Malcolm Weaver and hired him as their attorney. He called me just before I left for the jail, and said they wanted an accounting of everything spent out at the farm. He asked to see a copy of your agreement with Wally.

LEONARD: To have Wally here and managing my farm and cattle, I gave him a third interest in the cattle and all my assets besides the land.

GEORGE: I know.

LEONARD: How is Billy?

GEORGE: He's very depressed.

LEONARD: Did he ask to see me?

GEORGE: No.

LEONARD: Did you tell him I wanted to see him?

GEORGE: Yes.

LEONARD: And what did he say?

GEORGE: He didn't say anything. Uncle Virgil has lost all his money. He's broke. He asked to live on here. I told him he could. Is that all right with you?

LEONARD: Yes. (*GEORGE starts away.*) George.

GEORGE: Yes.

LEONARD: Do you know what I have in this package? Letters from Margaret to Wally—at least I've been told that's what's in here. I haven't been able to look at them.

GEORGE: Where did you get them?

LEONARD: From a man who had the room next to Wally's. Wally's parents asked him to pack his clothes for them. When he was doing it, he came across these letters. He called and asked if I wanted them. I told him that I did. He wanted money, of course.

GEORGE: And did you give him money?

LEONARD: Yes. I can't bring myself to even look at them. Would you see if it is really Margaret's handwriting?

GEORGE: I don't want to read them, Leonard.

LEONARD: I don't want you to read them. Just look at the handwriting. (*GEORGE looks at the letters.*)

GEORGE: Yes, it is her handwriting. (*LEONARD takes the package of letters and starts for the house.*) What are you going to do with them?

LEONARD: I'm going to destroy them. (*He continues on into the house. GEORGE follows after him.*)

GEORGE: I wouldn't do this, Leonard.

LEONARD: I'm not going to have these letters made public.

GEORGE: If it's ever discovered you're destroying evidence, it can make it very difficult for Billy.

LEONARD: I was read on the phone parts of the letters. I want them destroyed. (*He and GEORGE enter the house. He takes three or four of the letters and begins to tear them up. GEORGE reaches out and tries to stop him.*)

GEORGE: Don't Leonard. Please. I beg you not to do this. (*LEONARD moves away from him with the letters.*)

LEONARD: I'm going to destroy them. (*He tears them up in great anger. He finds a metal waste basket, puts the pieces of paper in there and sets fire to them. VIRGIL comes into the house and into the room. He seems very nervous and ill-at-ease.*)

VIRGIL: What are you burning? (*Neither of the brothers speak to him.*) The neighbors sure have brought in lots of food these last days, fried chicken, baked ham, potato salad, all kinds of pies and cakes. Can I bring you something to eat, Leonard?

LEONARD: No, sir. Thank you.

VIRGIL: George?

GEORGE: No, sir.

VIRGIL: There were so many flowers at the funeral. My goodness, I don't think I ever saw more flowers. Some people say it was the largest funeral they've ever had here. Mr. Charlie said he never remembered a larger one. (*EVELYN SPARKS, 65, comes into the yard. Her hair is dyed a vivid black. LEONARD sees her and goes out to her.*)

LEONARD: What do you want, Evelyn?

EVELYN: Has Harry Brightman been here?

LEONARD: I don't know who that is.

EVELYN: Had a room at my house. He's skipped out.

LEONARD: Why should that concern me?

EVELYN: Some valuable letters have been stolen from my room. I had hidden them there for safe-keeping. (*She pauses, looks at LEONARD. He doesn't say anything.*) The letters were to Wally Smith from your wife. Did he bring them here to you? (*Again LEONARD doesn't answer. GEORGE comes outside.*) George,I was asking Leonard about some letters from his wife to Wally Smith. Perhaps you've seen them. (*Neither GEORGE or LEONARD say anything.*) Well, I guess he wanted them for himself. I was sure he'd stolen them from me to sell to you. Well, it doesn't matter. I remember them very well. Wally and I used to get drunk together, and he'd read them to me. I've read them over many times since, so I don't really need them to be able to quote what was in there. They'll make interesting testimony at the trial. (*She starts out of the yard. She turns and comes back to them.*) What's it worth if I forget what I read in those letters. I can forget a lot of other things too. I can forget whether I was sober the night of the killing. If I remember, of course, that I was drunk, nothing that I've said around town would mean anything. And I saw plenty. (*A pause.*) I want money, boys. I want my share. I know to get Billy Dalton free, money will have to be spent. I know what happened when Lester Whyte murdered my boy. Money was spent, and the guilty went free. Do I get my share, boys? (*A pause. She looks at them. Neither of them says anything.*) Think it over. I'll be waiting at home to hear from you. (*She leaves.*)

GEORGE: Are you going to try and buy her off, too? (*VIRGIL comes outside to them.*)

VIRGIL: I thought the remarks made at the funeral by the preacher were very comforting. What was his name?

GEORGE: Brother Meyers.

VIRGIL: Oh, yes. I was introduced to him three or four times, but I can't remember names like I used to. I asked him what was the subject of the talk he gave and he said, "Blessed are the pure in heart for they shall see God." That is one of the Beatitudes. I used to know all the Beatitudes. Blessed are the meek for they shall inherit the earth. Blessed . . . I want to thank you boys for letting me stay on here. I know I did a terrible thing to you and even to your father. I refused to loan your father money once, and I was always afraid that because of that . . . (*A pause.*) . . . his death wasn't an accident. That's why I was so relieved when Leonard told me . . .

LEONARD: And I lied to you. He wasn't killed in any hunting accident.

He fixed it to look that way. He shot himself.

VIRGIL: Son.

LEONARD: That day when they brought his body home, I found a note in the pocket of his jacket saying what he had done and asking Mama to forgive him and I destroyed it. That's why I took sick, and I couldn't tell anybody what I'd found, not George or Mama. And I couldn't forgive him for leaving us all alone. For a long time after that, I was so ashamed of him and what he'd done that I couldn't stand to hear him even talked about. (*A pause.*) But lately I've wanted to know about him and why he did what he did. I've felt such compassion for him. (*He goes over to GEORGE.*) The night before we were to go hunting together that last time, we were in the kitchen cleaning our guns. Papa said to me, "I've failed you, boy." And then Mama came into the room and hurried me off to bed. But I didn't get to sleep, and I heard them quarreling and talking about money. I heard Mama say she was afraid, that it looked like poverty had been sent to her and her sons as a curse, and she had to be free once in her life of debt; that maybe they should turn the farm back to the bank. I must have gone to sleep then, because the next thing I remember was Daddy calling me and telling me it was time to get up if I was going. Then Mama came into the room and said it was cold, and I wasn't to go. (*A pause. He turns to GEORGE.*) I'm sorry I told you so abruptly that way about Daddy. I know that's why I've always had a particular feeling about the farm. It was with the insurance money he left that Mama was able to pay it off. (*LEONARD goes inside.*)

VIRGIL: It's a pretty day, isn't it?

GEORGE: Yes, sir.

VIRGIL: I'm glad it was a pretty day on the day of the little boys funeral. That was a sweet hymn they sang, "Jesus Loves Me." I remember singing it myself in Sunday School. How does it go?

GEORGE: Jesus loves me, this I know . . .

VIRGIL: Oh, yes. Yes. (*He begins to sing.*) For the Bible tells me so. Little ones to Him belong, They are weak but He is strong. (*MRS. TOLLIVER comes into the yard.*)

VIRGIL: I confessed to George and Leonard my secret, Lenora.

MRS. TOLLIVER: What is your secret?

VIRGIL: I'm broke. Bankrupt. I have no place to go. I threw myself at your sons' mercy, and they said I could live here. (*A pause.*) I've always known about Horace, too. Even when Leonard said that first day it wasn't true, I wanted to believe it, and yet I didn't believe it. (*He exits to GEORGE'S office.*)

GEORGE: Leonard told us just now that he knew Papa's death wasn't an accident. He said he had found a note in his hunting jacket that he destroyed. (*LEONARD comes outside. GEORGE goes to his office.*)

MRS. TOLLIVER: I've been to the cemetery.

LEONARD: Did you take the car?

MRS. TOLLIVER: No, I walked.

LEONARD: Tomorrow or the next day I thought we'd go over to Mr. Suskie's and look at some tombstones.

MRS. TOLLIVER: All right.

LEONARD: I just want something simple. Billy says he's resigning as County Attorney. I don't think he should do that.

MRS. TOLLIVER: Did you tell him how you felt?

LEONARD: How can I tell him? He won't see me. He won't see anyone but George. I asked George to tell him.

MRS. TOLLIVER: The doctor told Margaret last night about Billy. He said he's not sure she even understood. They have her so heavily sedated. I'm going to call now over to the hospital to see how she is. Have you eaten anything today?

LEONARD: No.

MRS. TOLLIVER: You'll make yourself sick if you don't try to eat something. Let me fix you some soup.

LEONARD: I'm just not hungry, Mama.

MRS. TOLLIVER: You haven't eaten for three days. You've gotten no sleep. (*She goes to him.*) George told me just now what you said about your father's death. That you found a note.

LEONARD: Yes, Ma'am. Which I destroyed. I'm sorry now I told George. You might as well have gone on believing it was an accident.

MRS. TOLLIVER: I've always felt it wasn't an accident.

LEONARD: Mama . . .

MRS. TOLLIVER: I always have, and all these years you thought you were protecting us from knowing the truth. I'm sorry you took this burden on yourself.

LEONARD: Why didn't you tell me, Mama?

MRS. TOLLIVER: I was never sure. I thought why burden you with something I wasn't actually sure of, and whenever his death was mentioned by anyone you'd leave the room. (*GEORGE comes out of his office.*)

GEORGE: T. L. Smith, Wally's father, just called. He said Evelyn Sparks told him you had some letters that belonged to Wally.

LEONARD: What did you tell him?

GEORGE: That I know nothing about it.

LEONARD: Then you lied.

GEORGE: Yes, I lied.

LEONARD: Why did you lie? For your brother? To save your brother from what he did? Mama, I paid a man some money for letters Margaret wrote Wally Smith. Evelyn Sparks says they were stolen from her room.

MRS. TOLLIVER: Where are the letters now?

LEONARD: I burned them. They were love letters, Mama, intimate and detailed. (*To GEORGE.*) Mama says she always felt daddy's death was a suicide. Did you know that?

GEORGE: Yes.

LEONARD: Did you think that, too?

GEORGE: Yes. When I was ten, a boy at school told me his father said it was a suicide. I was going to you to tell you what I'd heard, when Lonny told me not to. He reminded me how sick you had been after daddy's death and to ask Mama about it instead.

LEONARD: So you thought you were sparing me and I thought I was sparing you. I'm going now to the District Attorney and tell him about my tearing up Margaret's letters. I should know by now that tearing up letters doesn't change anything. (*He starts away. He pauses.*) Brother, will you come with me?

GEORGE: If you want me to. (*They start out. LEONARD pauses.*)

LEONARD: I can't go. You go for me. I can't bear to leave the yard.

GEORGE: Are you sure you want me to do this?

LEONARD: Yes. (*GEORGE exits. LEONARD sees a toy pistol and a ball under the shrubs by the house. He picks them up.*)

LEONARD: These were Leonard, Jr.'s. He liked to play here.

MRS. TOLLIVER: You look so tired, Leonard. Please get some rest.

LEONARD: I'll try, Mama. (*He starts for the house as the lights fade.*)

ACT II

SCENE 2

Four months later. There is a sign in the yard: "Apartment for Rent." MISS HELEN is sitting in front with VIRGIL.

VIRGIL: Why is it so quiet?

MISS HELEN: Is it so quiet? I can hear cars and trucks pass on the highway every now and then.

VIRGIL: Yes. I can hear cars and trucks on the highway; but it's so quiet here in the house and in the yard. It was quiet this way the night the two little boys died. It was quiet this way in my house in Goliad when my sister died. It's the quietness of death all around this house.

MISS HELEN: Don't say that, Virgil. Please, please don't say that. A boy is on trial for his life. Things are not going well.

VIRGIL: Who is on trial?

MISS HELEN: Billy. You remember?

VIRGIL: Do I know him?

MISS HELEN: Yes.

VIRGIL: I'm sure I do. Have I been sick again?

MISS HELEN: Yes.

VIRGIL: Was I sick long?

MISS HELEN: No, not too long.

VIRGIL: Where is everybody?

MISS HELEN: They're at the trial.

VIRGIL: Did I go to the trial?

MISS HELEN: No, you've been too sick.

VIRGIL: Did you go?

MISS HELEN: Every once in a while.

VIRGIL: How long is it going to last?

MISS HELEN: It's over today. The jury is out now, I believe. They're waiting for the verdict.

VIRGIL: I told the boys, Leonard and George, I was without funds and that I would like to live on here with them, and they told me I could. Their father wrote me three times before he died, asking me for money. I didn't even answer the letters. But I've been punished for anything wrong I did. Anything cold and unfeeling. About five years ago, without telling Sister, I began to invest in South Texas land. I wanted to surprise her with my profits. I surprised her all right. The land I bought and paid for wasn't the land I looked at. The land I gave our money for was all under water. I lost everything. In less than a month what had taken me and Sister a lifetime to get together. Sister never recovered from the shock. Just before she died, she told me she had saved three thousand dollars of her own; and I promised I wouldn't use it for anything but to get us buried back in Mississippi. I got her buried back there and a tombstone bought, though it isn't put up yet. I was going back there to supervise it when I got taken sick. I don't guess I'll ever get there now. It's a monument to us both. It says in beautiful lettering: "In Memory of Virgil and Sally Tolliver. Brother and Sister. Texas and Mississippi." (*A pause.*) Did I have another heart attack? Is that what caused my sickness?

MISS HELEN: No.

VIRGIL: What was I sick from this last time?

MISS HELEN: Well, you had a kind of nervous spell.

VIRGIL: How did I get nervous?

MISS HELEN: You thought we were trying to keep you from going to Mississippi to bury your sister. (*BERNICE comes in.*) Have they brought in a verdict yet?

BERNICE: No, but I got so nervous sitting there in the courthouse, I told George I couldn't wait any longer.

MISS HELEN: I don't know what the family would have done without George these past months.

BERNICE: I know.

MISS HELEN: In his own quiet way, he's turned out to be the mainstay of the family. Did Margaret take the stand this morning?

BERNICE: No, her doctor refused to let her go to the trial. (*MRS. TOLLIVER enters.*)

MRS. TOLLIVER: It's over. The jury found him guilty.

MISS HELEN: Oh, Lenora. Have they sentenced him?

MRS. TOLLIVER: Yes, he was given a suspended sentence. (*She goes into the house. MISS HELEN and BERNICE go in. LEONARD and LONNY come into the yard. They go into the house and to the front room. VIRGIL has dozed off sitting in his chair. LEONARD goes to the window and looks out. He seems very tired and much older.*)

LEONARD: I can't believe we won't be going back there tomorrow morning to listen to the arguments, the questions. I sat there watching the lawyers fighting, acting out their roles. I looked at Billy sitting there, and I thought, "My God, how a man's life can change in a day, a week, an hour, a second." I wanted to stand up and scream out to everybody, have compassion, have humility. Your lives, the fabric, the pattern, the bone, the essence can be destroyed overnight. Can be torn so to pieces that they can never be put together again. (*A pause.*) Lonny, would you go out in the kitchen and make a fresh pot of coffee for me? I don't want to go out there and see anyone now.

LONNY: All right. (*He goes. LEONARD takes off his suit jacket, loosens his collar and tie. He goes into the closet and hangs up the jacket of his suit. He comes out with a gun. He stands looking at it. GEORGE comes into the yard. He is carrying a briefcase and goes into the house and into the living room.*)

LEONARD: Remember this gun, George? I used it as a boy when I went hunting with Daddy. I found it the other night when I couldn't sleep and I was rummaging around. (*He puts the gun on the table.*)

GEORGE: How are you feeling, Brother?

LEONARD: I don't know. Relieved in some ways, I guess. Frankly, the last ten days I was so worried that they might sentence him to prison or even take his life. (*A pause.*) Did you talk to Billy?

GEORGE: Yes.

LEONARD: How was he?

GEORGE: Like he's been all through the trial, only answering questions that he's had to answer.

LEONARD: What is he going to do?

GEORGE: He'll go back to Houston this afternoon. He doesn't want to see you or Margaret for awhile, but after he's settled he'll write to us and let us know his plans. He wanted to know who was going to tell Margaret about the verdict. Do you know who will tell her?

LEONARD: No, I don't.

GEORGE: Won't you tell her, Leonard?

LEONARD: No, I will never see her again. She's to blame. Her whorish will is to blame . . . for the death of my boys; for the sentence of her brother. I'll tell her that. That's all I'll ever tell her. (*GEORGE opens the briefcase and brings out some papers.*)

GEORGE: I went by the office, and they asked if I would bring these over to you. Your secretary says they need your immediate attention.

LEONARD: Thank you. (*He takes them and holds them in his lap. He makes no attempt to look at them.*) I hope I can go back to the office sometime this week. If anyone had told me that for three months I would not go inside my office, that I would sit here in this room, staring out this window all night long, most nights . . . (*A pause.*) I don't know what I would have done without your help these last days, Brother. I just seemed incapable of any action or decision. But that's behind me now. I will begin vigorously to work again. I will bring some order into this chaos. Watch me. I was almost crazy with worry all during the trial. I am so afraid that my having given that man money for Margaret's letters was in some way the thing that clinched Billy's guilt for the jury.

GEORGE: Well, the prosecutor made much too much of that.

LEONARD: You're very kind. I don't agree. I know a jury. I know as a lawyer it would have been what I would have seized upon. If the crime were not premeditated, if they had nothing to hide, then why did his brother-in-law buy and destroy those letters? Why? (*A pause.*) Why did I, Brother?

GEORGE: To protect Margaret.

LEONARD: To protect myself. (*A pause.*) I can't walk down the street. I am the husband of a known adulteress. I am a cuckold. A fool. My brother-in-law has been convicted of murder defending my honor, his career ruined. I am mortified, ashamed . . . (*A pause.*) And the children? Their death has been forgotten. Fear and shame have not even allowed me the dignity of grief. Fear and shame . . . (*He stares* *down at the papers. He doesn't pick them up.*)

GEORGE: What do you want to do about the farm?

LEONARD: Why?

GEORGE: Lonny didn't speak to you?

LEONARD: No.

GEORGE: Eloise's father is almost well now. Her brother got Lonny a job, a good job, and he wants to leave for California right away.

LEONARD: Well, it doesn't matter. There's not much out there now. (*LONNY comes in with a cup of coffee for LEONARD.*) Why didn't you tell me about California, Lonny?

LONNY: I didn't want to worry you.

LEONARD: Are you happy about it, Lonny?

LONNY: Yes. Eloise wants to go badly, of course. She misses her family. And I'm looking forward to having a family.

LEONARD: You've gotten a good job?

LONNY: Her brother says he can get me one in a factory. (*LEONARD drinks his coffee. LONNY goes. LEONARD again tries to look at the papers. He pushes them aside.*)

LEONARD: I can't concentrate. Brother, take them and do what you can with them. This evening I'll look over what's left. (*GEORGE puts them back in the briefcase.*)

GEORGE: Would you like me to look for someone to take Lonny's place?

LEONARD: If you will.

GEORGE: Margaret's doctor called me yesterday. He says she's not getting any better.

LEONARD: When you're with her, what does she talk about?

GEORGE: Not much. She asked about Mama and Bernice.

LEONARD: Does she ask about me?

GEORGE: She did once.

LEONARD: What did she say?

GEORGE: She just asked how you were.

LEONARD: Does she mention our boys?

GEORGE: She can't talk about them. She begins to cry so uncontrollably . . . (*A pause.*) The doctor thinks Margaret is going to need psychiatric help. He thinks she should be taken to a hospital in Galveston.

LEONARD: Well, all right.

GEORGE: He says it will be very expensive.

LEONARD: How much will it cost?

GEORGE: I don't know. He just said that it was very expensive, and you should know that before consenting.

LEONARD: Do you think she should go?

GEORGE: If possible. She's getting no better here.

LEONARD: Then I want her to go. I don't care what it costs.

GEORGE: There's not a great deal of money left, Leonard. I've done the best I could in handling your business, but the settlement with Wally's family had to be done so quickly; and settling out of court this way, I know they got much more than they should have. To get the cash together for them, I had to practically give your cattle away.

LEONARD: I know. I don't care. Pay whatever there is and when the money is gone, sell what's left of the cattle, my rent houses. Sell it all if you have to. (*GEORGE closes the briefcase.*) When are you and Bernice getting married?

GEORGE: Probably next month some time. (*A pause.*) The Commissioner's Court decided instead of holding a special election to fill Billy's place, to appoint someone to take over his two year term. (*A pause.*) They asked me if I would consider the appointment.

LEONARD: Will you take it?

GEORGE: Yes.

LEONARD: Congratulations.

GEORGE: Thank you.

LEONARD: When will you begin?

GEORGE: Tomorrow or the next day. I can still help you at nights until you're ready to go back to the office.

LEONARD: Thank you. I'll be going tomorrow or the next day. (*GEORGE goes out of the room. LEONARD picks up the gun. He stands for a moment looking at it. LESTER WHYTE comes back to the corner and stands. LONNY enters.*)

LONNY: Didn't you want your coffee?

LEONARD: No. (*He sees LESTER WHYTE.*) Lonny, please go ask Lester Whyte to go some place else.

LONNY: All right, but you're going to have to look at him the rest of your life. You can't always have somebody running ahead of you and telling him to move.

LEONARD: I guess not. (*LESTER WHYTE leaves. LONNY takes the cup and goes out. LEONARD unloads the gun and puts it away. BILLY comes into the yard. LEONARD goes out to him.*) Saw you from the window. Will you come into the house?

BILLY: No, I can't stay. I went by the hospital twice. I wanted to go in and see Margaret. I wasn't able to. Have you seen her?

LEONARD: No.

BILLY: When you see her, will you tell her I'll write as soon as I get settled?

LEONARD: I will. Where will you go, Billy?

BILLY: I don't know.

LEONARD: What will you do?

BILLY: I've made no plans.

LEONARD: Do you need money?

BILLY: No.

LEONARD: If you ever need money, get in touch with me.

BILLY: Thank you. I know, Leonard, you spent a great deal of money on my defense. I'll pay you back some way.

LEONARD: I don't want repayment. Why wouldn't you testify, Billy? Evelyn Sparks admitted Wally Smith cursed you and reached for his gun first—Why?

BILLY: I had nothing to say except I killed Wally Smith, and everyone already knew that. (*MRS. TOLLIVER comes out of the house. She goes to LEONARD and BILLY.*)

MRS. TOLLIVER: Hello, Billy.

BILLY: Hello. I saw you everyday at the trial and I appreciated that. I'm sorry for all the anguish I've caused you all.

LEONARD: I'm sorry about the letters, Billy. I don't know why I destroyed them. If they had sent you to jail I would have felt responsible.

BILLY: Well, they didn't send me to jail, so . . .

LEONARD: No. I had such plans.

BILLY: I know . . . Goodbye. (*He goes.*)

MRS. TOLLIVER: I remember him when he was a boy just out of high school when his father died. He was so attentive to his mother. They were inseparable. She was always so proud of him. She told me once she couldn't have gotten through her life without him. I thought when he came back here how she would have been so proud of him.

LEONARD: He hated his father.

MRS. TOLLIVER: I know.

LEONARD: As much as I loved my father—He . . . (*A pause.*) Mama, the other night I found stuck away in a closet the gun I used when I went hunting with Papa. What happened to his gun?

MRS. TOLLIVER: I don't know. I don't think it was ever brought back home. I suppose it was left in the field after they found him.

LEONARD: I thought, Mama, just now what was to prevent me from going hunting and slipping under a barbed wire fence like Papa did.

MRS. TOLLIVER: Oh, Leonard, promise me . . .

LEONARD: I couldn't Mama. I tried, but I couldn't. (*A pause.*) Looks like rain. We could use a rain. It's been so dry.

MRS. TOLLIVER: Yes, hasn't it. Was the note your father left addressed to me?

LEONARD: No, Ma'am. Not to anyone.

MRS. TOLLIVER: Do you remember what it said?

LEONARD: No, Ma'am. It was so long ago. It was printed. I remember that. It was something about debts and responsibilities and asking our forgiveness.

MRS. TOLLIVER: Well, it doesn't matter now. (*She begins to cry.*) Oh, Leonard. Help me. Help your mother. I am so frightened. What's happening to us? The death of your two little boys. Wally's death. Your father's death. Have we committed some terrible sin? Are we being punished? Ever since your father's death, I've had to pretend courage and hide my fears. I can't any longer. I am in terror. I am in desperate terror. Help me, Leonard. Help your mother.

LEONARD: How can I help you, Mama? I can't help myself. How can I help you? One night when I couldn't sleep, I got up just before daybreak, and I went out to the cemetery, to the little boys' graves and I stood between Papa's grave and their graves, and I went back over all that happened, and I tried to imagine what it would be like if it had never happened. What it would be like for me now if Papa had never killed himself, or if I hadn't found his note and destroyed it; if George and I hadn't quarreled; if I hadn't brought Wally to work for me and Billy to live here. (*A pause.*) But you know what I wanted most to change? Not that my little boys did not die. Not that. But that I would have a chance to love them again. George tells me if you mention the name of our boys to Margaret, she cries uncontrollably. I don't cry, Mama. Mention them to me and I feel hurt and empty and tired, but I don't cry and I want to cry. (*A pause.*) George tells me Margaret's still very ill. The doctors think she should go to Galveston. Someone has to tell her about how the trial came out. (*A pause.*) Will you come with me? I think I want to go to see Margaret. Will you come with me?

MRS. TOLLIVER: All right, Leonard. (*They start out as MARGARET comes into the yard from the back. She seems ill and nervous and frightened. Her hair and clothing are disarrayed. MRS. TOLLIVER first notices MARGARET.*) Margaret . . . (*LEONARD turns and sees her. He is shocked by how she has changed.*)

MARGARET: They let me dress and sit up in my room this morning. I heard two of the nurses talking about the outcome of the trial, and I slipped away; I wanted to talk to Billy. I haven't seen him for four months. I went by his boarding house, but he was gone.

MRS. TOLLIVER: He left Harrison. He told George he'd be in touch with you all after he was settled. (*MARGARET sees the sign advertising the apartment. She looks directly at LEONARD for the first time.*)

MARGARET: What apartment are you renting?

LEONARD: Ours.
MARGARET: Why?
LEONARD: I need the money.
MARGARET: There are things I want in there that are very dear to me.
LEONARD: I won't dispose of anything until you've been consulted.
MARGARET: I started to go in just now. The front door was locked. I looked inside their bedroom window. (*She starts to cry.*) Oh, my God. Oh, my God. All their things are still there, like they left them that morning. Their clothes. Their toys. Don't touch them. I don't want them ever touched.
LEONARD: They can't stay there, Margaret. I could never live there again, could you?
MARGARET: No, I could never live there again. (*She seems overcome by a kind of exhaustion. MRS. TOLLIVER goes to her. She helps her down on the steps.*)
MRS. TOLLIVER: Sit down, honey. (*MARGARET is crying again now, quietly, almost to herself. MRS. TOLLIVER comforts her.*) Sh. Sh. Don't Margaret, don't. (*GEORGE enters from the house.*)
GEORGE: Hello, Margaret.
MARGARET: Hello.
GEORGE: They called from the hospital. They were very concerned about you. I told them I'd bring you back. (*MARGARET turns toward LEONARD.*)
MARGARET: Leonard, forgive me. (*LEONARD doesn't answer her. He goes into the house. MARGARET waits a beat and then she goes toward GEORGE.*) All right. All right. I'll go. (*She starts out of the yard. GEORGE follows after her as the lights fade.*)

ACT II

SCENE 3

Six months later. The lights are brought up. GEORGE's Attorney-at-Law sign is down as well as the sign about the apartment. LESTER WHYTE stands at the corner of the stage. MR.CHARLIE and MISS HELEN are in the front yard seated on the steps.

CHARLIE: Lester Whyte's wife died in Houston. They say she had been dead for two days before anyone found her. I heard uptown his daughter is bringing her body here tomorrow for burial. Nobody can figure if Lester has been told or not. Do you think he'll go to the funeral?

MISS HELEN: I wonder. (*VIRGIL comes out with his suitcase. He puts it down on the edge of the yard and sits on it.*)

CHARLIE: Where are you going with your suitcase, Virgil?

VIRGIL: Back to Mississippi if I can catch anybody going that way. Do you know anybody who could give me a ride?

CHARLIE: No.

VIRGIL: Well, I'm not going to get discouraged. I expect somebody will come along. (*He sits watching off the highway. CHARLIE looks at MISS HELEN.*)

MISS HELEN: (*Whispering.*) He started that yesterday. Packed his suitcase and came out here and sat most of the day and asked anybody who came by if they were going to Mississippi. George and Lenora spent an hour trying to get him to come back into the house, but they couldn't. (*MRS. TOLLIVER and LEONARD come out.*)

MRS. TOLLIVER: Virgil, come on back into the house now. (*He looks at her but doesn't answer.*)

MISS HELEN: Don't worry about him, Lenora. He won't go any place. Humor him.

MRS. TOLLIVER: He told me last night that all his family were alive and living in Mississippi. His mother, his father, his sister, his brother. Said he'd been carried off by gypsies years ago and that he was trying to get back to them.

MISS HELEN: Did you ever find out where his sister is buried?

MRS. TOLLIVER: No. He finally remembered they were born in a place called Oyster Bay, but when I wrote there to the postmaster to inquire if the sister had been buried there, the letter was returned saying there was no such town any longer on record.

MISS HELEN: How old is he?

MRS. TOLLIVER: I think about seventy-six.

MISS HELEN: Lonny leaves today.

MRS. TOLLIVER: Yes, we're waiting now for him to come tell us goodbye.

MISS HELEN: I hear Eloise is going to have a baby.

MRS. TOLLIVER: Yes, about the same time as Bernice and George expect theirs.

MISS HELEN: I wonder why they've never had children before. They've been married all these years.

LEONARD: I asked him that the other night, and he said neither of them wanted a child until they could offer him more of a future than he could find here. (*LONNY and GEORGE come in.*)

VIRGIL: Boys, are either of you going in the direction of Mississippi?
LONNY: No, sir.
VIRGIL: Where are you going?
LONNY: California.
VIRGIL: What time do you leave, Lonny?
LONNY: In a few minutes.
MISS HELEN: I hear you and Eloise are having a baby. Congratulations.
LONNY: Thank you. Before I go, I wonder if one of you all would tell me something about my mother. I just thought the other day my child is going to be curious about my parents and I have nothing to tell them.
MISS HELEN: I knew your mother. Her mother was the daughter of one of my father's slaves. My father let his slaves work for wages, and your grandmother was married to a man who was also one of our slaves. And your mother and I had the same last names for that reason.
LONNY: Do you remember what my mother looked like?
MISS HELEN: Oh, yes.
LONNY: Was she light or dark?
MISS HELEN: She was not a real dark woman, was she, Lenora?
MRS. TOLLIVER: No.
MISS HELEN: She was tall and thin, and as I remember, very quiet.
LONNY: Thank you.
MRS. TOLLIVER: Lonny postponed leaving for three months until Leonard could find someone to take his place out at the farm.
MISS HELEN: How old were you when you came to live with Lenora, Lonny?
LONNY: I was four when my Mama came to work. When Mama died and Miss Lenora took me in, I was seven. (*A pause.*) I slept in that room in there, (*He points towards GEORGE's office.*) every night until I was nineteen. I'll never forget your kindness to me, Miss Lenora. And Eloise will never forget it. (*He hands her a tray.*) This is to remember us both by. (*She opens it.*)
MRS. TOLLIVER: Oh, Lonny, it's beautiful. (*She takes his hand.*) Goodbye, Lonny.
LONNY: Goodbye. I'm going to miss you all. Goodbye, Miss Helen, Mr. Charlie.
CHARLIE AND MISS HELEN: Goodbye, Lonny. (*LONNY goes to VIRGIL.*)
LONNY: Goodbye, Mr. Virgil.
VIRGIL: Who are you?
LONNY: I'm Lonny.

VIRGIL: Oh, yes. Do you know my nephew, George Tolliver? He lives in the town of Harrison. He has an elder brother named Leonard.

LONNY: Yes, sir.

VIRGIL: If you see them, please give them this message. Tell them I have a mother and father, sister and a brother in Mississippi. I haven't seen them for many years, because gypsies stole me away when I was a boy, but I want to get back to them now, and these people are holding me here against my wishes, because they want my money.

LONNY: Yes, sir. I have to go. (*LEONARD goes to LONNY.*)

LEONARD: (*Shaking hands with LONNY.*) Goodbye, Lonny. (*LONNY waves goodbye to the group. He and GEORGE go off together.*)

CHARLIE: All the nigras are leaving, going to California or Detroit or Chicago.

MRS. TOLLIVER: Margaret is coming home from the hospital today.

MISS HELEN: Is she?

MRS. TOLLIVER: We hired Herman to go to Galveston early this morning to get her.

MISS HELEN: Where will she stay?

MRS. TOLLIVER: Here with us until she is rested and can make plans for herself. I am going to stay in the front room. I'm going to give Margaret mine, because it's quieter and more secluded. It's very hard for Leonard, I know, to have her here. I'm sure you know they're separated, but there is nothing else we can do. Their apartment is rented now. Billy can't have her with him, and she can't be alone for a while. (*BERNICE comes into the yard. She has pink roses.*)

BERNICE: Good afternoon, Mr. Charlie. Hello, Miss Helen, Uncle Virgil. (*She hands the roses to MRS. TOLLIVER.*) I brought these for Margaret.

MRS. TOLLIVER: They're lovely. I know she'll appreciate them. (*CHARLIE starts out of the yard.*)

MISS HELEN: Where are you going, Charlie?

CHARLIE: I don't know. Going for a walk. Just restless. (*He goes.*)

MISS HELEN: It's our brother's birthday today. Though Charlie doesn't like to talk about him, I'm sure he remembers and it's upsetting him. (*MARGARET comes into the yard. She has a suitcase. She seems nervous and thin. MRS. TOLLIVER goes to her.*)

MRS. TOLLIVER: Hello, Margaret. Welcome home.

MARGARET: Thank you.

MRS. TOLLIVER: Bernice brought these roses for you.

MARGARET: Thank you. (*BERNICE goes to her.*)

BERNICE: Hello, Margaret.

MARGARET: Hello, Bernice. (*MISS HELEN goes to her.*)

MISS HELEN: Hello, Margaret.

MARGARET: Hello, Miss Helen. Hello, Uncle Virgil. I hear our apartment is rented.

MRS. TOLLIVER: Leonard wrote you that, didn't he, Margaret?

MARGARET: Oh, yes. He asked me for my permission. He said he would take out for me anything I wanted, but I didn't want anything except a few personal things. Did nice people rent it?

MRS. TOLLIVER: I think so.

MARGARET: Do I know them?

MRS. TOLLIVER: No, they just moved here. He's with an oil crew.

MARGARET: Then they won't live here long. People on oil crews never stay long in one place. Do they have any children?

MRS. TOLLIVER: No.

MARGARET: Then what did they want with such a large apartment?

MRS. TOLLIVER: They're expecting a child.

MARGARET: Oh. I didn't think there were children. The yard looked so neat and uncluttered.

MRS. TOLLIVER: Bernice and George are expecting a baby, Margaret.

MARGARET: I'm very happy for you, Bernice.

BERNICE: Thank you.

MISS HELEN: And Lonny and Eloise.

MARGARET: That's nice.

MRS. TOLLIVER: Come on inside, Margaret. I know you're tired after your trip. I'm going to let you have my room. You'll be quiet there.

MARGARET: Where will you stay?

MRS. TOLLIVER: Here in front.

MARGARET: I don't want to uproot you.

MRS. TOLLIVER: I don't mind. I want you to have a nice rest.

MARGARET: Thank you. (*They go inside.*)

BERNICE: I'm going over to George's office to tell him Margaret is here. (*She goes. VIRGIL looks over at MISS HELEN.*)

VIRGIL: Who was that lady that just came?

MISS HELEN: That was Margaret, Leonard's wife.

VIRGIL: Where has she been?

MISS HELEN: In Galveston.

VIRGIL: Enjoying the sea breezes.

MISS HELEN: No, I think she was in a hospital. (*MISS HELEN gets up.*)

VIRGIL: Where are you going?

MISS HELEN: To my room. (*MISS HELEN exits to her room. VIRGIL goes off left. LEONARD comes into the yard. He stands looking. MARGARET comes back down the hall and onto the porch. LEONARD turns towards the house. He sees her.*)

MARGARET: Hello, Leonard.
LEONARD: Hello, Margaret. When did you get here?
MARGARET: Just a while ago.
LEONARD: You're looking well.
MARGARET: Thank you. I'm feeling better.
LEONARD: I'm sorry I had to ask you to come back here to recuperate.
MARGARET: It's all right. I know these last months you've spent a lot of money.
LEONARD: I'm afraid I've had to. There's not much left.
MARGARET: Did my illness cost you a great deal?
LEONARD: Well . . .
MARGARET: I know it did. And did you pay for all Billy' s lawyers and his defense?
LEONARD: Yes.
MARGARET: And I remember at the time being told that he had the best, so I know that was expensive.
LEONARD: It was. He says he will pay me back some day, and I'm sure he will.
MARGARET: You don't have any money left?
LEONARD: No.
MARGARET: Was it my illness and Billy's defense that took all your money?
LEONARD: No. If you remember, I had a partnership agreement with Wally Smith and his family sued me. They made excessive demands but I thought it wiser to settle out of court; and the settlement was costly. I had to sell off the cattle and my rent houses, finally.
MARGARET: Your father's farm, too?
LEONARD: No, I have that left.
MARGARET: My driver told me you had gone back to the office.
LEONARD: About six weeks ago I began to go back. (*A pause.*)
MARGARET: You're thin, Leonard. You look older.
LEONARD: Well, I'm forty now.
MARGARET: Are you? You had a birthday while I was away, and I didn't remember. Forgive me. I've been very preoccupied.
LEONARD: That's all right.
MARGARET: Herman told me you had a monument put up for the boys.
LEONARD: Yes, a very simple one, but I think you'll like it.
MARGARET: I'm sure I will. (*A pause.*) George and Bernice are married now?
LEONARD: Yes.
MARGARET: Bernice was here when I arrived. She brought me a bouquet of pink roses.

LEONARD: That was very nice.

MARGARET: Leonard, your mother has given me her room, and I don't want to hurt her feelings, but I don't like it back there. It's too quiet. I wonder if I could have the front room and let her take her room back. I'm supposed to rest some in bed each day and at least while I'm resting I could watch the street and the people coming in and out of the house.

LEONARD: All right. Just go in there. I'll tell Mama. She won't mind.

MARGARET: Thank you. (*He starts away.*) Leonard . . . (*He pauses.*)

LEONARD: Yes?

MARGARET: I would like your forgiveness.

LEONARD: I can't give you that. I can give you money, take care of you, find a place for you to live.

MARGARET: I've forgiven you.

LEONARD: For what? What have you to forgive me for? For the death of my boys? For . . . (*A pause.*) I'm sorry. It's a mistake. We shouldn't try to see each other. It's too painful. I'll live some place else until you're stronger and I can find you a place of your own. (*He starts away.*)

MARGARET: Leonard . . . (*He turns again.*) Forgive me. Please, forgive me.

LEONARD: I forgive you. (*MARGARET takes up the suitcase that has been left in the hall and goes into the front room with it. LEONARD goes into the other part of the house. MARGARET puts the suitcase on the bed and begins to unpack. She takes some dresses into the closet. When she comes out, she has LEONARD's hunting rifle. She stands for a moment examining it. MRS. TOLLIVER comes down the hall. MARGARET hears her and quickly puts the gun in the closet. MRS. TOLLIVER knocks on the door.*)

MARGARET: Yes? (*MARGARET opens the door.*)

MRS. TOLLIVER: Leonard says you prefer this room.

MARGARET: I do if it's all right with you.

MRS. TOLLIVER: Why, certainly.

MARGARET: Thank you.

MRS. TOLLIVER: You have your suitcase?

MARGARET: Yes.

MRS. TOLLIVER: Let me unpack for you.

MARGARET: No, I have very little, I prefer doing it myself.

MRS. TOLLIVER: I'll clean out the closet and move my clothes back in my room.

MARGARET: Later, if you don't mind. I'm very tired now after my trip. I'd like to have some rest.

MRS. TOLLIVER: Certainly. (*She closes the door and goes back down* *the hall. MARGARET comes back into the room. She begins to unpack her suitcase. GEORGE comes into the yard. LEONARD comes out of GEORGE'S old office.)*

GEORGE: Bernice says Margaret is here.

LEONARD: Yes, she's in your old room.

GEORGE: How is she?

LEONARD: She seems very nervous. I know coming back is a terrible strain on her.

GEORGE: We'll do what we can to make her feel at home. I saw Lonny drive away. It gave me a funny feeling. I can't believe I'm not going to see him every day. Lonny saw me through a very difficult time in my life.

LEONARD: I know he did. (*A pause.*) George, I'm going away.

GEORGE: When?

LEONARD: As soon as I can.

GEORGE: For how long?

LEONARD: Forever, I suppose.

GEORGE: Where will you go, Brother?

LEONARD: I think I'd like Canada.

GEORGE: Canada?

LEONARD: Yes. I've thought so often of Palmer Evans leaving here to manage that big ranch out there. I want to go some place where I'm not known and I know no one. I'll sell the farm and give part of the money to Margaret, so she can live how she wants, and where she wants. Maybe you could take over the lease of my office . . . my secretary, I'll sell you my furniture.

GEORGE: I don't think I'd have any use for it, Leonard, for awhile. I'm planning to run again for County Attorney.

LEONARD: I didn't know what your plans were about County Attorney.

GEORGE: I would like to talk over with Bernice about our buying the farm though.

LEONARD: I don't think you could afford that, George. I'll need cash for that, and I'm going to ask for a great deal.

GEORGE: How much?

LEONARD: Five hundred dollars an acre.

GEORGE: No, I can't pay you that. (*A pause.*) However, Leonard, I do feel you should consider that I sold my half of the farm to you for considerably less, and consequently, I feel . . .

LEONARD: The circumstances were very different.

GEORGE: Not for me, Leonard.

LEONARD: For everybody. For everybody. Don't you have enough now? You have a wife. A law practice. You're expecting a child. You're

County Attorney. You have exactly what you want. Are you so greedy? What else do you want? This house? The land? Do you want me to give it to you? All right, I will. I'll give it to you, because I'm afraid of your wishes. God knows in what black, terrible manner you'll bring about . . . (*GEORGE starts out of the yard. LEONARD runs after him.*) George, I'm sorry. I didn't mean that. I swear to God, I didn't mean that. I'm glad for whatever you have. You've worked hard, and you've got what you deserve. Take the land for exactly what I paid you for it.

GEORGE: Leonard . . .

LEONARD: Please forgive me, Brother. I'm half crazy; I don't know what I'm doing or saying.

GEORGE: All right. (*He starts away.*)

LEONARD: Don't go away.(*He goes to him.*) You're still angry.

GEORGE: No, I'm not. (*GEORGE goes inside the house. LEONARD goes inside. LEONARD knocks on MARGARET'S door. She locks the door. She takes the gun out of the closet and loads it.*)

LEONARD: I want to tell you something, Margaret. (*A pause.*) Can you hear me? I'm going to Canada to live. I'm selling my farm to George. I'll give most of the money to you, and you can go where you like. (*A pause.*) Did you hear me? (*CHARLIE comes into the yard. He sees MARGARET in the room holding the gun. She has her back to the yard and faces LEONARD at the door, so she doesn't see CHARLIE. He goes quietly across the yard, goes to LEONARD in the hall.*)

CHARLIE: (*Whispering.*) Margaret has a gun in there.

LEONARD: (*Whispering.*) Go tell George. He's in with Mama. (*CHARLIE goes.*) Margaret? You heard what I said about Canada? And about selling the farms. Please open the door now, so we can discuss it. I have to make my plans. I want to go very soon.

MARGARET: Go away, please. I'm resting.

LEONARD: You're not resting. You're there by the door. Let me in. I know you have a gun in there. Put it down and open the door.

MARGARET: No, I won't.

LEONARD: Then I'm going to break down this door.

MARGARET: You do, and I'll shoot myself.

LEONARD: Margaret . . .

MARGARET: I will. Don't try to come in here.

LEONARD: Please put the gun away.

MARGARET: I don't want to live.

LEONARD: Yes, you do.

MARGARET: What have I to live for? To become a cripple with arthritis in some Houston boarding house like Lester Whyte's wife? I've nothing to live for. I want to die.

LEONARD: I meant it when I said that I forgive you.

MARGARET: No, you didn't. I had to beg you to get you to say it. You're telling me this now because you feel sorry for me, and you want to get here and take my gun from me . . .

LEONARD: Think of Billy . . .

MARGARET: Billy doesn't care anything about me any more. He didn't come to see me once in Galveston.

LEONARD: I do. I care about you.

MARGARET: No, you don't. Don't lie to me.

LEONARD: Come to Canada with me. We'll start our life there again. We'll live on a farm or a ranch. We'll work hard; we'll rest at nights. I don't rest at night now, Margaret. Sometimes I think I'm going to lose my mind if I don't sleep. I get in my car and I ride all night long like Brother used to. Remember? (*GEORGE and CHARLIE quietly come in the other door. They grab MARGARET. She screams. They take the gun. CHARLIE opens the door, and LEONARD comes in. MARGARET struggles to free herself, but they are too strong for her.*)

MARGARET: Leave me alone. All of you. Go away and leave me alone. All of you. Go away and leave me alone. (*GEORGE and CHARLIE go out. GEORGE has the gun. LEONARD still holds MARGARET. She has stopped struggling.*) I'm tired. I'm so tired. I was kept under lock and key there in Galveston. There was a girl down the hall who screamed in terror all night long. Everybody had somebody. Even the girl that screamed. She had a mother and a father, but I had no one . . . except attendants, doctors, nurses. My father died all alone. No one went near him except to take him food and water. Not Billy. Not Mama. When they went into his room, they wouldn't speak. They didn't ask him how he felt, or what he wanted, or would he like something to read. Not a word would they speak to him. Silence. Every night when they left me alone in my room at the hospital, I knew I was going to die like my father did. Alone. Lonely. I'm tired. I'm so tired. (*LEONARD gently leads her to the couch. She sits down. He sits beside her, holding her. Then he helps her to stretch out on the couch. She is exhausted. She closes her eyes. He watches her for a moment and then starts out of the room. She opens her eyes.*) Leonard . . . (*He comes back into the room.*)

LEONARD: Yes, Margaret?

MARGARET: Don't leave me, please. Please stay here.

LEONARD: All right.

MARGARET: Even if I sleep and close my eyes, don't leave me.

LEONARD: I won't.

MARGARET: I can rest if I know you're here beside me in the room. If I'm alone, I can't rest. I have to rest, Leonard.

LEONARD: I know.

MARGARET: I'm tired. I'm so tired. I can get well if I can only rest.

LEONARD: I won't leave. I promise.

MARGARET: Where's Lonny?

LEONARD: Gone to California. He and Eloise left today. Did Billy write you he had a job now?

MARGARET: No.

LEONARD: He's working on an oil boat in the Gulf. One of his friends in the Magnolia legal department got it for him. (*She closes her eyes. LEONARD puts a cover over her. VIRGIL gets up out of his chair in the yard, picks up his suitcase and comes into the house and into the living room.*) Shh.

VIRGIL: What's wrong son?

LEONARD: Margaret's asleep.

VIRGIL: Oh. Where am I going to stay?

LEONARD: You'll share the room over there with me.

VIRGIL: Oh. (*A pause.*) Well, it don't look like I'm going to get a ride today. I'm real discouraged.

LEONARD: Yes, sir. (*VIRGIL goes across the room carrying his suitcase. He stops by MARGARET's bedside.*)

VIRGIL: Is she the one been in Galveston?

LEONARD: Yes, sir.

VIRGIL: I once spent three days there with Sister. We stayed at the Buccaneer Hotel. It was criminal the prices they charged. I said to Sister . . .

LEONARD: Sh . . .

VIRGIL: (*Whispering.*) I said to Sister, "Let's get out of here before they take all our money." (*He picks up his suitcase and goes. MARGARET gives a sudden frightened scream. She sits up. LEONARD takes her and holds her. She opens her eyes.*)

LEONARD: It's all right. You just had a bad dream.

MARGARET: I have them all the time. Always the same one. I hear Horace and Leonard, Jr. calling to me from the river and I can't get to them. (*She closes her eyes again.*) I'm tired. I'm so tired.

LEONARD: Margaret, when you were sixteen and I was eighteen, and we first became secretly engaged, I wanted so to please you in all things. Sitting here now, watching over you, looking at you asleep and sorrowing, I wanted again so to please you.

MARGARET: I need you, Leonard. I want to sleep. (*LEONARD gets up. She lies again on the couch, then faintly she sings:*) Go tell Aunt Rhodie, Go tell Aunt Rhodie, Go tell Aunt Rhodie . . . That's the song

I used to sing to Leonard Jr., and to Horace I sang . . .

LEONARD: Go to sleep. (*She closes her eyes again. GEORGE comes into the room. He motions to LEONARD to meet him outside. GEORGE goes out to the yard. LEONARD watches MARGARET to be sure she is asleep and then goes out to GEORGE.*)

GEORGE: I just wanted to tell you before I go that I want you to sell your farm for all you can get.

LEONARD: George . . .

GEORGE: If you can get a thousand dollars an acre, I want you to have it. I'm sorry I talked just now in a way I had no right to. I can't realistically consider buying that land at any price. I would have to borrow from the bank and with the new election just a year off, I'll need the money I can get together for that. So will you please forget I ever mentioned it to you and go sell it for all you can, and don't worry the least about me.

LEONARD: Couldn't you buy half the farm back? Your half, I mean.

GEORGE: I don't see how.

LEONARD: I wouldn't require any cash. You could pay me so much a month; make it over as long a period as you like.

GEORGE: I thought you needed cash. I thought the whole purpose of this was to get as much money as you could, so you could leave for Canada.

LEONARD: Maybe I won't go. It came to me as I was sitting there by Margaret, that I was leaving out of shame and that's no reason to go any place. To go like Lonny did to California, or any place to better yourself, or to be with your family, is one thing. But my family is here. My father is buried here, and my boys. My brother lives here, and his wife and my mother . . . (*A pause.*) Just now Margaret sat up in bed screaming. When I woke her she told me she heard the boys calling to her. Brother, sometimes I wake up at night and hear those two little boys calling to me out of that water to save them, and I can't save them. They've gone down in that water forever. (*A pause.*) But I can try to save myself and their mama, and that can count for something. (*A pause.*) Mama told me when I took Billy into my law firm it broke your heart. Did it?

GEORGE: I guess so. It seemed at the time anyway. But don't lose any sleep over it. It's mended very well.

LEONARD: I'm going to ask Margaret to resume our marriage. She needs me.

GEORGE: I expect she does.

LEONARD: She's never needed me before, and I never needed her before. I do now.

MARGARET: (*Calling.*) Leonard. Leonard.

LEONARD: I'm coming. I'm just out in the yard. (*LEONARD goes into the bedroom. GEORGE leaves.*)

LEONARD: Here I am. Now go on back to sleep. (*She closes her eyes. VIRGIL comes into the room. LESTER WHYTE comes into the yard.*)

VIRGIL: See that old man out there. He killed his wife's lover. He walks the streets all night.

LEONARD: Yes, sir.

VIRGIL: Once when I was still in South Texas I had this dream. It was just as plain to me. I dreamt I was a boy still, eight or nine, and this Preacher was there and I was crying. He kept saying, "Forgiveness," and I kept crying, and he kept saying, "Forgiveness."

LEONARD: Forgiveness?

VIRGIL: That's all he said. Forgiveness. And I woke up to tell my mama and papa about the dream, and of course, they weren't there. No one was there, and I was alone. Who was there to forgive? (*VIRGIL sits beside LEONARD.*) Forgiveness. That's all he said. But what was there to forgive, except myself, or ask forgiveness of? Nobody. Nobody. Except myself. (*A pause.*) Who are you, son? Leonard or George?

LEONARD: Leonard.

VIRGIL: Are you the oldest or the youngest?

LEONARD: The oldest.

VIRGIL: Who am I? Horace or Virgil?

LEONARD: Virgil.

VIRGIL: Am I the oldest?

LEONARD: Yes, sir.

VIRGIL: I broke my brother's heart, and he died. By his own hand, he died. Did you break your brother's heart?

LEONARD: Yes, sir.

VIRGIL: And did he die?

LEONARD: No, sir. He is alive, and his heart has mended very well.

VIRGIL: Are you alive?

LEONARD: Yes, sir, and my heart is broken.

VIRGIL: Who broke it?

LEONARD: I did.

VIRGIL: George?

LEONARD: No, sir. Leonard.

VIRGIL: Do you think it will mend?

LEONARD: I hope. In time. (*VIRGIL leans his head back on the chair. He closes his eyes. LEONARD is watching MARGARET as the lights fade.*)

NIGHT SEASONS

NIGHT SEASON premiered at the American Stage Company in Teaneck, New Jersey on February 26, 1993. It was directed by Horton Foote with the following cast:

LAWRENCE: Devon Abner
MR. CHESTNUT: Lewis Arlt
MERCER: George Bamford
ROSA: Jo Ann Cunningham
LAURA LEE: Hallie Foote
SKEETER: Frank Girardeau
THURMAN: Michael Hadge
MR. BARSOTY: Howard Hensel
MR. WEEMS: James Pritchett
DOLLY: Barbara Sims
JOSIE WEEMS: Jean Stapleton
DELIA: Karen Trott
DORIS: Beatrice Winde

Characters

JOSIE WEEMS
MR. WEEMS, Josie's husband
THURMAN WEEMS, Josie's oldest son
LAURA LEE WEEMS, Josie's daughter
SKEETER WEEMS, Josie's youngest son
DOLLY, Josie's niece, Rosa's first cousin
ROSA, Josie's niece, Dolly's first cousin
DORIS, a practical nurse for Josie
MERCER HADLEY, Dolly's husband
LAWRENCE, Josie's nephew, Dolly's brother, Rosa's first cousin
DELIA, Thurman's wife
MR. CHESTNUT, Laura Lee's fiance
MR. BARSOTY, Laura Lee's beaux

Setting

Harrison, Texas 1917–1963. The play moves back and forth in time between the years 1917 and 1963, taking place in the various living areas of the Weem's family. A hotel bedroom, waiting room and dining room and the bedroom and the living room of their later small apartment. They are a wealthy family, who choose to live in the simplest of circumstances. The furnishings around them are utilitarian and non-descript. We also visit now and then the living room of Mrs. Weems' niece, Dolly. She lives, too, very modestly, but does so out of necessity.The lighting should be a series of cross fades, rarely blacking out, and we should see the action go from area to area as the play progresses. Up stage center is a huge birthday card wishing Josie a Happy 93rd Birthday. The card is made of scrim. Barsoty and Rosa appear behind the scrim as they sing their songs.

NIGHT SEASONS

ACT I

At Rise JOSIE WEEMS, 93, is seated in a wheelchair. Near her is a practical nurse, DORIS, a black woman, 78. Today, November 9, 1963 is JOSIE's birthday. DOLLY, JOSIE's niece, enters. She has a small present for JOSIE.

DOLLY: Has Aunt Josie had many callers today?
DORIS: No'm. Not too many.
DOLLY: Have Cousin Thurman and Cousin Skeeter been over?
DORIS: Mr. Thurman has. Mr. Skeeter telephoned.
DOLLY: Here's a card from Cousin Rosa.
DORIS: She's still in Austin ain't she?
DOLLY: Yes. She works in a cafeteria there. She never gets home anymore. She gets a week's vacation but she says she's so tired she only wants to stay in her room and rest.
DORIS: I use to love to hear Miss Rosa sing.
DOLLY: So did I. (*ROSA, another niece of JOSIE's, appears behind the scrim. She sings "Roses of Picardy." She has a pleasant, sweet, soprano voice.*)
ROSA: (*Singing.*) ROSES ARE SHINING IN PICARDY IN THE HUSH OF THE SILVER DEW (*ROSA disappears.*)
DORIS: I seen them moving Miss Rosa's old house yesterday.
DOLLY: Yes, Cousin Thurman sold it for four thousand dollars. (*ROSA again appears.*)
ROSA: (*Singing.*) ROSES ARE FLOWERING IN PICARDY BUT THERE'S NEVER A ROSE LIKE YOU (*ROSA disappears.*)
DORIS: Miss Rosa's Mama raised you didn't she?
DOLLY: Yes. She raised me and my brother—Lawrence.
DORIS: He's dead isn't he?
DOLLY: Yes, he's been dead now a long time.
DORIS: Mr. Lawrence married Miss Alice Temple didn't he?
DOLLY: Yes.
DORIS: Miss Rosa never married?
DOLLY: No. (*The piano is heard in the distance playing LAURA LEE's theme. LAURA LEE WEEMS walks slowly across the stage.*)
DORIS: Miss Laura Lee never married. I never understood that. She was so pretty and popular, too.

DOLLY: Yes, she was.

DORIS: She had a lot of beaux didn't she?

DOLLY: As a young girl she did.

DORIS: Sure did. I know she did.

DOLLY: When she got older she had two very serious suitors. Mr. Barsoty and Mr. Chestnut. (*The old woman stirs around in the wheelchair. DOLLY notices this. JOSIE has opened her eyes.*)

DORIS: She's awake. Did you have a nice rest, Aunt Josie? Happy Birthday. And I hope you have many, many more.

JOSIE: Oh, don't wish me that, Honey.

DOLLY: I have a present for you.

JOSIE: Thank you, Honey.

DOLLY: It's not so much really. It's just a handkerchief. (*She opens it.*) Lavender. I remembered it's your favorite color.

JOSIE: Where is Lawrence? (*DOLLY doesn't answer. LAWRENCE appears behind the scrim.*) Is your brother Lawrence here Dolly?

DORIS: No'm. Miss Josie. Mr. Lawrence is dead. You remember that?

JOSIE: Oh, yes. Who died first Lawrence or Laura Lee? (*LAWRENCE disappears.*)

DORIS: Lawrence.

JOSIE: Did Laura Lee die before or after Mr. Weems?

DOLLY: She died after Uncle, Aunt Josie.

JOSIE: Laura Lee always accused me of interfering in her life. That's why she never married, she said. "I never stopped my niece Dolly," I said. How old are you, Dolly?

DOLLY: Seventy.

JOSIE: My God . . . My God. I'm ninety-three. Did you know that? How old was Lawrence when he died?

DOLLY: Forty-two.

JOSIE: Mr. Weems was sixty-five when he died. Laura Lee was sixty. And I'm ninety-three. Did Rosa sing at your funeral, Dolly?

DOLLY: Not at my funeral, Auntie. I'm not dead yet. At my wedding. Remember?

JOSIE: Oh, yes. Thurman tried to talk sense into Mercer before the wedding he told me. He always worried so about you marrying Mercer. We all did. (*The lights on upstage center are lowered and the lights are brought up downstage right. MERCER HADLEY is there. THURMAN WEEMS, JOSIE's oldest son, small, wiry, a constant worried look on his face, enters.*)

THURMAN: Mercer . . .

MERCER: Morning, Thurman.

THURMAN: Dolly told Mama you had a little luck come your way.

MERCER: Sure did.
THURMAN: How much did your Uncle leave you?
MERCER: Twenty thousand dollars.
THURMAN: I hope you're gonna be wise and invest it.
MERCER: Dolly and I want to have a nice honeymoon.
THURMAN: Mercer put it all away. Fix it so you can't gamble.
MERCER: Did Dolly tell you we planned to go to New Orleans on our honeymoon? We'll stay a week.
THURMAN: You do gamble. You . . .
MERCER: (*Interrupting.*) Rosa is going to sing at our wedding.
THURMAN: I heard you spent forty dollars for a silk shirt to be married in.
MERCER: I did. (*A pause.*) But I'm not gambling. Whoever said I was gambling is a liar. You can tell them I said so. (*He leaves. THURMAN sighs and leaves as the lights fade. The lights are brought up downstage left. JOSIE gets out of her wheelchair. She is now in her midfifties. She enters down stage left. She is joined by LAURA LEE WEEMS, JOSIE's daughter, who is doing her nails—buffing them. She is a handsome woman, and dresses very simply but in excellent taste. THURMAN comes in. It is LAURA LEE's room in the Harrison Hotel.*)
JOSIE: Dolly had another little girl last night. Sister and I are going over to see her in a few minutes. (*She looks up at him.*) What's the matter, son? You look depressed . . .
THURMAN: I am. (*He sighs. He looks up at LAURA LEE.*) Do you have a date tonight, Sister?
LAURA LEE: Yes.
THURMAN: What time?
LAURA LEE: Six. (*She finishes her nails.*) He's picking me up at the hotel after we finish supper.
THURMAN: Mr. Chestnut?
LAURA LEE: Yes.
THURMAN: Sister, I wish he'd get himself another job.
LAURA LEE: Why?
THURMAN: It hurts me to have to say to people when they ask me what your beaux does . . . to have to say he's a baker.
LAURA LEE: He's a gentleman—I tell you that.
JOSIE: Where's Delia, son?
THURMAN: She's out in the car.
JOSIE: Why don't you ask her to come in?
THURMAN: She won't. She's mad about something. (*Again he sighs.*) Did you know Mercer wasn't at home last night when Dolly had her baby?

Did Dolly tell you that?

JOSIE: No.

LAURA LEE: I don't think she would tell us that. She has pride, you know. Mother made it very clear she didn't want her to marry him.

JOSIE: That was before he inherited the twenty thousand dollars.

THURMAN: Mercer doesn't have twenty thousand dollars now.

JOSIE: I guess not. The way they bought clothes and that honeymoon trip to New Orleans.

THURMAN: He's lost it all. Every cent . . . He lost ten thousand dollars gambling in the past week.

JOSIE: (*Alarmed.*) Good God, Thurman . . .

THURMAN: He has not a dime. Not a red cent. (*MR. WEEMS, JOSIE's husband, comes in.*)

JOSIE: Mr. Weems, Mercer has lost all of his money . . . gambling . . .

MR. WEEMS: Well, they live in a house.

THURMAN: A rented house.

MR. WEEMS: But it's a house. Where do we live? In two hotel rooms. What good does money do us? I could own the finest house in town: we had a beautiful home . . .

JOSIE: (*Ignoring her husband.*) How do you know this, son?

THURMAN: Everyone in town knows it. It's the first thing I heard when I opened the bank this morning. (*DELIA WEEMS, THURMAN's wife, comes in. She has a pretty face, but her discontent is immediately apparent.*)

DELIA: How much longer are you going to be, Thurman?

THURMAN: (*Snarling at her.*) Why?

DELIA: You told me five minutes.

THURMAN: Well, I may be longer than five minutes. God Damn it . . . I may be twenty minutes or thirty minutes. We have something serious to discuss in our family.

LAURA LEE: Mother, are we going over to see Dolly?

JOSIE: I guess so. Mercer has gambled all their money, Delia.

DELIA: Thurman told me.

JOSIE: I don't know what they're going to do now.

DELIA: Maybe he'll have to go to work like everybody else.

JOSIE: Could you give him a job at the bank, Mr. Weems? (*He is pouting and doesn't answer.*) Mr. Weems?

MR. WEEMS: No.

JOSIE: Why not? He's been trained as a bookkeeper. He used to keep books over at the gin.

THURMAN: Mercer is drunk half the time now, Mother. Nobody is going to hire him anyplace now.

JOSIE: Then what's going to happen to Dolly?

THURMAN: I don't know.

DELIA: I don't have a bit of sympathy for her. She knew what he was before she married him.

THURMAN: You never have sympathy with anybody. Do you?

DELIA: I'm not a sentimental fool like you. If that's what you mean.

THURMAN: I don't care what you mean. I don't give a God Damn about what you mean . . .

DELIA: I'm sure you don't. And I don't give a God Damn about you either. Only I'm telling you this. You're not helping Mercer by giving him money.

THURMAN: I'm not giving him money.

DELIA: Don't lie to me. I saw you . . .

THURMAN: I loaned him money. God Damn it. I loaned him money.

DELIA: You'll never get it back. You know that. (*A pause.*) How much did you loan him?

THURMAN: It's none of your damn business.

DELIA: Oh, it's none of my damn business?

THURMAN: No.

DELIA: Yes, it is some of my damn business. As long as I have to live in that stinking rent house I live in, and scrape and save the way I do on the money you give me to feed us. It is my damn business. And I'll make it my damn business. Because I'm not going to live my life like your mother and father and your sister in a ugly hotel room . . . having to eat dinner every night in the hotel dining room with a bunch of homeless old maids. (*THURMAN walks out. She screams after him.*) Don't you walk out on me. You come back here . . . Thurman . . . You come back here. (*She turns to them in a fury.*) He has the rottenest disposition of anyone I know. (*She turns to them.*) Why do you allow him to act so? Why do you allow him? (*She leaves. JOSIE sighs and shakes her head in distress. A pause.*)

LAURA LEE: They should never have gotten married.

JOSIE: I guess not. (*A pause.*) What time is it, Mr. Weems? (*MR. WEEMS takes a gold pocket watch out of his pocket.*)

MR. WEEMS: Four o'clock.

JOSIE: Do you think we have time to go over to see Dolly, Sister, before supper?

LAURA LEE: I don't know.

JOSIE: Do you want to walk over with us, Mr. Weems?

MR. WEEMS: No, thank you. (*LAURA LEE goes to her father.*)

LAURA LEE: Do you know that Thurman offered Mr. Chestnut a position at the bank, father?

MR. WEEMS: Yes.
LAURA LEE: Was it your idea?
JOSIE: Now, sister . . .
LAURA LEE: Was it your idea, Father?
MR. WEEMS: No . . .
LAURA LEE: Was it Thurman's?
MR. WEEMS: I don't think so.
JOSIE: It was mine, Sister. Now we all like Mr. Chestnut fine, but your father and your brothers worry about his owning a bakery. He does his banking with them. They know how little he has. What kind of future is there in owning a bakery in a small town? Do you know all that he has in the bank is . . .
LAURA LEE: I don't care what he has in the bank. Do you hear me? I don't care . . .
JOSIE: All right, Miss Lady . . . Don't care . . . Don't care . . . (*A pause.*) Sister where is the present we were going to take Dolly's baby? (*LAURA LEE walks over to a table and gets it. She hands it to her mother.*)
LAURA LEE: I don't want to go now.
JOSIE: Why?
LAURA LEE: I don't feel well.
JOSIE: What's wrong?
LAURA LEE: I don't know. I just don't feel well.
JOSIE: I wonder how much Thurman loaned Mercer? Do you know, Mr. Weems?
MR. WEEMS: No. Want me to drive you over?
JOSIE: No, I'll walk.
MR. WEEMS: It's hotter'n blazes out there.
JOSIE: I have my parasol. (*She gets it and opens it with a snap. She goes on out.*)
LAURA LEE: Father, put your foot down. Stand up to her. You have all the money you want. If you want a home get yourself a home. (*A pause.*) Why did you ever sell our home in the first place?
MR. WEEMS: I don't know.
LAURA LEE: It was such a beautiful home, father.
MR. WEEMS: I know. (*A pause.*) I think often of how it happened. How did I ever allow myself to agree to it? I guess it was when she got so sick that time and we took her to Galveston for her operation. They didn't expect her to live . . . and when she survived the operation they told me she would have to be very careful for many years to come. So, I brought her on back home and I got her as many servants as she wanted. But she quarreled with them all. She was so particular

how things were done, none of them could stand it. I came home one day to find her cleaning the house, to get it like she wanted . . . and I told her she would have to stop working this way because it would kill her, if she didn't and she said then to sell the house and get her something she could take care of without killing herself, and I said that wasn't necessary we'd get her more servants. She said she couldn't take the Negroes anymore, they made her nervous and I said I'd get her a White woman and she said no they were all lazy and shiftless . . . and they would resent her giving them orders. (*A pause.*) And so we compromised. We shut up the house for six months and moved to the hotel until she got her strength back. And then, she wouldn't go back. She said at first she would go back to a smaller one-story house, so I sold our big house and we began to look for a smaller one . . . she's never found anything, of course, that pleases her. She never will. (*A pause. MR. BARSOTY, appears behind the scrim upstage.*)

MR. BARSOTY: (*Singing.*) OH, DON'T YOU REMEMBER SWEET ALICE, BEN BOLT, SWEET ALICE WITH HAIR—SO BROWN.

MR. WEEMS: I got a card from Barsoty yesterday. (*A pause.*) You got one too, didn't you?

LAURA LEE: Yes.

MR. BARSOTY: (*Singing.*) SHE WEPT WITH DELIGHT WHEN YOU GAVE HER A SMILE, (*ROSA joins him behind the scrim.*)

ROSA AND BARSOTY: (*Singing.*) AND—TREMBLED WITH FEAR AT YOUR FROWN?

MR. WEEMS: Mine came from New Orleans. Where did yours come from?

LAURA LEE: New Orleans.

MR. BARSOTY: (*Singing.*) IN THE OLD CHURCH—YARD IN THE VALLEY, BEN BOLT,

ROSA AND BARSOTY: (*Singing.*) IN A CORNER OBSCURE AND ALONE, (*From where she is sitting, LAURA LEE joins ROSA and BARSOTY in singing.*)

LAURA LEE, ROSA, AND BARSOTY: (*Singing.*) THEY HAVE FITTED A SLAB OF—GRANITE SO GRAY, AND SWEET ALICE LIES UNDER THE STONE; (*LAURA LEE stops singing.*)

MR. WEEMS: When you and Rosa and Barsoty sang "Sweet Alice Ben Bolt" I never heard anything lovelier. He's been gone three years. He said once he left he would never come back, and he never has. (*A pause.*) He didn't say on my card what he was doing. Did he on yours?

LAURA LEE: No.

MR. WEEMS: Mr. Barsoty was your one beaux your mother approved of you marrying.

LAURA LEE: That's because she knew I didn't want to marry him.

MR. WEEMS: Why didn't you want to marry him? He came from a fine family; he was always so attentive to you. Your brother liked him; your mother liked him; I liked him. Why didn't you want to marry him?

LAURA LEE: I don't know. I just didn't want to marry anyone then. When he asked me that last time he said if I refused him, he'd never ask me again, but would leave and never come back . . . I didn't believe him. He had said that before and he always came back.

BARSOTY: (*Singing.*) THE MILL HAS GONE TO DECAY, BEN BOLT,

MR. WEEMS: Is this the first card you've had from him since he left?

LAURA LEE: Yes.

ROSA AND BARSOTY: (*Singing.*) AND A QUIET NOW REIGNS ALL AROUND. (*Again LAURA LEE joins BARSOTY and ROSA in the singing.*)

LAURA LEE, ROSA, AND BARSOTY: (*Singing.*) SEE THE OLD RUSTIC PORCH, WITH ITS ROSES SO SWEET LIES SCATTER'D AND FALLEN TO THE GROUND; (*LAURA LEE, ROSA, and BARSOTY stop singing. ROSA and BARSOTY disappear.*)

LAURA LEE: Father, what's to become of Dolly and Rosa?

MR. WEEMS: Your mother and your brother will always take care of them.

LAURA LEE: Father?

MR. WEEMS: Yes.

LAURA LEE: Promise me one thing: That I will never be dependent on mother or my brothers. Promise me that?

MR. WEEMS: You never will be. I put a thousand dollars in a savings account for you every now and then. (*A pause.*) Do you want to know what you're worth at present?

LAURA LEE: What?

MR. WEEMS: Ten thousand dollars. (*She kisses him on the cheek.*)

LAURA LEE: Thank you.

MR. WEEMS: Never tell your mother or your brother. They wouldn't approve. Sister, are you going to marry Mr. Chestnut?

LAURA LEE: I don't know, father.

MR. WEEMS: He's a nice man. Quiet. I only hope he's not a fortune hunter.

LAURA LEE: Why do you say that?

MR. WEEMS: No reason. I just worry about it, sometimes. (*ROSA and BARSOTY appear.*)

LAURA LEE, ROSA, AND BARSOTY: (*Singing.*) AND OF ALL THE FRIENDS WHO WERE SCHOOLMATES THEN, THERE ARE ONLY YOU AND I. (*As the lights fade on the area down left . . . they are brought up on the area down right. It is the living room of the house MERCER and DOLLY rent. MERCER is seated in a chair holding a baby.*)

JOSIE: (*Calling off stage.*) Dolly . . .

MERCER: Come in, Aunt Josie . . . (*She comes into the area.*) Dolly is sound asleep. I'll wake her.

JOSIE: No, don't do that, son. (*She looks at the baby.*) She's a pretty baby. How much does she weigh?

MERCER: Eight pounds.

JOSIE: Were you here when she was born?

MERCER: No.

JOSIE: Have you named her?

MERCER: Mary . . .

JOSIE: I've heard distressing news, Mercer.

MERCER: Yes, Ma'am . . .

JOSIE: Why didn't you invest your money like you promised? (*A pause, he doesn't answer.*) I begged you to, son. Thurman begged you to.

MERCER: Yes, Ma'am. And I should have. I realize that now, of course.

JOSIE: How much did you lose, son?

MERCER: Ten thousand.

JOSIE: My God! That's a fortune!

MERCER: Yes, Ma'am.

JOSIE: Was that all you had?

MERCER: Yes, Ma'am. Every penny.

JOSIE: What will you do now, son?

MERCER: That's a good question. I hope to get myself a job keeping books. You know I used to keep the books over at the gin.

JOSIE: I remember. How many bookkeepers are needed in this town, son?

MERCER: Not many, I guess. (*A pause.*) I spoke to Thurman about my keeping books at the bank and he said he would like to help me out, but that he was going to have to give a job to Laura Lee's beaux. I didn't know Mr. Chestnut was a bookkeeper.

JOSIE: I don't think he is. He's going to have to go into Houston and go to business school.

MERCER: Is that what he's going to do?

JOSIE: That's what he will have to do if he's going to work at the bank. (*A pause.*) Mercer, do I smell liquor on your breath?

MERCER: I don't think so.

JOSIE: I think I do, son.

MERCER: Well, you might at that. I did have a drink early this morning when I came home and found the baby here. That unnerved me, and so I had a drink to settle me down. But that was almost eight hours ago, and I'm surprised you can still smell anything at all on my breath.

JOSIE: Who won your money, son?

MERCER: It wasn't anyone from around here. Mr. Burgess—he is from Galveston. Everyone from around here lost. Not as much as I did, but they all lost. Mr. Albert Murray lost, Little Bobby Tate lost, Lawrence lost. (*A pause.*) Oh, I'm sorry I said that. I said that without thinking. I promised Lawrence I wouldn't ever tell you he was there.

JOSIE: How much did Lawrence lose?

MERCER: I don't know.

JOSIE: Didn't he try to stop you? (*A pause.*) What does he think is going to happen to his sister now that her husband has lost all his money?

MERCER: Lawrence is getting married. Did he tell you?

JOSIE: No. Who is he marrying?

MERCER: Alice Temple.

JOSIE: What's he going to marry on? He doesn't have a nickel. Once he gets one he starts gambling. (*LAWRENCE, JOSIE's nephew, comes in. He's the age of MERCER and THURMAN.*)

LAWRENCE: Hello, Aunt Josie.

JOSIE: Hello, Lawrence. (*He goes to the baby.*)

LAWRENCE: Is this my new niece? What's her name?

MERCER: Mary.

LAWRENCE: Aunt Josie. Alice Temple and I are going to be married. (*A pause.*) Are you pleased?

JOSIE: She's a lovely girl. She is beautiful. Yes, I'm pleased.

LAWRENCE: Her family aren't pleased. I said to Alice last night "I know I don't have anything, but I must say for the wife of a former saloon keeper to carry on like your mother does . . . "

JOSIE: Don't you think you'd better get yourself a job now, before you think about marrying?

LAWRENCE: I have myself a job. I begin next week. I'm going to clerk for Mr. Abott in his grocery store.

JOSIE: How much are you going to make?

LAWRENCE: He's starting me at fourteen dollars a week.

JOSIE: Can you support a wife on that?

LAWRENCE: She's going to work too. She is going to teach music. (*She gets up.*)

JOSIE: I brought this for the baby. Tell Dolly I'll be over tomorrow to see her.

MERCER: All right, Miss Josie. (*She goes.*)

LAWRENCE: Did Aunt Josie hear about your loss?

MERCER: Yes.

LAWRENCE: How did she take it?

MERCER: She was upset. She was real upset.

LAWRENCE: Did you tell Dolly?

MERCER: I didn't have to. Someone had already told her.

LAWRENCE: How did she take it?

MERCER: You know how your sister is. She never says anything. I told her I was very sorry, and she said she knew that. I told her I'd be getting a job now.

LAWRENCE: Do you have any money?

MERCER: Twenty-five dollars I borrowed from Thurman.

LAWRENCE: Can you loan me some of it?

MERCER: How much?

LAWRENCE: Ten dollars.

MERCER: Sure. (*Lights fade downstage right and are brought up, up center. JOSIE is asleep. DOLLY and Doris are near her. SKEETER, JOSIE's youngest son, comes in. He is small and wiry like his father.*)

DORIS: Hello, Mr. Skeeter.

SKEETER: Hello, Doris.

DOLLY: Hello, Skeeter. She's sound asleep.

SKEETER: She been asleep all afternoon?

DOLLY: No. She's been awake part of the time.

SKEETER: Here. (*He hands her flowers.*) Put these in water for her. (*DORIS takes them and goes on off. He goes over to the bed, JOSIE opens her eyes and looks at him.*) Hello, Mama.

JOSIE: Hello, son.

SKEETER: It's Skeeter.

JOSIE: I know who you are.

SKEETER: Lovella said she'd come over after supper. She had to go to Houston today. Delia come over?

JOSIE: No. Thurman said she'd be over too this afternoon. She had her bridge club. Who entertained Delia's bridge club today?

DOLLY: Ada Cox.

JOSIE: Oh, yes. (*DORIS comes in with the flowers.*)

SKEETER: Happy Birthday, Mama!

JOSIE: Oh, thank you, son. (*He also takes a red poppy out of his pocket and pins it on her.*)

SKEETER: And I brought you a poppy. They're selling them for Armistice Day.

JOSIE: Thank you. (*She looks up at him.*) Mrs. Andrews was over to see me yesterday and she said "Skeeter is so quiet; he never says a word, and he never smiles about anything." I said, "You can thank the First World War for that. As a young man, before he went to France, he was laughing and talking and joking all the time, and then when the Armistice was signed and he came home we never heard him laugh much again, or smile . . . nor talk a whole lot. But he still has the disposition of a Saint, I said.

DOLLY: Potter Reavis, Hugh's brother that was shell-shocked, died yesterday in Austin in the Veteran's Hospital.

JOSIE: How old was he?

DOLLY: I don't know. How old would you say he was, Skeeter?

SKEETER: About sixty-five.

JOSIE: I'm ninety-three. How old are you, son?

SKEETER: Sixty-seven.

JOSIE: That's right. (*DELIA and THURMAN come in.*)

DELIA: Happy Birthday! (*She hands her a slice of cake wrapped in a napkin.*) Ada Cox sent you this from the party. I didn't have time to buy you a present, but I will tomorrow. Anything you want in particular?

JOSIE: Not a thing in this world. How was the party?

DELIA: It was lovely.

JOSIE: What kind of refreshments did she serve?

DELIA: Creamed chicken in patty shells, molded salad, cake and ice cream for dessert. I had terrible hands all afternoon. (*She rubs her head.*) I have a splitting headache.

THURMAN: What are you telling us that for?

DELIA: I'm not telling you that for any reason.

THURMAN: This is Mother's birthday. Can't you for five minutes think of anyone but yourself? (*He takes some papers out.*) I brought these over for you to sign, Mother.

JOSIE: What are they, son?

THURMAN: Just the last few papers putting the rest of your land in Skeeter and my name.

JOSIE: Put them here and I'll sign them tomorrow.

THURMAN: Don't forget. (*To DOLLY.*) That stupid lawyer should have had this all done five years ago, when we made the other transfers. He claims he had never heard of this land until this week. (*To his mother.*) You'll have to live three years longer mother, to keep the government from getting a big part of this. (*To DOLLY.*) We learned our lesson when Laura Lee died. She left no will, of course, she was so young she didn't expect to die.

DELIA: She was sixty when she died. I don't think that's so young.

THURMAN: Well, she'd never been sick in her life and we certainly never expected her to die. It seemed young to me.

DELIA: Sixty isn't young. Plenty of people die at sixty.

THURMAN: God Damn it, Delia. That's not the point. Nobody cares whether you think sixty is young or not. What the hell's the matter with you? Do you have to disagree with everything anybody says?

DELIA: I'm just expressing an opinion. I have a right to express an opinion.

THURMAN: I don't want to hear your damn opinions. I'm sick of your damn opinions.

DELIA: And I'm sick of yours, too. (*A pause.*) What were you saying before?

THURMAN: How the hell do I know what I was saying before? You get me so rattled, I can't think. You're always disagreeing with everybody like a God Damn Bolshevik.

DELIA: You were talking about Laura Lee and her will.

THURMAN: Oh, yes. Well, all I wanted to tell Dolly was that since sister left no will, the government held everything up forever. They got a terrible amount, too. Right away, I began to fix mother's and mine so they can't touch it. All they do is waste it anyway. Just give it away to worthless people.

JOSIE: Just give it away?

THURMAN: So, you better live three more years.

DOLLY: How old is your mother, Doris?

DORIS: A hundred. Born right at the end of slavery times. I can't read and write but she can. Mrs. Hood taught her when she was ten years old to read and write.

DELIA: Didn't you go to school?

DORIS: No, Ma'am. I been working for white people since I was eight. You don't have to know how to read and write to clean and cook.

DELIA: I think we'd all live longer if we didn't worry about money and the government.

THURMAN: What the hell do you know about money and the government? You've never had to worry about anything all your life. I give you everything you want.

DELIA: I've never gotten anything out of you without a torndown fight.

THURMAN: God Damn it, haven't you got the finest house in town?

DELIA: I like my house . . . but it took ten years of fights to get it.

JOSIE: I got a card from Rosa, son. (*Dolly hands it to him. He reads it aloud.*)

THURMAN: (*Reading from the card.*) "Bluebirds are the symbol of true happiness, they say, So that's why there are bluebirds On your special card today, To hope that on your birthday You'll be happy as a song, And everything that's finest Will be yours the whole year long." (*THURMAN puts the card down and turns to his mother.*) I'm surprised Cousin Rosa didn't call up today and wish you a Happy Birthday.

DELIA: She probably can't afford to call up on the phone. She makes very little working at that cafeteria, I'm sure.

THURMAN: Mama's done a lot for her, you know. We all have.

DELIA: What have you done?

THURMAN: Well, before she went to Austin to go to work we gave her a hundred dollars every month. Just like we did Dolly.

DELIA: She's been gone fifteen years. You haven't given her anything since she left.

THURMAN: How do you know what we've given her? We've had to help out many a time.

DELIA: How?

THURMAN: Two operations . . . for one thing. I don't think she needed either one of them. In my opinion she's a terrible hypochondriac. (*He gets up.*) Let's go home, Delia. I'll be back to see you tonight, Mama. (*He goes out.*)

DELIA: (*Calling after him.*) Thurman, don't be so rude. You left without saying good-bye to Dolly or Skeeter.

SKEETER: Don't worry, Delia. We're used to him. (*She leaves.*)

DOLLY: They'll kill each other one day.

SKEETER: No, they won't. They'll kill everybody else first. (*He gets up.*) I'm going, Mama.

JOSIE: Will you be back tonight, son?

SKEETER: I'll try. (*He leaves.*)

JOSIE: I'd forgotten all about Laura Lee's money. That she didn't have a will. Do you remember how much she had when she died?

DOLLY: She had the lot for her house . . . I know that. And then she had the money to build the house, someone said, and I never knew how much more.

JOSIE: When Mr. Weems died, he left everything to me, but taxes weren't so high then. But he'd been putting aside money for Laura Lee all that time, too. Were Rosa's operations serious? I can't remember.

DOLLY: I don't know, Auntie, how serious they were. (*The lights are brought down on JOSIE's area and are brought up downstage right. ROSA is there. THURMAN enters.*)

THURMAN: Mama told me you'd be in town today, Rosa. How much do you need?

ROSA: A hundred and fifty dollars. I hate to ask you all for this, Thurman. But the doctor says I need another operation. I feel terrible all the time, so I suppose I need something. I wouldn't ask you at all if I wasn't desperate.

THURMAN: All right. You sure you need it now?

ROSA: I'm afraid so.

THURMAN: All right. How long are you staying here?

ROSA: I'm taking the bus back this afternoon.

THURMAN: I see.

ROSA: How's Aunt Josie?

THURMAN: She's fine.

ROSA: And Laura Lee?

THURMAN: Fine.

ROSA: I think often of the good times we used to have here. Laura Lee was always so pretty and popular and had so many beaux. I think my favorite was always Mr. Chestnut.

THURMAN: Yes? I'll send you the check to Austin tomorrow.

ROSA: Thank you. (*The lights down right fade as the lights are brought up downstage center as LAURA LEE's theme is heard on the piano. LAURA LEE is seated in the hotel lobby. MR. CHESTNUT comes in. He's in his early thirties, quiet, pleasant-looking.*)

LAURA LEE: Did you have your talk with Father and Thurman, Mr. Chestnut?

MR. CHESTNUT: Yes. Do you know they want me to go to business school in Houston for six months before I start work at the bank?

LAURA LEE: They mentioned something about it to me.

MR. CHESTNUT: They didn't to me before.

LAURA LEE: They didn't?

MR. CHESTNUT: No. They said if I would sell my bakery and come to work at the bank, they would agree to our marriage. Well, I sold the bakery and when I went over this afternoon to talk about my new job, they said Mr. Jackson had felt . . .

LAURA LEE: Mr. Jackson?

MR. CHESTNUT: Yes. They said since he was the President of the bank they had to clear everything with him and that he felt that I would be of more use at the bank if I had a business course first. They want me to enroll for six months in Houston.

LAURA LEE: Before or after we marry?

MR. CHESTNUT: Before. That means we'll have to wait six months before our marrying.

LAURA LEE: Father said the bank wanted to pay for it. Did they tell you that?

MR. CHESTNUT: Yes.

LAURA LEE: That was kind and thoughtful, wasn't it? It shows they are very interested in you. We own a lot of the bank stock, you know, our family, that is. I know when Father retires as Vice President, Thurman hopes to become Vice President, and when Mr. Jackson retires as President, he hopes to become President. I'm sure when Thurman becomes Vice President, they'll give you his place as Treasurer and when he becomes President, you'll become Vice President. (*She takes a house plan out of her purse)* I found this house plan in Holland's magazine that I like a whole lot. Don't you? *(He takes the house plan and looks at it*) Father says he'll give it to us as a wedding present.

MR. CHESTNUT: What does a house like that cost?

LAURA LEE: Three thousand.

MR. CHESTNUT: I have nothing, you know. I sold my bakery so quickly and took a loss on that. (*A pause.*) I don't want the bank to send me to business school, Laura Lee. I really don't want to be obligated to them in that way. I'd prefer putting myself through business school. I'll get myself a job working at a bakery in Houston. I'll save my money and educate myself.

LAURA LEE: How long will that take?

MR. CHESTNUT: I don't know. Longer than six months, certainly. (*A pause.*) I must tell you I didn't appreciate being told about the business school after I sold my bakery. I'm no fool, you know. I'm a good businessman. I would certainly think I could count change in a bank. And I don't want your father giving us a house. I don't want a house from him. (*A pause.*) I want you to marry me now. Now!. . .

LAURA LEE: Do you want me to live in Houston with you, while you work for a bakery and go to business school?

MR. CHESTNUT: Yes.

LAURA LEE: My heavens! I can't say yes or no . . . right off this way. I'll have to think about it.

MR. CHESTNUT: Please, marry me.

LAURA LEE: I want to marry you, but there's a great deal to consider, Warren.

MR. CHESTNUT: Please marry me now, Laura Lee . . . Please . . .

LAURA LEE: Maybe . . . after you're settled in Houston. (*A pause.*)

MR. CHESTNUT: Will you go to the dance with me tomorrow night?

LAURA LEE: If you'd like. (*A piano off stage plays a waltz. LAURA LEE and MR. CHESTNUT get up and start dancing.*)

LAURA LEE: I have money of my own. Father has been putting it in a savings account for me over the years. I can build us a house.

MR. CHESTNUT: I don't want you to spend your money. I want you to come and live in Houston on what I make.

LAURA LEE: I have to think . . . You go on to Houston. I need time to think. (*LAURA LEE kisses him and leaves as the music ends. JOSIE enters joined by ROSA carrying many packages, and crosses into downstage center—talking all the while.*)

JOSIE: I can never find anything I want in this town. The poorest selection of merchandise I have ever seen. Alice Temple came by to see me yesterday. She said she was going to have to leave Lawrence if he didn't stop his gambling. I said I couldn't blame her. I've tried every way in the world to get Dolly to leave Mercer, but she won't do it. "Think of your children," I told her. "He hasn't worked in five years. He's drunk half the time. He's no self-respect. He doesn't stay home when he drinks, but he wanders around the streets so everybody can see him." I worry sometimes. I think more about Dolly and Lawrence than I do my own children. Alice says she wanted Lawrence to move to Houston. She thought it would get him away from his cronies here, and he'd have an easier time there. I agreed with her about that. Mrs. Temple sold all her property here and bought a duplex in Houston, so she could have a little income. "Are you going to continue to live with your mother?" I asked her. "Yes," she said. Well, that will never work out, I thought to myself. Mrs. Temple despises Lawrence. I asked Dolly and Mercer to come have supper with us tonight at the hotel. I'm giving her fifty dollars a month, you know. They'd starve otherwise. Thurman said I shouldn't give them money. He said I should put them in one of our rent houses and give them groceries. He says Mercer always finds the way to get the money out of her. What do you think?

ROSA: I don't know. I wish I had been trained to do something, Auntie. It worries me so. I don't know what will happen to me when Mother dies. Why didn't they insist that I get training of some sort?

JOSIE: I think they always expected you would marry.

ROSA: Well, I haven't.

JOSIE: Don't mention it to Laura Lee, but Mr. Chestnut got married yesterday in Houston. We read an account of the wedding in the Chronicle last night. I don't blame Sister for not marrying him. He turned his back on the bank here and he insisted she come and live in Houston while he worked in a bakery. Of course, her father and Thurman almost had a fit when they heard that . . . and . . . (*LAURA LEE comes in.*)

LAURA LEE: Hello, Miss Rosa . . .

ROSA: Hello, Miss Laura Lee . . .

LAURA LEE: Hello, Mama.
JOSIE: Hello, Laura Lee. (*MR. WEEMS comes in.*)
LAURA LEE: Hello, Father.
MR. WEEMS: Hello, Daughter. Hello, Rosa.
ROSA: Hello, Uncle.
JOSIE: I've invited Mercer and Dolly for supper, as soon as they get here we'll go into the dining room.
LAURA LEE: I'm playing bridge tonight.
JOSIE: Who with?
LAURA LEE: Lillian Burger, Christine Hamilton, and Ada Cox. They're all wonderful players. Rosa, I'll have to teach you to play.
ROSA: Oh, I'm too stupid to learn, Honey.
JOSIE: I never cared for it. I could never sit still that long. (*DOLLY comes in.*)
DOLLY: Hello, Cousin Rosa.
ROSA: Hello, Cousin Dolly.
DOLLY: Hello, Auntie. Hello, Cousin Laura Lee. Hello, Uncle.
JOSIE: Where's Mercer?
DOLLY: He's not well. He has a terrible cold.
JOSIE: Who's staying with the children?
DOLLY: My neighbors. I have a very sweet neighbor. She has no children and she just loves mine. (*MERCER comes in. He is very drunk.*)
JOSIE: Hello, Mercer. We weren't expecting you. We thought you were home sick.
MERCER: I'm not sick. Who told you I was sick?
DOLLY: I did, Mercer. And I think we better go home now.
MERCER: No. I've come to take you to the dance.
DOLLY: I'm not going to any dance, Mercer. So go on home, please.
MERCER: Laura Lee, are you going to the dance?
LAURA LEE: No, I'm not. I'm playing bridge tonight.
MERCER: I'm going dancing. (*He starts to dance. DOLLY grabs him.*)
DOLLY: I think I'd better take him home. I'm so sorry, Auntie.
JOSIE: That's all right, Dolly.
DOLLY: Come on, Mercer. (*She takes him by the arm. She starts to help him out. He pulls away from her and goes to LAURA LEE.*)
MERCER: Old Chestnut. Old Chestnut. He fooled us all. He fooled us all. He gave up the sweetest girl in town. I think he's crazy, Laura Lee . . . I just want you to know that. I'm going to give him hell the next time I see him. I always liked old Chestnut, too. Of course he couldn't sing like Barsoty . . . but I liked him . . . Quiet . . . A hard worker . . .
DOLLY: Come on, Mercer. I'm sorry, Laura Lee. He doesn't know what he's saying.

LAURA LEE: Yes, he does. I think he knows very well what he's saying. (*She goes on out downstage left.*)

DOLLY: Come on, Mercer. Now, please come on. (*She leads him out.*)

ROSA: I can't stand unpleasantness of any kind. Oh, Dear, Auntie . . . I can't. I can't . . .

JOSIE: Mr. Weems, go up and see if Laura Lee is all right. (*MR. WEEMS enters downstage left. LAURA LEE is there.*)

MR. WEEMS: Sister. . . (*BARSOTY appears behind the scrim.*)

BARSOTY: (*Singing.*) SHE WEPT WITH DELIGHT WHEN YOU GAVE HER A SMILE, AND TREMBLED WITH FEAR AT YOUR FROWN (*BARSOTY disappears behind the scrim. She looks up at her father. She has been crying. She wipes her eyes.*)

LAURA LEE: It's all right father. You go on back. I'll be there in a little.

MR. WEEMS: Mercer was drunk.

LAURA LEE: I know he was drunk, but I know he said drunk, what everyone else in town is saying, drunk or sober. (*BARSOTY appears again behind the scrim.*)

BARSOTY: (*Singing.*) IN THE OLD CHURCH—YARD IN THE VALLEY, BEN BOLT, IN A CORNER OBSCURE AND ALONE, (*BARSOTY disappears behind the scrim.*)

LAURA LEE: You were wrong, father, and Thurman was wrong and mother was wrong. I wish I'd married him.

MR. WEEMS: We were only thinking of what was best for you. We always had your best interest at heart.

LAURA LEE: Did you? I'm thirty-three, father. I'm embarrassed to go to dances now, the women my age are all married. What's to become of me, father? Am I to live out my life in this hotel room? Playing bridge at night with other lonely women? Is that how I'm to spend my life?

MR. WEEMS: I'm going to insist that your mother move into an apartment at least, so we'll have a living room and can entertain people. And I want you to start taking some trips. I think you should go to West Texas this summer to get away from the heat or to Galveston. I want you to have at least a two week vacation.

LAURA LEE: When can we move into an apartment?

MR. WEEMS: I'll go speak to your mother about it now. Would that make you happy?

LAURA LEE: Yes. It would. (*She picks up a magazine.*) Show her this. Here are my plans for a house. Tell her that's what I really want us all to have. And I know you do, too.

MR. WEEMS: She won't consent to that, I'm afraid. But she will, I believe, move back into an apartment. You stay here. Let me try. (*He goes back to JOSIE and ROSA.*)

JOSIE: How's Sister?
MR. WEEMS: She's all right.
JOSIE: Is she going to have supper with us?
MR. WEEMS: I don't know. She didn't say. (*A pause.*) Josie . . .
JOSIE: Yes.
MR. WEEMS: She wants us to move into an apartment so she can have a living room that she can entertain in.
JOSIE: Well . . . I don't know, Mr. Weems, I'm awfully happy here at the hotel.
MR. WEEMS: Josie, we're getting an apartment. I promised daughter we would.
JOSIE: There are no apartments here.
MR. WEEMS: They're going to put one up somewhere over on Caney. I'm going to reserve one of them for us. (*LAURA LEE comes in.*) We're going to move to an apartment. I was telling your mother . . .
JOSIE: (*Interrupting.*) We'd better go get our supper.
LAURA LEE: What I really want is a house.
JOSIE: Well, I don't.
LAURA LEE: My own house. I have money of my own now.
JOSIE: Sister, you want to live by yourself?
LAURA LEE: Yes.
JOSIE: We'll talk about that another time. Let's have supper now. (*A pause.*) How much have you given her?
MR. WEEMS: It's none of your business, Josie.
JOSIE: (*To LAURA LEE.*) How much has he given you?
LAURA LEE: That's none of your business, mother. (*They go out as the lights fade. JOSIE crosses to her wheelchair. The lights are brought up, up center. JOSIE is asleep again. DORIS and DOLLY are there.*)
DORIS: Miss Dolly, I want to ask your advice about something. My friends all tell me I don't get paid enough.
DOLLY: What do you make here?
DORIS: Twelve dollars a week . . . an' I do everything.
DOLLY: I know you do. I just don't know what they pay people here now.
DORIS: My friends get twenty-five dollars a week.
DOLLY: Then I think you should tell them that.
DORIS: Should I ask Mr. Thurman?
DOLLY: I wouldn't. I'd ask Mr. Skeeter.
DORIS: Yes, Ma'am. I thought maybe I should ask Miss Josie, but I don't like to worry her, sick as she is. Miss Josie says she is going to remember me when she's gone. She says she's going to reward me for all my faithfulness. (*SKEETER comes in.*)
DOLLY: She's back asleep now. I was just going. Tell Aunt Josie I'll be by

to see her tomorrow. (*She goes.*)

DORIS: Mr. Skeeter, I think I should have a raise.

SKEETER: What do you make now?

DORIS: Twelve dollars a week.

SKEETER: What would you like?

DORIS: My friends that do this kind of work all get twenty-five dollars a week now.

SKEETER: Let me talk to Mama about it.

DORIS: Yes, Sir. (*A pause.*) You gonna be here a little while, Mr. Skeeter?

SKEETER: A little while.

DORIS: Then I think I'll take me a walk for a few minutes.

SKEETER: All right.

DORIS: I won't be long.

SKEETER: Take your time. (*She goes. JOSIE opens her eyes.*)

JOSIE: Doris?

SKEETER: She's gone for a walk. It's Skeeter, Mama. Can I do anything for you?

JOSIE: No, thank you. Just sit here by me. (*He does so.*) I came here in 1890. I was twenty–three and a bride. I came from the coast and I was used to rainy weather, but I never saw before or since rain like we had that year. The streets were mud. The cotton crops failed. The cane crop failed. There were hard times for everybody. I was sick a great deal in those days. As a matter of fact, son, I never thought I'd live to see fifty. I thought Mr. Weems would certainly outlive me. And I've outlived him by years.

SKEETER: Mama, I'm giving up rice farming.

JOSIE: Are you losing money at it, son?

SKEETER: No, but I'm not making any either. I do well to break even and it's very hard work, Mama.

JOSIE: What will you do, son?

SKEETER: I will go back to work at the bank. Thurman is finding a job for me.

JOSIE: Well, if that's what you want to do. (*A pause.*) I think Thurman is very disappointed with Mr. Jackson. I am too. I don't think he's ever going to retire and turn the Presidency over to him.

SKEETER: Doesn't look like it. Mama, are you satisfied with Doris?

JOSIE: Tolerably.

SKEETER: She asked for a raise.

JOSIE: How much?

SKEETER: She wants twenty-five dollars a week.

JOSIE: She's not worth it. None of them are. I've never known any help white or black worth that kind of money. You have to watch over them all the time and make them redo half of what they've done. (*DORIS comes in.*) Doris. You can just pack your bags and go right now. I won't raise you one penny. You do nothing but sit here and cook a little food for yourself. Get on out now.

SKEETER: You can't stay here by yourself though, Mama.

JOSIE: Oh, yes I can. I won't be robbed blind. I won't be. (*She struggles to get out of the wheelchair. SKEETER takes hold of her.*)

SKEETER: Mama.

JOSIE: No, I can't. I can't stay by myself at all. Pay her. Let her rob us. Pay her. If that's how she wants to repay us for all these years of friendship. (*Lights fade and come up downstage left in LAURA LEE's room. LAURA LEE is there. LAWRENCE enters right and stands upstage with his back to the audience. JOSIE gets up from wheelchair and goes to LAURA LEE.*)

LAURA LEE: Lawrence was here.

JOSIE: Where is he now?

LAURA LEE: I don't know. He said he'll be back.

JOSIE: How does he like Houston?

LAURA LEE: I don't think too well. He said he and Alice made a mistake moving in with Mrs. Temple.

JOSIE: They can always move out.

LAURA LEE: He can't now. He's lost his job.

JOSIE: I hope he's looking for another one.

LAURA LEE: He's very discouraged.

JOSIE: Had he been drinking?

LAURA LEE: I don't think so.

JOSIE: Dolly said he was drunk the other night and called Mercer from Houston and told him he was depressed and didn't want to live and he was going to kill himself. Dolly says Mercer says that he's always threatening that when he's drunk. Thurman says he came into town one night last week drunk and stood in the Courthouse Square hollering on the top of his lungs that he needed money. (*LAWRENCE comes in.*)

LAWRENCE: Hello, Aunt Josie.

JOSIE: Hello, Nephew.

LAURA LEE: Excuse me. (*LAURA LEE exits.*)

JOSIE: Sister says you and Mrs. Temple aren't getting along.

LAWRENCE: She despises me. She wants to break up our marriage.

JOSIE: Thurman says you came into town the other night and stood at the Courthouse Square yelling: "I need money, I need money."

LAWRENCE: Yes Ma'am I was drunk. I won't do that again. I've stopped drinking.

JOSIE: Have you stopped your gambling?

LAWRENCE: Yes.

JOSIE: Son, that's not what Mrs. Temple says. She says you leave Alice alone night after night . . . while you carouse in Houston. She says that's why you can't keep a job. She says you have broken Alice's heart . . . You're killing her.

LAWRENCE: She's a liar. If I leave it's because I can't stand listening to her any longer. I need some money. Will you loan me a little money, Aunt Josie? Until I get back on my feet and find another job?

JOSIE: I haven't any money, son, except what Mr. Weems gives me. I don't feel I can ask him for any more for my family. He supports Dolly now and Rosa.

LAWRENCE: I'll pay you back . . . interest.

JOSIE: I can't do it, son. We're doing now all we can. Besides I think a man has to learn to stand on his own two feet. (*A pause.*) Dolly said Mercer told her you'd threatened to kill yourself. Now, you know talking that way is just foolishness— (*LAWRENCE is crying.*) Now son, you're gonna land on your feet, yet—now go on back to Houston to your wife and get a job. Be a man, son—try and be man—look at your cousins. Look at Thurman and Skeeter. Their fathers has money, but they never ask for a penny. They work like they were both poor boys. Now you go back to your wife and child and be a man.

LAWRENCE: Yes, Ma'am. (*He goes. JOSIE goes as the lights fade. LAWRENCE has gone directly to his spot upstage. He stands with his back to the audience. Yelling in great anguish.*) I need money! I need money! I need money! (*He turns and leaves the stage as his light fades. LAURA LEE's theme is heard as the lights are brought up on DOLLY's area down right. DOLLY is there. LAURA LEE enters.*)

LAURA LEE: Lawrence came by the apartment last night looking for me but I was out playing bridge. Do you know what he wanted?

DOLLY: I'm afraid he wanted to borrow money. He seemed desperate and Aunt Josie and Thurman won't loan him any. I don't blame them of course. They're having to help me and Mercer now. I gave him what I could spare. It wasn't much.

LAURA LEE: Do you know where he is now?

DOLLY: I think he went back to Houston.

LAURA LEE: I'll try to get hold of him. I'm going over to Christine's to play bridge. If you hear from him, tell him I want to help in anyway I can.

DOLLY: Thank you cousin. (*LAURA LEE leaves as the lights fade and we hear LAURA LEE's theme being played. LAWRENCE comes in and stands upstage and yells in great anguish:* "I need money! I need money! I need money!" *He goes. The lights are brought up on LAURA LEE's area downstage left. LAURA LEE is there. SKEETER enters.*)

SKEETER: Mama?

LAURA LEE: Mama's not here, brother. Can I do anything for you?

SKEETER: No. I have a little time to kill. I just wanted to say hello.

LAURA LEE: I'm glad to see you Skeeter. Come on in and visit with me. How's rice farming?

SKEETER: Well it goes on. Not much to do out at the farm this time of year. Do you know that I've been rice farming for ten years?

LAURA LEE: Is that possible?

SKEETER: A lot of my friends are going into the oil business. They're giving up rice farming. Did you play bridge this afternoon?

LAURA LEE: I've just come from playing. I think I'm going to the picture show tonight.

SKEETER: What's playing?

LAURA LEE: To tell you the truth, I don't know.

SKEETER: I haven't been to a picture show in I don't know when. When I work all day out at the rice farm I'm so tired when I get home, all I want to do is go to bed.

LAURA LEE: You get up early, too, don't you?

SKEETER: Oh, yes. I'm up at five every morning. I'm out at the farm by day break. What time do you wake up?

LAURA LEE: It depends. I haven't been sleeping so well lately. I have trouble falling asleep some nights and then when I do get to sleep I wake up and I have a hard time getting back to sleep.

SKEETER: Are you feeling all right?

LAURA LEE: Yes, I feel all right. I just don't sleep most nights.

SKEETER: Mama says Lawrence has been in town again asking for money. Mama and Thurman turned him down. He hasn't come to me and Mama says if he does not to give him any. I hope he doesn't ask me for money. I'd hate to have to turn him down. Has he asked you for money?

LAURA LEE: He came here looking for me the other night. I expect that's what he wanted. I wasn't home.

SKEETER: Would you have given him money?

LAURA LEE: Yes I would.

SKEETER: To tell you the truth so would I. Do you like the apartment?

LAURA LEE: I like it well enough. It's better than being at the hotel.

SKEETER: I used to like to go to the picture show you know when I was a kid. I went every Saturday. I loved the serials and the cowboy pictures and I liked the comedies. You know that cross-eyed man. What was his name? Ben Turpin. I liked him a lot. He used to make me laugh. (*DOLLY enters*.)

DOLLY: Where's Aunt Josie?

LAURA LEE: Uptown shopping. (*DOLLY cries*.) What is it Dolly? Has something happened to the children? To Mercer?

DOLLY: It's Lawrence. He killed himself. Mrs. Temple just called me from Houston. (*ROSA appears behind the scrim*.)

ROSA: (*Singing*.) NEARER, MY GOD, TO THEE. NEARER TO THEE. (*ROSA disappears*.)

SKEETER: I'll go find Mama and tell her. I'm so sorry Dolly. He leaves.

DOLLY: They're going to bury him in Houston. The funeral is day after tomorrow to give us time to go there.

LAURA LEE: I tried to reach him in Houston, but no one knew where he was. Oh, my God. Oh, my God. Poor Lawrence. Poor Lawrence. Poor Lawrence.

DOLLY: They asked Rosa to sing at the funeral. Can I drive over with you all? Mercer isn't well again. I'm not going to take the children. They're too young to understand. I'm going to have another baby, Laura Lee. I'm ashamed to tell Aunt Josie. I know Thurman and Skeeter will be cross with me. I pray this will be my last. Will they have trouble getting a preacher for the funeral services since Lawrence committed suicide?

LAURA LEE: I don't think so.

DOLLY: My poor, poor brother. Mrs. Temple says Alice is prostrated with grief. She found the body. He had hung himself. He had threatened a number of times to kill himself. I didn't believe his threats. I just thought he wanted sympathy.

LAURA LEE: Poor Lawrence. Poor, poor Lawrence. (*The lights are dimmed downstage left, but they are still visible. The lights center are brought up full; THURMAN comes in*.)

THURMAN: I just came in to say goodnight. How does she feel? How do you feel, Mother?

JOSIE: I'm all right, son. I'm very tired.

THURMAN: Do you know what I was thinking coming over here? We're rich. I have a million, three hundred thousand dollars in assets. Mama has eight hundred thousand dollars.

SKEETER: I'm not rich.

THURMAN: You're not rich as we are, but you have a half million dollars in assets. I figured it up coming over here. That's one thing about working in a bank. You know everybody's assets. Mama, you have eight hundred thousand dollars in assets. Don't that make you happy? I knew I was going to be rich the day Mr. Jess Turner came into the bank and said he wanted to give me 5% on his oil royalties.

"What for?", I said. "Because you treated me fair and square." He said, "I can't read or write and you gave me wonderful advice and showed me how to invest my money, so I wouldn't be taken advantage of. I try to be fair to everybody. I give them good advice. I tried to advise poor old Lawrence, you know. But he wouldn't listen. (*ROSA appears behind the scrim.*)

ROSA: (*Singing.*) THERE LET THE WAY APPEAR STEPS UNTO HEAVEN (*ROSA disappears.*)

JOSIE: Rosa doesn't sing at funeral's anymore. Wonder who they'll get to sing at my funeral.

THURMAN: Damn it. Do you understand Mr. Jackson? He's half dead. You'd think he'd retire and let me be the President of the damn bank. It gets me so upset, I don't sleep.

JOSIE: Skeeter quit rice farming.

THURMAN: I know that, Mama.

JOSIE: He's going back to work at the bank. I'm ninety–three. I've outlived my mother, my father, my sister, my brother, my nephew Lawrence, my daughter.

THURMAN: We're still here, Mama. And Dolly is and Rosa.

JOSIE: Try to get Rosa to sing at my funeral. Just this one last time.

THURMAN: I'm sure she will, Mama. If she knows you want her to.

JOSIE: I do. (*ROSA appears behind the scrim. LAURA LEE and DOLLY from downstage left join ROSA in singing.*)

LAURA LEE, DOLLY, ROSA: (*Singing.*) OUT OF MY STONE GRIEFS BETHEL I'LL RAISE; SO BE MY WOES TO BE NEARER, MY GOD, TO THEE, NEARER, MY GOD, TO THEE, NEARER TO THEE.

JOSIE: I remember Lawrence's funeral. They asked Rosa to sing, but she was so overcome with grief when the time came she couldn't sing by herself, so Dolly and Laura Lee joined in with her. It was all spontaneous. But I think it was the loveliest thing I ever heard at a funeral. Lawrence's sister and his two first cousins singing. Then we all joined in. Remember?

ROSA: *(Singing.)* OR IF ON JOYFUL WING

LAURA LEE, DOLLY: (*Join ROSA singing.*) CLEAVING THE SKY, SUN, MOON, AND STARS FORGOT UPWARD I FLY STILL ALL MY SONG SHALL BE NEARER, MY GOD, TO THEE, NEARER, MY GOD, TO THEE, NEARER TO THEE. (*Curtain.*)

ACT II

Later that night. The lights are brought up on upstage center area. JOSIE and DORIS are alone. JOSIE is in her wheelchair. She is awake. DORIS asleep in the chair. The alarm clock rings.

JOSIE: Doris . . . (*DORIS doesn't hear her at first.*) Doris . . . (*DORIS opens her eyes. She gets up and goes over to her.*)

DORIS: Yes, Ma'am?

JOSIE: What time is it? (*DORIS looks at the clock, turning off the alarm.*)

DORIS: Five o'clock in the morning.

JOSIE: Five o'clock in the morning?

DORIS: Yes, Ma'am. Now go on back to sleep.

JOSIE: I'm trying. (*She closes her eyes. DORIS closes hers.*) I can't sleep.

DORIS: You want a drink of water?

JOSIE: No. Where are those papers Thurman brought over here for me to sign?

DORIS: You signed them and he took them away.

JOSIE: He says I have to live three more years to have them effective. (*A pause.*) Talk to me, Doris.

DORIS: What do you want to talk about?

JOSIE: Where's that scrapbook Laura Lee used to keep? (*DORIS goes over to a corner of the room.*) Did you find it?

DORIS: Yes, Ma'am.

JOSIE: Read it to me.

DORIS: Read you what?

JOSIE: Read me what's in the scrapbook.

DORIS: Miss Josie, I can't read. You know that.

JOSIE: Bring it here. (*She does so.*) Hold it for me so I can see the pages. (*She does so.*) You know what's on the first page? An announcement of the birth of Dolly's last child. (*The lights are brought up, down right. DOLLY is in her living room holding a baby. MERCER enters.*)

MERCER: How are you feeling?

DOLLY: I'm all right, Mercer. Laura Lee is coming over.

MERCER: What about Aunt Josie?

DOLLY: No.

MERCER: Is she still mad at us for having the baby?

DOLLY: She'll get over it.

MERCER: Laura Lee comes over a lot. Don't she?

DOLLY: Yes she does.

MERCER: Why do you think she comes over here so much?
DOLLY: I think she's lonely.
MERCER: Lonely?
DOLLY: Yes and we have become very close since Lawrence's death.
MERCER: We're not lonely, God knows. Not with four children.
DOLLY: No, we're not lonely. (*LAURA LEE comes in with a present. She goes and looks at the baby.*)
LAURA LEE: Hello, Mercer.
MERCER: Hello, Laura Lee.
LAURA LEE: Hello, Dolly. I brought you a little present.
DOLLY: Thank you, cousin.
LAURA LEE: What a fine looking boy.
MERCER: It's time we had a boy after three girls. Don't you think?
LAURA LEE: Yes. I do.
MERCER: Dolly, I'm going uptown to get some cigarettes.
DOLLY: All right, Mercer. (*He leaves.*)
LAURA LEE: Let me hold him. (*She takes the baby.*) Can I do anything for you?
DOLLY: No. Thank you. I'm managing fine. Is it warm out?
LAURA LEE: Not bad. I've just come from the bank. It was a pleasant walk. Do you know Mrs. Reeves that's had all the trouble with her son?
DOLLY: Yes.
LAURA LEE: Well, she sent word to me yesterday asking if I'd come over to her house. I went and she told me that her boy was in trouble again and she was going to have to sell her house cheap to get money to help him. She is selling it very cheap. It's just a simple little cottage, really, but it is all I want or need. I told her I would buy it.
DOLLY: That's nice.
LAURA LEE: I told father and Thurman that I wanted them to arrange it for me. He's a good little boy. (*She hands the baby back to DOLLY.*)
DOLLY: Yes he is.
LAURA LEE: Did you know that Mr. Chestnut is married now and has four children? (*BARSOTY appears behind the scrim.*)
BARSOTY: (*Singing.*) OH, DON'T YOU REMEMBER SWEET ALICE, BEN BOLT
DOLLY: Yes, I'd heard that.
BARSOTY: (*Singing.*) SWEET ALICE WITH HAIR SO BROWN,
LAURA LEE: I'm thirty-eight now. I was thirty-eight my last birthday. I'll be thirty-nine my next birthday. I'll . . .
BARSOTY: (*Singing.*) SWEET ALICE WITH HAIR SO BROWN. SHE WEPT WITH DELIGHT WHEN YOU GAVE HER A SMILE AND

TREMBLED WITH FEAR AT YOUR FROWN

LAURA LEE: Guess who I got a letter from yesterday?

BARSOTY: (*Singing.*) SHE WEPT WITH DELIGHT WHEN YOU GAVE HER A SMILE AND TREMBLED WITH FEAR AT YOUR FROWN (BARSTOY disappears.)

LAURA LEE: Barsoty. He said he would be riding through here today on business, and he would like to stop and see me. I wrote him back and told him I would see him. I asked him to meet me over here. Do you mind my doing that?

DOLLY: No.

LAURA LEE: I don't want Mother or Father or my brothers to know anything about this.

DOLLY: I'll not tell them. (*LAURA LEE starts out as the lights fade and the lights are brought up downstage center. JOSIE, THURMAN, and MR. WEEMS are there in the Weems apartment living room. LAURA LEE comes in.*)

THURMAN: Laura Lee, Mother and Father and I have been discussing the Reeve's house. I don't think it's worth what she's asking for it.

JOSIE: It's a common little house, honey. Four thousand is robbery for a house like that.

THURMAN: I offered her twenty–five hundred dollars. She turned me down. She's greedy.

LAURA LEE: Who told you to do that? I told you I wanted to buy that house.

THURMAN: I know, I know.

LAURA LEE: I am going to buy that house. I have the money.

JOSIE: How much money do you have?

LAURA LEE: None of your business.

JOSIE: How much have you given her, Mr. Weems?

MR. WEEMS: I'm not going to tell you, Josie.

THURMAN: It's not a whole lot. I can tell you that.

JOSIE: How much?

THURMAN: I can't tell you, Mother, without father's permission.

JOSIE: Why did you do this behind my back? Why?

MR. WEEMS: Because I want her to have a house, if she wants a house.

JOSIE: Then let's get a decent house. Let's don't buy old Mrs. Reeves' shack. Build us a house, Mr. Weems.

LAURA LEE: I don't want to live with you. I want my own house.

JOSIE: Laura Lee . . .

LAURA LEE: And I'm going to buy the Reeves' house and you're not going to stop me.

JOSIE: Laura Lee . . .

THURMAN: Dolly had another baby last night. A boy.

JOSIE: I know, I know. (*DELIA comes in. She has some letters.*)

THURMAN: What do you want?

DELIA: Don't take that tone with me. (*She hands him a letter. He reads it quickly.*)

THURMAN: When did you get this?

DELIA: Never mind. I have more, too. (*A pause.*) Do you know what this is? That's a love letter from a girl named Christine Murray, who lives in Corpus. Your son has been having an affair with her. A twenty-year-old girl. Did you ever hear of anything as despicable in your life? You want to be the bank President? I'll fix you so you'll never be able to hold up your head in this town again. How long have you been seeing this slut? Answer me? (*He walks out. She hands the letter to LAURA LEE.*) Read it. I have twenty more besides.

LAURA LEE: I don't want to read it. (*Delia hands it to MR. WEEMS. He reads it.*)

DELIA: Isn't that disgusting? Aren't you proud of him? Do you know it has been going on for two years? He has been sneaking over there for two years and seeing that little slut.

MR. WEEMS: What can we do?

DELIA: What can we do? What can he do?

MR. WEEMS: What can he do?

DELIA: He'd better do something, or I'm going to ruin him. He has money, you know. He has quite a bit of money now.

JOSIE: I don't think he's got all that much.

DELIA: Don't lie to me. That'll get you nowhere with me. You know he's very prosperous. (*THURMAN comes in.*)

THURMAN: I want to say that I'm very sorry. I don't know why I've acted this way. I'm very ashamed. I've never done anything like this before and I swear to you it will never happen again. (*A pause. DELIA takes the letter from MR. WEEMS.*)

DELIA: How long were you seeing her?

THURMAN: I don't know. Six months.

DELIA: You're a liar. You've been seeing her two years. I warn you. I know everything, Thurman. I went over to Corpus and I got everything out of that girl.

THURMAN: If you know everything, why are you asking me?

DELIA: Because I want your parents to see what a liar you are. I want your sister and your mother and your father to see what a horror you really are. Do you know what he did to you today? He told Mrs. Reeves that you wouldn't pay her price for the house, that it was way too much, and then he told one of his bank customers who is buying up rent property that he thought he could get it for a thousand dollars less than she asked you, and he went over to see her and she sold him the house.

LAURA LEE: Did you, Thurman?

THURMAN: I just didn't think it was a good buy for you, Sister.

LAURA LEE: Now, you find me another house.

THURMAN: I will . . . I will . . . (*To DELIA.*) Are you satisfied now? You've humiliated me in front of my mother and father and sister, are you satisfied?

DELIA: No.

THURMAN: Are you going to ruin me? Is that what you're going to do? (*A pause.*) What do you want, Delia? Do you want a divorce?

DELIA: No . . . I don't want a divorce.

THURMAN: Then what do you want?

DELIA: I want many things. I want a house. I want to build the finest house around. I want it handsomely furnished. I want you to put money in my own name to do with as I please. I want you never to see that girl again.

THURMAN: You know I don't have as much money as you seem to think.

DELIA: You have plenty of money. And I don't want you once to complain about the price of anything I ask for. For if you do, if you do, then I will get a divorce. I'll take everything you have. People despise you in this town. Did you know that? Because of your position at the bank you've had power over most of the people here. And you've behaved arrogantly to them, shown them your contempt when they had to come to you for money. They would be so happy to know about all this. And I would be so happy to tell them. And I will, if you once object to anything I ask. (*To JOSIE.*) I want you to read these.

JOSIE: I don't want to read them. (*She gives her the letters.*)

DELIA: I insist. (*DELIA goes.*)

JOSIE: What got into you, son?

THURMAN: I don't know. I don't know. (*A pause.*) I apologize to you both. I'm very sorry. (*The lights are brought up down stage left. LAURA LEE is there. THURMAN goes to LAURA LEE. JOSIE and MR. WEEMS remain in their area.*) Please forgive me, Sister. I thought I was doing the best thing for you. I thought this wanting a house was just a whim that would pass. I'll go to the man that I got to buy the house and see if he won't let you have it. And if he won't . . . I swear to you I'll find you another one.

LAURA LEE: They're not so easy to find you know at that price.

THURMAN: We'll find you one. (*A pause.*) Do you really want to live by yourself?

LAURA LEE: Yes, I do.

THURMAN: Won't you be lonely by yourself?

LAURA LEE: No.

THURMAN: I got a nice note from Barsoty. He said he was coming through here today on business. He said he hoped to have a visit with you and afterwards he'd come by the bank and say hello. (*A pause.*) I don't think he's done much with his life. He's a travelling man, you know. But he's always changing jobs. I looked up his credit rating. It wasn't much. But anyway he's a nice fellow and I'll be glad to see him. (*A pause.*) Old Chestnut is doing pretty well. I looked his credit rating up and I was surprised. He has a wife and four children. (*A pause.*) I better go on home before Delia does something crazy. I'll never hear the last of this, you know. Never. (*He goes. LAURA LEE comes back into the downstage left area.*)

JOSIE: I'm amazed, Sister. Mr. Weems thinks Thurman is worth over half a million dollars. Did you have any idea he was worth something like that?

LAURA LEE: I really don't care, Mother. I'm so appalled at what is happening between him and Delia. That's all I can think about . . . And he'd better be careful with Delia, you know. She will ruin him . . . She will certainly ruin him.

JOSIE: She says she wants us to read all those letters.

LAURA LEE: Don't read them, Mother.

JOSIE: I don't want to read them, but she's insisting . . . Don't worry about a house, sister, we'll build us a house.

LAURA LEE: I don't want to live with you. I want my own house.

JOSIE: Let's don't discuss it now. I told Mr. Weems earlier I think maybe we shouldn't help Dolly anymore as long as she stays with Mercer . . . And I wish you'd stop going over there.

LAURA LEE: I'm not going to stop going over there, Mother.

JOSIE: I wish I had never permitted that marriage. I blame myself for giving my consent.

LAURA LEE: I think they would have married anyway, Mother. (*LAURA LEE exits.*)

JOSIE: You're very quiet, Mr. Weems. (*A pause.*) Why are you so quiet?

MR. WEEMS: I have nothing to say. Nothin' at all. (*He goes out. JOSIE goes to her wheelchair as the lights fade and the lights are brought up downstage right. DOLLY is there. LAURA LEE comes in.*)

DOLLY: You look very pretty, Laura Lee.

LAURA LEE: Thank you.

DOLLY: Is that a new dress?

LAURA LEE: Yes. (*She reaches into a package and takes out three girl's dresses.*) I got these for your girls.

DOLLY: Aren't they beautiful!
LAURA LEE: I think they'll look pretty on them.
DOLLY: Thank you. That's very thoughtful of you.
LAURA LEE: I bought a dress for you, too.
DOLLY: I don't need a dress.
LAURA LEE: Yes, you do.
DOLLY: I never go anywhere.
LAURA LEE: You go to church. You can wear it there.
DOLLY: Thank you. Thank you so much. What time are you expecting Barsoty?
LAURA LEE: Three. He said he would be here at three promptly.
DOLLY: I can't wait to show the dresses to the girls. (*She exits as the lights are dimmed and the lights are brought up, center. JOSIE and DORIS have fallen back asleep. JOSIE wakes with a start.*)
JOSIE: Doris . . . Doris . . . wake up . . . (*DORIS opens her eyes.*) What time is it?
DORIS: Five-thirty.
JOSIE: Turn the page for me. (*DORIS does so.*) Look here. You know what that is?
DORIS: That's Mr. Thurman as a young man, and Mr. Skeeter, and Miss Delia, and Miss Laura Lee, and who is this gentleman?
JOSIE: Barsoty.
DORIS: Who's that?
JOSIE: One of Sister's beaux. He was always my favorite. He came from a lovely family. (*DORIS looks closely at the picture.*) I wonder where in the world he is now. I don't remember if he is alive or dead. Rosa and sister and Barsoty used to sing trios together . . . Over at Rosa's house. We never had a piano. You know I'm lonesome for Rosa. Let's call her up on the telephone.
DORIS: You can't call her up this time of night, Miss Josie.
JOSIE: Thurman said he was going to ask Rosa to sing at my funeral. Now you don't let him forget after I die.
DORIS: No, Ma'am. (*A pause.*) May I ask you a question now? You're always saying you're gonna leave me something after you've gone. Are you gonna really leave me something?
JOSIE: Yes, I am. Of course I am.
DORIS: I would appreciate that. How much you think you're gonna leave me?
JOSIE: I'm not going to tell you.
DORIS: Miss Laura Lee always said she was going to leave me something, but she didn't leave me a thing.
JOSIE: She didn't leave anybody anything; because she didn't leave a

will.

DORIS: You have a will?

JOSIE: Certainly I have a will.

DORIS: And it is in your will about you leaving me something?

JOSIE: Why certainly. (*A pause.*) When Lawrence died and Mr. Weems died Rosa sang "Nearer My God To Thee." I think that's what I want her to sing at my funeral, too.

DORIS: I want a lot of songs sung at my funeral. I want "Buelah Land," "Amazing Grace," "Swing Low Sweet Chariot," "Shall We Gather at the River.."

JOSIE: We don't sing those songs at the Episcopal Church. We don't even sing "Nearer My God To Thee" there. Rosa just started singing that on her own. Would you sing it for me now?

DORIS: I can't sing, Miss Josie. I can't sing at all.

JOSIE: Can you pray?

DORIS: Yes, I can pray.

JOSIE: Then pray. I feel very funny.

DORIS: Maybe I ought to call the doctor.

JOSIE: Maybe you should. (*The lights are brought up down stage right. DORIS goes. JOSIE closes her eyes as the lights fade. LAURA LEE and DOLLY are still there. LAURA LEE looks at her watch.*)

DOLLY: What time is it now?

LAURA LEE: A quarter of four.

DOLLY: Maybe he's late getting here.

LAURA LEE: He must be.

DOLLY: Maybe he went by your apartment.

LAURA LEE: Maybe, but I told him to come here.

DOLLY: When was the last time you saw Barsoty?

LAURA LEE: Oh, it's been a long time.

DOLLY: I always liked him. Aunt Josie did too. She told me that . . .

LAURA LEE: Mother gets on my nerves terribly, Dolly. I'm ashamed of myself for behaving the way I do sometimes, but the very sight of her irritates me so I can hardly stand it. She wants me with her every place: she follows me around; I have absolutely no privacy at all. I swear, that's why I play bridge so much just to be able to get away from Mother. Yesterday, I started playing bridge at ten. I played until twelve. Then I went home for dinner and I started playing again at two. I played until six. Then I went home for supper and I started playing again at eight. I played until eleven. (*A pause.*) I don't think Mr. Barsoty is going to come after all.

DOLLY: Maybe he got lost, maybe he couldn't find our house. (*MERCER comes in.*)

MERCER: Laura Lee. Laura Lee. Laura Lee, your father had a heart attack uptown just now. They've taken him home.

LAURA LEE: Oh, Mercer!

MERCER: I was standing in front of Ruegeley's drugstore talking to Mr. Henry, when this man came up and said "Did you hear about Mr. Weems? He had a heart attack and they've taken him home."

DORIS: Dolly, I'm scared. Come with me. (*She and LAURA LEE hurry off as the lights fade. The lights are brought up down stage center in the WEEMS apartment living room. DELIA, SKEETER and THURMAN are there. LAURA LEE and DOLLY come in.*)

LAURA LEE: Where's father?

THURMAN: Now don't be alarmed, Laura Lee, we think he is going to be all right. The doctor is in with him now. I was never so shocked by anything in my life. I had been talking over at the bank with Barsoty. He had come by to see me: he wanted to borrow some money. We had a long talk, and he explained what he wanted the money for, but I didn't think we could loan it to him. I explained to him why, and I told him I'd always liked him and it was not easy to say "No." He's a nice fellow, you know, and he said he understood and he thanked me for taking all the time I had with him, and then, just as he left, Abe Kendricks came running into the bank and told me about father. I got Mrs. Sweeney to call Skeeter and Delia. I came right over here. I thought you'd be here. (*JOSIE gets out of her wheelchair and enters the area left.*)

SKEETER: How is he, Mother?

JOSIE: He's resting. He's going to be all right. The doctor is staying on a few minutes longer, but he says there's nothing to worry about.

SKEETER: Can he go on working?

JOSIE: He said we'll wait a few days before we make a decision about that.

THURMAN: I was telling Laura Lee I heard the news. Barsoty had come in to see me about a bank loan . . .

JOSIE: Barsoty?

THURMAN: Yes. He hasn't changed a whole lot. Looks about the same. He seemed in good spirits. I don't think he's all that prosperous, though. He asked a lot of questions about you and Laura Lee. I said you both were just fine. I told him father was fine, too. Of course I hadn't heard the news then. (*A pause.*)

LAURA LEE: Can I go in and speak to father?

JOSIE: I don't think you better yet, Sister. The doctor will tell us, he says, when we can see him. (*A pause.*)

DOLLY: I'm glad he's gonna be all right. I better get home to my children. (*DELIA opens some blueprints she has with her.*)

DELIA: Here are the plans for my house. (*She shows them to LAURA LEE.*)

JOSIE: Could I see them, please? (*LAURA LEE hands them to JOSIE.*) How much is it costing?

DELIA: At least forty thousand.

THURMAN: No, it's not, Delia. I am not going to spend forty thousand dollars on a house.

DELIA: Aren't you?

THURMAN: No . . . I told you twenty-seven thousand five hundred is my limit. She's talking to a fancy architect in Houston and of course he'll charge her double for everything.

DELIA: You go to hell. I am spending what I want on the house and what I want to furnish it. You have Miss Murray to thank for that, Mister. You have absolutely no say in it whatsoever now. And don't be too sure it's going to be forty thousand. The architect said it could go so high as sixty thousand and I said that's just fine with me. And he said, "How will your husband feel?" and I said, "My husband has nothing at all to say about it." (*Off stage BARSOTY calls.*)

BARSOTY: (*Calling.*) Mrs. Weems . . . Mrs. Weems . . . (*THURMAN goes to greet him.*)

THURMAN: Barsoty. Come in. (*BARSOTY enters.*)

BARSOTY: Thurman. Hello, Mrs. Weems, Skeeter, Delia, Laura Lee. (*He shakes hands with all of them except LAURA LEE.*) I went over to Dolly's to see Laura Lee and Mercer told me about Mr. Weems. I'm awfully sorry. I do hope it's not serious.

JOSIE: It's serious, I guess, Barsoty, but the doctor thinks he will be well again . . . just be careful that's all . . .

BARSOTY: Laura Lee, I was late getting over to Dolly's because of a business meeting I had with Thurman at the bank. (*ROSA appears behind the scrim.*)

ROSA: (*Singing.*) IN THE OLD CHURCHYARD IN THE VALLEY, BEN BOLT, IN A CORNER OBSCURE AND ALONE . . . (*ROSA disappears.*)

BARSOTY: Well, it's good to see none of you sweet people have changed. I've always had such happy memories of the time I spent here in old Harrison with you all.

JOSIE: We think of you, too, son. Mr. Weems was so pleased when he got your card two or three years ago.

BARSOTY: (*To LAURA LEE.*) I was hoping you could have supper with me, but I suppose under the circumstances . . .

JOSIE: Go ahead and have supper with him, Sister. We all have to eat. Your father is going to be all right.

LAURA LEE: Well . . .
JOSIE: Go eat at the hotel, and if we need you we can always call you.
LAURA LEE: Well, all right.
BARSOTY: Nice to have seen you all again.
JOSIE: Nice to have seen you Barsoty. (*He and LAURA LEE go out. DELIA, THURMAN, SKEETER and JOSIE exit as the lights fade and are brought up again down center. LAURA LEE and BARSOTY come in. They sit.*)
BARSOTY: What would you like?
LAURA LEE: Nothing. I'm not very hungry. I'm still very nervous about father.
BARSOTY: Maybe you shouldn't have come.
LAURA LEE: No, it's all right. I'm glad to be out of the apartment.
BARSOTY: How long have you lived there?
LAURA LEE: Too long. I'm going to build me a house . . . soon.
BARSOTY: Are you?
LAURA LEE: I'm trying to find me a lot.
BARSOTY: How large a lot do you want?
LAURA LEE: Oh, just a small lot. I don't want a large yard to take care of. (*A pause.*) Where do you live now?
BARSOTY: I'm on the road. My headquarters are in Shreveport.
LAURA LEE: Do you have a house there?
BARSOTY: No, I rent a room. (*A pause.*) I'm surprised you never married, Laura Lee.
LAURA LEE: And I'm surprised you never married. (*A pause.*) Do you like your work?
BARSOTY: Pretty well. Matter of fact, I'm hoping to change. I want to go into business for myself. That's why I was here talking to Thurman. I was hoping to get the bank interested, but he didn't think they would be.
LAURA LEE: You'd better order some supper.
BARSOTY: To tell you the truth, I'm not so hungry myself. (*A pause.*) I'm very disappointed about Thurman. I was hoping he would be able to get the bank to help. (*A pause.*) Your mother looks well. She hasn't changed.
LAURA LEE: No.
BARSOTY: Mercer tells me he's been having a rough time.
LAURA LEE: Yes.
BARSOTY: And he told me about Lawrence. I was awful sorry to hear that.
LAURA LEE: Yes, it was very sad.
BARSOTY: That's a most becoming dress.

LAURA LEE: Thank you.
BARSOTY: Is that new?
LAURA LEE: Yes. I bought it to wear to parties this Spring.
BARSOTY: You still play bridge?
LAURA LEE: Yes. What kind of business are you hoping to start?
BARSOTY: A trucking business. I want to build up a trucking fleet to haul cotton back and forth over the Coast.
LAURA LEE: How much money do you need?
BARSOTY: Enough to buy two trucks to get me a start.
LAURA LEE: Are they expensive?
BARSOTY: Yes, they are new. But I know of two second-hand ones in very good condition that I can get much cheaper.
LAURA LEE: I'd like to loan you the money.
BARSOTY: You would?
LAURA LEE: Yes.
BARSOTY: Do you have money?
LAURA LEE: Yes, money my father has given me. It's been put in a saving's account over the years.
BARSOTY: What would your father say? Or Thurman? About you loaning me money?
LAURA LEE: It's my money. It's in my name. (*A pause.*)
BARSOTY: Thank you, but I couldn't take it from you. (*A pause.*) I knew you had money. Thurman told me the exact amount. When I heard it I thought, well, maybe she'll loan it to me for old time's sake. (*A pause.*) But I couldn't take it from you. I couldn't ever take it from you . . . If the business failed and I lost your money . . . Like I lost you a long time ago . . . I lost you and you lost me. How many years ago? (*A pause.*) You were engaged to marry a man named Chestnut. Why didn't you marry him?
LAURA LEE: I don't know.
BARSOTY: I'm engaged to be married. I have been for three months now. She's very jealous of you. She doesn't know I'm here. (*A pause.*) Thank you again, so much, but you understand why I can't borrow the money. You understand. (*A pause.*) I keep telling Mildred, that's my fiancée, how silly she is to be jealous of you. "How many years since I've seen her, Mildred?" I said. (*ROSA appears behind the scrim.*)
ROSA: (*Singing.*) OH! DON'T YOU REMEMBER THE WOOD, BEN BOLT, NEAR THE GREEN SUNNY SLOPE OF THE HILL. (*LAURA LEE cries. ROSA disappears.*)
LAURA LEE: I'm sorry. Forgive me. I just thought of father . . . if anything should happen to him. I don't know what I'd do. I'd be very lost

without father. (*JOSIE, DELIA, and THURMAN come in.*)

THURMAN: Mind if we join you?

BARSOTY: No, sit down. (*He and THURMAN bring more chairs. DELIA and JOSIE sit.*)

JOSIE: I just want a cup of coffee. (*ROSA appears behind the scrim.)*

ROSA: (*Singing.*) THE MILL HAS GONE TO DECAY, BEN BOLT, *LAURA (LEE and BARSOTY sing with ROSA. They remain seated at the table.*)

ROSA, BARSOTY, AND LAURA LEE: (*Singing.*) AND A QUIET NOW REIGNS ALL AROUND. (*ROSA disappears.*)

THURMAN: Well, it's like old times having Barsoty here with us. Isn't it?

JOSIE: It certainly is. Mr. Weems and I often talked about the times you and Rosa and Laura Lee used to sing trios together. You're travelling Thurman tells me?

BARSOTY: Yes, Ma'am. What kind of a house are you going to build Laura Lee?

LAURA LEE: Just a very simple one. (*She laughs.*) One I can afford.

DELIA: Is that a dig at me?

LAURA LEE: No. Certainly not.

DELIA: Thurman and I are building a house, too.

THURMAN: She's building it. I'm not. I'm just paying for it.

DELIA: And it's not going to be modest, I tell you that. It will cost as much as I can make it.

THURMAN: You have a sweet disposition, Delia.

DELIA: And so have you.

THURMAN: We haven't seen Barsoty in I don't know how long and you have to start a fight. (*A pause.*) And don't start pouting now. I can take anything but that.

DELIA: You go to hell.

THURMAN: You go to hell yourself. (*She slaps him.*)

DELIA: Don't tell me to go to hell. Have you forgotten yourself? Have you forgotten what I have on you? Did you tell your friend, Barsoty, how you've been acting?

THURMAN: Come on, Delia, please . . . (*A pause.*)

BARSOTY: I'll have to go. I have a long ride ahead of me tonight. Can I take you home, Laura Lee?

LAURA LEE: That's all right. I'll ride home with Thurman.

BARSOTY: Well, good-night again, folks. Nice to have seen you all.

JOSIE: Goodbye, Barsoty. Goodbye.

THURMAN: If you're down this way again stop by and see us.

BARSOTY: Thank you, I will. (*He leaves.*)

JOSIE: You never know, do you? I would never have thought Chestnut would amount to a thing and that Barsoty would set the world on fire . . . and it's just the opposite. Well, I'm glad you didn't marry him now, Sister . . . since he hasn't amounted to anything. I wonder why he hasn't amounted to anything?

THURMAN: I don't know, Mother. You can't figure something like that out. Some men amount to something and some men don't. (*He looks at his watch.*) We'd better get on back to the apartment. (*He gets up and starts out. JOSIE follows after him.*)

DELIA: I didn't want to come here in the first place. I felt you two should be left alone. (*A pause.*) I'm sorry for what I did to make a scene. (*A pause.*) Maybe he'll come back to see you.

LAURA LEE: I don't want him to come back to see me. I don't think he came here to see me in the first place. I think he came here hoping to borrow money. I felt very sorry for him. I wanted to give him money but he wouldn't take it from me. (*JOSIE comes back.*)

JOSIE: Come on, Laura Lee, you're holding us up.

LAURA LEE: Go on without me.

JOSIE: We can't go on without you. You can't walk home alone at this time of night.

LAURA LEE: (*She screams at her.*) Leave me alone, Mother, and get out of here.

JOSIE: Why are you so cross with me lately, Sister?

LAURA LEE: (*She continues to scream.*) Because you irritate me. The very sight of you irritates me. Get out of here and leave me alone. (*LAURA LEE gets up and leaves.*)

JOSIE: Did you ever hear anything like that?

DELIA: I think she's disappointed.

JOSIE: About what?

DELIA: Mr. Barsoty.

JOSIE: Why?

DELIA: Well . . .

JOSIE: (*Interrupting her.*) Oh, nonsense. There's nothing to be disappointed about. She should be glad she never married him. Look at poor Dolly. (*They go on out as the lights fade. The lights are brought up downstage left. LAURA LEE is there cutting out pictures from magazines. JOSIE comes in.*) Has Thurman been by this evening?

LAURA LEE: Not yet.

JOSIE: He's been here every night since your father's funeral. I certainly appreciate that. I thank you for staying home with me so much.

LAURA LEE: That's all right, Mother. I haven't felt like going out much myself.

JOSIE: We got a lovely letter from Barsoty. He asked to be remembered especially to you. He said he borrowed some money and was going into his own business.

LAURA LEE: That's nice.

JOSIE: He says he's getting married. She's a trained nurse. They've gone together for over a year. She's been married once before he says. (*THURMAN comes in. He kisses his mother.*) I do appreciate you coming by here, son.

THURMAN: I enjoy the visits, Mother.

JOSIE: Have you started your duties as Vice President?

THURMAN: I did today. (*LAURA LEE is crying. She leaves the room.*)

JOSIE: She cries all the time since Mr. Weems died. She is grieving so for him. (*A pause.*) Did you ask her about postponing the building of her house?

THURMAN: I will.

JOSIE: Tell her I'm too nervous to think of anything right now. But in six months or so when I'm over the shock of your father's death, I will certainly think about building a house for the two of us. (*A pause.*) Son, how much had your father put aside for Laura Lee?

THURMAN: She has forty thousand dollars in a savings account and five thousand in a checking account.

JOSIE: Forty-five thousand dollars. That's a fortune. I hope she doesn't do anything foolish. (*JOSIE goes to her wheelchair. LAURA LEE comes back in.*)

THURMAN: Sister . . . (*He takes her in his arms.*) Sister . . . Sister . . . (*She wipes her eyes.*) I think you and mother should go out to Kerville. You've always enjoyed yourself there playing bridge. Mother asked me to speak to you about your house. She said will you wait a while before building it? She doesn't want to be left alone. You understand that. When she's over her grief, she wants to build a house with you if that's what you still want.

LAURA LEE: That's not what I want. I don't want to live with mother.

THURMAN: You can't tell her that now, Sister. Wait a while. You know you've never lived by yourself, Sister. It wouldn't be easy for either of you or mother living by yourself. At least if you build a house together you could have enough space, so you wouldn't be in each other's way. You wouldn't need to be crowded like you are here in the apartment.

LAURA LEE: I have my house all picked out.

THURMAN: I know, well, don't worry about it now. But do give it some thought. Miss Nannie Stanfield tried to live by herself and then a man started peeking in her window and she had to give up and go live at the hotel. (*He leaves. LAURA LEE puts pictures in her scrap-*

book. The lights are lowered. LAURA LEE's music theme is heard. LAURA LEE walks around the room. The lights are brought up. Once again she goes to her scrapbook. DELIA comes in.)

DELIA: Where's your mother?

LAURA LEE: She's gone uptown shopping.

DELIA: (*Laughing.*) Merchants hate to see her come into the store. She drives them crazy. She wants to see everything in the store, before she makes up her mind what to buy and then when she finally decides on something and brings it home, she always brings it back the next day to exchange it for something else. Have you decided to go ahead and live with your mother?

LAURA LEE: Oh, I guess so. She's all alone.

DELIA: Do you think you'll ever really get her out of this apartment?

LAURA LEE: She says she's ready to move. I'm paying for the house and the lot. The house is to be in my name.

DELIA: Has Thurman finished searching the title for your lot?

LAURA LEE: Not yet.

DELIA: It's been almost a year.

LAURA LEE: I know it. I've waited this long, I guess I can wait a while longer.

DELIA: Have you decided on your final plan?

LAURA LEE: I want this one. (*She hands a picture to DELIA.*) But mother thinks it's too many rooms to keep clean. So I guess it will be this smaller one. (*She hands another picture to DELIA.*) You know Mother is such a fanatic about keeping a house clean. She has to scrub and clean every minute of the day. I don't really see any reason to be quite so particular do you?

DELIA: No. (*BARSOTY and ROSA appear behind the scrim.*)

BARSOTY AND ROSA: (*Singing.*) AND DON'T YOU REMEMBER THE SCHOOL, BEN BOLT, WITH THE MASTER SO KIND AND SO TRUE? (*They disappear. LAURA LEE picks up a clipping. She hands it to DELIA.*)

LAURA LEE: Barsoty died in Galveston. I saw this in the Chronicle. He'd been married just a year. (*DELIA reads it. DELIA looks up from the clipping.*)

DELIA: Do you mind if I ask you a personal question?

LAURA LEE: No.

DELIA: Were you in love with him?

LAURA LEE: (*Laughs.*) I guess so. At one time.

DELIA: What about Mr. Chestnut?

LAURA LEE: I don't know.

DELIA: Did you break off the engagement or did he?

LAURA LEE: I did.

DELIA: Why?

LAURA LEE: I was scared to go to Houston and try to live on what he made then. Mr. Chestnut cut a ring I gave him in half and sent it back to me after I said I couldn't marry him.

DELIA: He's very successful now, I hear.

LAURA LEE: I've heard so, too.

DELIA: I saw in the Houston paper where his daughter was making her debut this season.

LAURA LEE: I read that.

DELIA: Well, I've got to go meet Thurman. (*DELIA exits as the lights fade. LAURA LEE remaining in her area. The lights are brought up center as JOSIE continues to stare at the scrapbook. DORIS comes back in.*)

DORIS: Doctor says he'll be here right after breakfast. He says you'll last until then, he's sure.

JOSIE: I expect I will. (*A pause. She points back at the scrapbook.*) I never saw so many house plans in my life. One story houses, two story houses. I had agreed to let her build a house, but, then, (*A pause.*) The War came . . . Before Thurman could get the title cleared on the lot she wanted to buy. And once the War started everybody knew it was a bad time to build anything, so we never talked about it. All she did was play bridge, morning, noon, and night, and so I thought she'd forgotten all about a house. Then the War was over and one day she began again. She brought out plans and pictures of the house and I said to myself . . . it's crazy . . . She's sixty and I'm eighty–three and we'll no sooner get a house built then I'll die. But I never said that aloud, I swear. I only thought it. Thurman agreed with me. But he was the one that said aloud, "What in the world do two old women want with a house?" I didn't. But anyway, unfortunately Delia heard him say it and you know how mean she has always been. She could hardly wait, of course, to repeat the remark to sister. (*LAURA LEE has remained seated left all the while, putting away the clippings in the scrapbook. JOSIE gets out of her wheelchair and enters the down left area. LAURA LEE ignores her when she enters.*) How was the bridge party, Laura Lee? (*LAURA LEE doesn't answer her.*) Who was there? (*LAURA LEE still doesn't answer or make any sign of recognition that her mother is in the room.*) What's the matter with you, Laura Lee? If I've said or done anything . . . (*Still LAURA LEE pays no attention to her. JOSIE goes over to her and hands her the package she has been holding.*) Here. I bought you this slip for your birthday. Happy Birthday! I got it on sale, but Beatrice said if it didn't fit you or if you didn't like the color, I could still return it. (*LAURA LEE takes the package and throws it across the room.*)

LAURA LEE: Did you tell Delia that you didn't see any sense in two old women building a house?

JOSIE: No. I didn't say that.

LAURA LEE: She said you did.

JOSIE: Well, I didn't say it, thank you. But now that the remark has been made I must say I agree.

LAURA LEE: I'm not old. You're old.

JOSIE: You're sixty.

LAURA LEE: I'm not old.

JOSIE: You're sixty, Laura Lee. You're sixty. (*LAURA LEE looks at JOSIE. The two women stand there staring at each other as if mesmerized. JOSIE leaves. LAURA LEE sinks to the floor. JOSIE comes back in and goes to her.*) Oh my God, Oh my God. Laura Lee what's wrong. Get up off the floor. Please, get up off the floor. Laura Lee . . . I'm sorry I ever said what I did. I know you think I've ruined your life. Delia has told me often enough you've told her that and I'm sorry you feel that way. You can have anything you want, believe me . . . Anything I have. I'll build you a finer house than Delia and Thurman. Only, please get up off this floor. Please . . . Please. (*She screams.*) Thurman! Thurman! Thurman! (*As she goes to her wheelchair and sits.*) But she couldn't get up. I called her brothers. And they came over and helped her up. And they called the doctor and he took her to the hospital and then we brought her back home and we got you to come and nurse her. (*DORIS goes from the area upstage center to the area downstage left. LAURA LEE is in the wheelchair.*)

DORIS: (*To LAURA LEE.*) You look a whole lot better today. Of all the White girls I watched growing up . . . I always thought Miss Laura Lee Weems was the sweetest and prettiest.

LAURA LEE: I'm feeling better, Doris.

DORIS: I'm glad. Mr. Thurman called to say that your lot has been bought. He said he has a clear title for it now. He says for you to hurry up and get well so you can start building you a house.

LAURA LEE: You live with your mother?

DORIS: Yes, Ma'am.

LAURA LEE: How can you live with your mother in that house you live in?

DORIS: Lot's more of us lived there at one time. My mother, my two children, my grandson and his wife and four children. (*She laughs.*) We managed. I just try to keep cheerful. My son gets discouraged. He says, "Mama, I don't like to see you and Sissy," that's what we all call my Mama, Sissy, "living in this old shack, it leaks when it rains, it's so cold in the Winter. I want you all to have a nice house." "Well, you're gonna make yourself sick worrying about it." I tell him. "We're gettin' along. We don't worry about it. You go ahead and worry about your own self . . ."

LAURA LEE: Your roof leaks?

DORIS: (*Laughing.*) It sure does. And now the front porch and the steps are rotting.

LAURA LEE: Well, we're going to do something about that. When I get better, I'm going to find me a carpenter and I'm coming out there and we're going to fix the roof of your house and the front steps and the porch. (*A pause.*) Maybe we shouldn't wait until I get better. March is almost here. It always rains so in March. (*A pause.*) You love your mother?

DORIS: Yes, Ma'am.

LAURA LEE: I wish I did. I despise my mother. I wish I didn't. It makes me feel so bad. I know it's wrong to feel this way. (*She is crying.*)

DORIS: Sh, now. Sh . . . don't get upset now. You've been doing so well.

LAURA LEE: Bring me my checkbook.

DORIS: Yes, Ma'am. (*She gets it and brings it to her.*)

LAURA LEE: I think five hundred dollars will take care of a new roof and porch don't you?

DORIS: Oh, yes, Ma'am. We didn't pay but five hundred dollars when we bought the house.

LAURA LEE: Get my fountain pen, please. (*DORIS goes to get it. LAURA LEE closes her eyes. Her head falls forward. DORIS comes back with the fountain pen.*)

DORIS: Miss Laura Lee . . . Miss Laura Lee. (*She goes to her. She sees she is dead.*) May God rest your soul in peace. (*The lights are brought down. DORIS goes back upstage center to JOSIE. The lights are brought up. THURMAN comes in.*)

THURMAN: I couldn't sleep, so I got in the car and began to ride around, then I saw your lights on here, and I thought I'd see if you're all right.

JOSIE: I'm pretty good.

DORIS: She wasn't feeling too well a few minutes ago, but I called the doctor and he said there was nothing to worry about. He said he'd be here early this morning.

JOSIE: Why couldn't you sleep, son?

THURMAN: Just before bedtime, Mr. Jackson's son called me. Mr. Jackson was taken to the hospital. He said he was going to have to resign as president of the bank. He said, "I'm president now."

JOSIE: I know that makes you happy.

THURMAN: I don't know. I guess it does. Maybe it's come too late. I'm seventy. I don't know. If it had happened ten years ago, but now. I'm not sure I care now. (*He picks up the scrapbook.*)

JOSIE: That was your sister's. She cut out all kinds of things: History about Harrison, Texas and the South. Birth announcements, wedding announcements, the writeup in the paper when Mr. Weems died and when poor Lawrence died . . . and on every other page there are plans or pictures of a house she wanted to build at one time or another. Nothing about herself though, except her obituary. I put that in myself. There's room for one more. I guess that will be mine. (*A pause.*)

DORIS: It's going to be a pretty day.

THURMAN: We need rain. The cotton farmers are all begging for rain.

JOSIE: I've never understood why Laura Lee didn't want music or flowers at her funeral. She always loved pretty things so. (*DOLLY comes in.*)

DOLLY: Good morning.

THURMAN: Good morning, Dolly. You're up early.

JOSIE: She's like me. We're both up at 5:30. I like to get an early start so does Dolly.

DOLLY: I sure do. (*She hands JOSIE a newspaper.*) I brought you the Houston paper.

JOSIE: Thank you.

DOLLY: I thought I'd sit here with you while Doris fixed your breakfast.

JOSIE: All I want is a cup of coffee. Would you like some breakfast, son?

THURMAN: No, thank you. I'll eat up at the restaurant. (*He gets up.*) I'll look in again this afternoon, Mama. (*He leaves.*)

JOSIE: Thurman has been made president of the bank. Mr. Jackson has been taken sick and has to retire.

DOLLY: I know that makes him happy. (*DORIS gets up.*)

DORIS: Do you want a little breakfast, Miss Dolly?

DOLLY: I've had mine, thank you. Had it an hour ago. (*DORIS goes.*)

JOSIE: Put that scrapbook away, Dolly. (*DOLLY puts it away.*)

DOLLY: This was Laura Lee's.

JOSIE: Yes. I don't believe in saving things, as you know, but I just couldn't somehow ever throw that out. She's dead and here I am. I think living has been my punishment. (*A pause.*) I never could see why Sister disliked this apartment so. I've been happy enough here.

DOLLY: There's a notice in the paper that Mr. Chestnut died yesterday.

JOSIE: How old was he?

DOLLY: It didn't say. But he was very rich, you know. A millionaire. He had a beautiful house in River Oaks. It was always open in the Spring, when they had the azalea trail.

JOSIE: Thurman is a millionaire, too, you know.

DOLLY: I know. We're all so proud of him.

JOSIE: Did you ever see Mr. Chestnut's house in River Oaks?

DOLLY: No. I saw a picture of it once, though. It looked like a big plantation house, except it wasn't because it was in the middle of Houston. Who do you think Laura Lee loved the most? Barsoty or Mr. Chestnut?

JOSIE: I don't know. (*A pause.*) I'm awfully tired, Dolly. I just don't want to think about anything anymore. Barsoty is dead, isn't he?

DOLLY: Oh, yes. He died before Laura Lee did. (*DORIS comes in with a cup of coffee.*)

DORIS: Here's your coffee.

JOSIE: Thank you but I don't want it. You drink it. (*A pause.*) Living is to be my punishment, I think. (*LAURA LEE, ROSA, and BARSOTY appears behind the scrim.*)

LAURA LEE, ROSA, AND BARSOTY: (*Singing.*) GRASS GROWS ON THE MASTER'S GRAVE, BEN BOLT, THE SPRING OF THE BROOK IS DRY. (*They disappear.*)

JOSIE: I hear music. I hear long ago, forgotten music . . . Sister and Rosa and Barsoty. (*A pause.*) How long did Thurman say I had to live?

DORIS: Something about three years.

JOSIE: Oh, yes. Three years. I reckon you can stand anything for three years. (*She closes her eyes. LAURA LEE, ROSA, and BARSOTY appear behind the scrim.*)

LAURA LEE, ROSA, AND BARSOTY: (*Singing.*) AND OF ALL THE FRIENDS WHO WERE SCHOOLMATES THEN THERE ARE ONLY YOU AND I . . . (*ROSA and BARSOTY slowly disappear. LAURA LEE lingers a moment longer and then disappears. A spotlight is on JOSIE as she listens to the singing and then all lights are dimmed and the stage is dark.*)

DIVIDING THE ESTATE

DIVIDING THE ESTATE premiered at the McCarter Theatre, New Jersey, on March 28, 1989. It was directed by Jamie Brown with the following cast:

DOUG: Thomas Martell Brimm
EMILY: Julie Corby
IRENE: Debora Jeanne Culpin
SON GORDON: Edmund Davys
LEWIS: Jay Doyle
SISSIE: Ginger Finney
STELLA: Jane Hoffman
LUCILLE: Annette Hunt
MARY JO: Kimberly King
LUCY: Mary Martello
BOB: Jerry Mayer
CATHLEEN: Théa Perkins
MILDRED: Beatrice Winde

DIVIDING THE ESTATE was subsequently produced at the Great Lakes Theatre Festival in Cleveland, Ohio on October 11, 1990. It was directed by Gerald Freedman with the following cast:

EMILY: Elizabeth Atkeson
MILDRED: Erma Campbell
CATHLEEN: Bellary Darden
BOB: Jack Davidson
LUCILLE: Elizabeth Franz
MARY JO: Jennifer Harmon
LUCY: Annalee Jefferies
SON GORDON: Brian Keeler
STELLA: Nan Martin
LEWIS: Logan Ramsey
IRENE RATLIFF: Christine Segal
DOUG: W. Benson Terry
SISSIE: Lucinda Underwood

Characters

SON GORDON
STELLA GORDON
LUCILLE
MILDRED
DOUG
LEWIS
LUCY
CATHLEEN
SISSIE
EMILY
MARY JO
BOB
IRENE RATLIFF

Setting

Place: Harrison, Texas. Time: 1987.

DIVIDING THE ESTATE

ACT I

SCENE 1

A living room in the GORDON house. It is an old-fashioned, comfortable room. Through double doors you can see the dining room with a table being set for dinner by three black servants, a man and two women. They appear and reappear at different times setting the table, arranging flowers. The year is 1987. SON Gordon, 35, is alone in the room reading a paper. His mother, LUCILLE, and his grandmother, STELLA, enter. LUCILLE, a noticeably nervous woman, has STELLA by the arm. SON rises when they enter.

SON: Grandmother, here—take your chair.

STELLA: No, Son, I'll sit over here.

LUCILLE: Now, Mama, Son doesn't mind you having that chair. He knows it's where you always sit. (*SON goes to STELLA and leads her to the chair he was sitting in. MILDRED, one of the black women, comes into the room.*)

MILDRED: How many coming for dinner?

LUCILLE: Let's see . . . Mama and me and Son and Brother, and . . .

STELLA: Where is Brother?

LUCILLE: I don't know. I haven't seen him since breakfast. Go see if you can find him, Sonny. Tell him Mama was asking for him.

SON: Yes, Ma'am. (*He goes.*)

MILDRED: You still haven't answered my question, Miss Lucille. How many are coming to dinner?

LUCILLE: Well, let's see. There are the four of us, and Sister and her two children, and Bob . . .

STELLA: Are Mary Jo's girls bringing their husbands?

LUCILLE: No, Mama. Heavens, they are both divorced. Now, you remember that.

STELLA: I don't remember it at all.

LUCILLE: My God, Mama. Of course, you do. Sissie divorced her husband last fall, and Mary Jo and Bob had Emily's marriage annulled a week after she was married.

STELLA: Did they marry boys from here?

LUCILLE: No, they were both Houston boys.
STELLA: Were they well connected?
LUCILLE: Who?
STELLA: The boys my granddaughters married.
LUCILLE: They were both lazy and no good, according to Mary Jo and Bob, but they came from lovely families.
STELLA: Which child was it had that awful tragedy on the night of her wedding?
LUCILLE: I don't know what you are talking about, Mama.
STELLA: Yes, you do, too. One of the girls' husbands blew his brains out on their wedding night.
LUCILLE: No, Mama. That wasn't Sissy or Emily's husband.
STELLA: Whose husband was it?
LUCILLE: That was Cousin Gert Stewart's daughter's husband—I forget her name.
STELLA: Clara Belle?
LUCILLE: No, that's the oldest girl.
STELLA: Catherine Lee?
LUCILLE: Yes, she is the one.
STELLA: Why did that happen? Did he leave a note?
LUCILLE: No. Gert just said it was an accident.
STELLA: An accident?
LUCILLE: Yes—that he was cleaning his gun, and he was laughing, and he said, "If I didn't think you loved me, I'd kill myself," and the gun accidentally went off and she ran to him screaming, and held him and blood was running all over her beautiful wedding gown—you remember, that wedding gown had been in Gert's family for generations. Her great, great-grandmother had brought it with her from Virginia.
STELLA: What was he doing cleaning his gun on his wedding night?
LUCILLE: No one knows, Mama. That is just one of those great mysteries.
MILDRED: Wasn't Miss Lucy invited for dinner?
LUCILLE: Oh, yes. That's right.
MILDRED: And that will make nine.
LUCILLE: Yes. (*MILDRED starts away.*) Mildred . . .
MILDRED: Yes'um.
LUCILLE: You had better set ten places, just in case. I keep thinking I've invited someone else.
MILDRED: You probably invited five more, if I know you.
LUCILLE: Oh, I hope not. Well, we always have plenty of food, that's one thing.

MILDRED: Mr. Son is after me about the grocery bills again. I said, "Mr. Son, I don't make up the menu. Speak to your Mama."

STELLA: There is only one way to economize, and that's to have a garden and grow your own vegetables. (*DOUG, an old black man comes into the dining room.*) Kill your own hogs, have a cow and calves and chickens. There is no reason why this place can't be self-sufficient again.

LUCILLE: My God, Mama—be sensible. We're living in the middle of the town on a highway. You can't keep pigs and chickens and cows here now.

STELLA: Doug . . .

DOUG: Yes, Ma'am.

STELLA: Come in here.

DOUG: Yes, Ma'am. (*He enters into the living room.*)

STELLA: I want you to put in a garden again. I want you to get some pigs, and some chickens and cows . . .

DOUG: Miss Stella, I'm an old man. I can't do that anymore.

STELLA: Well, find somebody who can.

DOUG: You can't find people to do work like that no more, Miss Stella. And if you find them, you couldn't afford their wages.

STELLA: How old are you, Doug?

DOUG: Ninety-two.

STELLA: When did you come to work here?

DOUG: When I was five years old. Your papa brought my mama in from the farm after my daddy was killed by one of the bulls, and she cooked for you all.

STELLA: Henrietta?

DOUG: Yes'um. I remember the day you was born and the day you got married, and the day your husband, Mister Charles, died.

STELLA: Charlie wasn't my husband, Doug. He was Lucille's husband—Donald was my husband.

DOUG: Yes'um that's how it was. I remember all of it. (*He leaves. MILDRED leaves.*)

STELLA: Did I hear you say Lucy is coming?

LUCILLE: Yes.

STELLA: Who invited her?

LUCILLE: Son.

STELLA: You know I have never understood why our young men here are always attracted to school teachers. Do you realize how many of the young men here married school teachers? Both the Courtney boys, Mr. Jackson, Lewis Fraley—oh, there are so many. (*A pause.*) She's very modern, I think. She's always giving lectures. I cannot stand the way she lectures you. She thinks she knows the answer to everything—why we no longer find it profitable to grow cotton here, why the chemical plants are poisoning our environment here on the Coast, why the Mexicans are coming in droves from Mexico, why . . .

LUCILLE: Well, Mama, I find her very sensible and down to earth. And personally I'm grateful Son has found someone like Lucy, after all he went through with his first wife.

STELLA: Why do you think Olive Louise divorced Son?

LUCILLE: Now, Mama, we've been over this a thousand times and you know very well I don't know the answer to that.

STELLA: Why does Son think she did?

LUCILLE: I don't know. We've never discussed it with him. All I know was he was very hurt and upset.

STELLA: I'm going to ask him.

LUCILLE: Don't you dare.

STELLA: I'd certainly like to know. Maybe one day I'll ask Olive Louise.

LUCILLE: You can't ask her, Mama. She's dead. Heavens!

STELLA: Oh, that's right. She certainly is. Bless her heart. Well, I wish someone would tell Lucy to stop acting like an encyclopedia.

LUCILLE: Oh, Mama, the poor thing has to talk about something. All we ever talk about is our family and friends. That must be very boring to her. This is not her family and these are not her friends.

STELLA: Doesn't she have any family?

LUCILLE: Of course she does, Mama, but if she talked about them, we wouldn't know who in the world she was talking about.

STELLA: I don't care for over-educated women. I never have. (*LEWIS enters—he is STELLA'S son and LUCILLE'S brother.*)

LUCILLE: Did Son find you?

LEWIS: No.

LUCILLE: He went looking for you.

STELLA: Where were you?

LEWIS: I took a walk downtown.

STELLA: Lewis . . .

LEWIS: Yes, Mama.

STELLA: I smell liquor on your breath. Have you been drinking?

LEWIS: Yes, Mama.

STELLA: So early in the morning?

LEWIS: Yes, Mama.

STELLA: I don't allow liquor in this house.

LEWIS: I know that, Mama. I don't drink it in this house. (*DOUG has reappeared in the dining room.*)

DOUG: Miss Ida Belle Coons was a Coke fiend. She drank Coca Colas all day long.

LEWIS: Nobody wants to hear about Ida Belle Coons, Doug.

DOUG: Mrs. Coons's cook told us that Mrs. Coons banned Coca Colas from the house, but Miss Ida Belle would slip out of the house and go over to the Texaco filling station and buy her cokes. The cook said she would slip out at seven in the morning and be there waiting for the filling station to open.

STELLA: Merciful God.

DOUG: Coca Colas are bad for you if you drink too many. Mr. Leroy had the lining of his stomach eaten out from drinking Coca Colas, everybody says.

STELLA: That's the truth . . .

DOUG: And I tell you another thing . . .

LEWIS: All right Doug, that's enough.

DOUG: Yessir. You know I can read and write and do the multiplication table—your Mama taught me. I never went to school, but your Mama did and she say to me—she wasn't more than twelve—"How old are you?" "Twenty-two," I say, "And you can't read or write?" "No, Ma'am," I says. "Then I'm going to teach you," she says, and she did. I knows all the books in the Bible—Genesis, Exodus . . .

LEWIS: All right, Doug. We know you do.

DOUG: I read in the Bible every morning and every night.

LEWIS: Hush up, Doug.

DOUG: Do you read your Bible?

LEWIS: I said hush up, Doug. (*DOUG leaves.*)

STELLA: Lewis, you promised me.

LEWIS: I know, Mama, but I've broken my promise.

STELLA: Why?

LEWIS: Because I am very nervous today. (*A pause.*) I wanted to go on record as saying I am for immediately dividing the estate.

STELLA: Why?

LEWIS: Because . . .

STELLA: You would run through your share in a day . . .

LEWIS: Then I'll run through it. (*SON enters.*) But I'm tired of having pittances doled out to me by my nephew every month.

STELLA: Pittances. You have a house, three wonderful meals every day. Servants to wait on you hand and foot, four hundred dollars every month, a car . . . (*MILDRED reappears.*)

MILDRED: Miss Lucille, did you tell Doug he couldn't serve the food today?

LUCILLE: Not yet—

MILDRED: Well, you better tell him. He's bound and determined. I told him Cathleen was going to serve and he said he'd break both of her arms if she tried.

STELLA: Why can't Doug serve?

LUCILLE: Because his hands shake and tremble, Mama. He spilled gravy all over Miss Ida Cox last time she was here for dinner. (*DOUG comes out followed by CATHLEEN.*)

DOUG: Miss Stella, this fresh thing says she is going to serve your dinner today and not me. You tell her she is wrong.

LUCILLE: She's not wrong, Doug. We've retired you now, you know that.

DOUG: I don't want to be retired.

LUCILLE: Well, you are, so be quiet.

STELLA: Don't talk to Doug that way, Lucille.

LUCILLE: Please, Mama—

STELLA: I want him to serve the dinner.

LUCILLE: Mama, how—

STELLA: I said he's going to serve that dinner.

LUCILLE: All right, Mama. Cathleen, let him have his way. (*They go back to the kitchen.*)

SON: (*Singing to himself.*) Rock of ages, Cleft for me . . .

STELLA: Why are you singing that, Son?

SON: I don't know, it just came into my head, so I sang it.

STELLA: Is this teacher you go with religious?

SON: Yes, I think she is. She is no fanatic. She's not there every time the Church doors open, but she goes to Church.

STELLA: Which one?

SON: Methodist.

STELLA: Does she know you are a Baptist?

SON: Yes.

STELLA: Of course, in my day that was a very serious matter if one was a Baptist and one was Methodist. Now, of course, it doesn't seem to matter. Baptists marry anybody and anything—Methodists, Catholics, Lutherans, Holy Rollers . . .

LEWIS: I just love the way everybody in this family changes subjects. I made a statement earlier about dividing the estate.

STELLA: That's just because you've been drinking, Lewis. That's how you always talk when you're drinking.

LEWIS: I am sick and tired of having to go to my nephew for the least thing. Son, I need ten dollars or fifteen or twenty. Why? Because I spent my allowance too soon this month. Why? Because it is none of your God damned business is why.

STELLA: Lewis, Lewis, just shut up. Shut up if you have to talk that way. Thank God, we have Son is all I say. Thank God, Son is willing to devote his life to keep this estate in operation. This estate has taken very good care of us all these years, hasn't it? It took care of my mother and father, me and my family. It took care of my grandfather and grandmother.

LEWIS: These are difficult times. Cotton is too expensive to grow these days.

STELLA: Don't talk to me about difficult times. We got through the depression, when people were abandoning their land, selling it all over this county, but my father held on to our land, scraped together the money to plant cotton every year, pay our taxes and keep body and soul together. Just look at what is surrounding us. Fruit markets and fast food restaurants. That's what happens when you sell your land. Of course, the sight of all that squalor is all you've ever known, Son, but when your Mother and Uncle were growing up this was a lovely, quiet street. Beautiful homes—

LUCILLE: Son knows that Mama—

STELLA: Fine, gracious, lovely homes.

LEWIS: People sold because they needed money.

STELLA: Too bad. (*A pause.*) I'm not feeling well. I'm going to my room.

LUCILLE: Now, Mama. Mama, please don't go—you're going to spoil everything.

STELLA: I know what you're all up to. Plotting behind my back. The minute I'm dead you'll sell this house, divide the land and it will all be gone. Well, you'll never do it while I'm alive. I tell you that. (*She leaves.*)

LUCILLE: Brother, why in the world— (*A pause.*) My God, my God.

LEWIS: I need some money.

SON: For what?

LEWIS: Never mind. I just need money—

SON: Uncle, I've already given you two advances, you know.

LEWIS: It's not your money.

SON: I'm aware of that.

LEWIS: Then just give it to me and shut up.

SON: How much do you want?

LEWIS: A large sum.

SON: How much?

LEWIS: You can deduct it from my share of the estate.

SON: How much, Uncle Lewis?

LEWIS: Ten thousand dollars.

SON: Ten thousand dollars! My God, Uncle Lewis, the estate can't afford shelling out money like that.

LEWIS: You're not giving me anything—I said to take it off my share of the estate.

SON: I gave you fifteen thousand dollars last year.

LEWIS: You gave me nothing—I took it out of my share of the estate.

SON: Do you know how much you already owe the estate?

LEWIS: No, but I bet you do.

SON: You're God damned right I do.

LUCILLE: Son . . . Son . . .

SON: Two hundred thousand dollars.

LEWIS: I don't believe it.

SON: It's there in black and white.

LEWIS: How much has Mary Jo taken?

SON: Plenty.

LEWIS: How much?

SON: I can't tell you off-hand. (*A pause.*)

LEWIS: Just don't argue and give me the ten thousand dollars.

SON: I'm not going to do it. Not until the end of the year and we can see how we stand. I may have to borrow money to pay the taxes again.

LEWIS: Goddamnit, it's my money. (*LUCY enters.*)

LUCY: Good morning. I hope I'm not late.

SON: No, our Houston kin aren't here yet.

LUCY: What a day—what a lovely day!

LUCILLE: Yes, it is.

LUCY: I was over at the Historical Museum just now looking for some pictures of the town for an article I'm writing for the *Houston Post*. I had never seen pictures of this street before they paved it. It was simply beautiful. It's too bad that so many of the lovely old houses have been torn down. I'm glad you've saved this one. Have you heard about the restoration plan for our town?

LUCILLE: I've heard something about it.

LUCY: This could be a beautiful town, you know, if the buildings were restored. (*She laughs.*) Oh, well—Son, I'm sure, is tired of hearing me go on about this.

LUCILLE: Are they busy up town?

LUCY: No, it's very quiet.

LUCILLE: It used to be so busy in town on Saturdays, and so crowded you could hardly walk down the sidewalk.

LEWIS: Are you going to give me the money, Son?

SON: I can't now, Uncle.

LEWIS: I want it now.

SON: You can't have it now.

LEWIS: I want to have it now.

LUCY: Maybe I should go . . .

SON: No, stay. This goes on all the time.
LEWIS: Jesus Christ, you sonofabitch. (*He gets up and starts out.*)
LUCILLE: Lewis . . .
LEWIS: Go to hell. I'm going to a lawyer and have those books examined. I want to see just how much I do owe. I don't trust your son, lady. (*He goes.*)
LUCILLE: Excuse me. (*She goes.*)
SON: Don't get upset over anything he says—he's been drinking. He can be a terror when he's drinking. And he wants money. You see, he gambles. He's a terrible gambler and so he always loses, and he gets into debt and then he has to borrow from the estate to pay his debts.
LUCY: Does he have a job?
SON: No.
LUCY: Has he ever had a job?
SON: One or two. But then he'd get on a drunk and get fired.
LUCY: Does he help you out at the farms?
SON: No. He tried managing them right after my grandfather died, but he got things so screwed up that my grandmother took everything away from him and asked my father to take over.
LUCY: He's never married?
SON: No. He's had plenty of lady friends, but none the family felt he should marry.
LUCY: The family?
SON: My grandmother and grandfather.
LUCY: What was wrong with them?
SON: Well, you know Miss Pearl Davis?
LUCY: Yes.
SON: She was one of them.
LUCY: What's wrong with her?
SON: They thought she was after his money. And I've heard about the others. I never knew them. (*DOUG comes out.*)
DOUG: Son, I have to lie down.
SON: All right, Doug.
DOUG: Those women out in the kitchen are trying to conjure me. (*MILDRED comes out.*)
MILDRED: Mr. Son, don't believe a word he says he's just old and mean.
DOUG: She and Cathleen been conjuring me, Son. They won't rest until I'm dead.
MILDRED: You ought to be ashamed of yourself talking that way—nobody is studying you, old man. Nobody in this world. Cathleen is crying out there because of your foolishness. You have her so upset, old man, with all this conjure talk she is a nervous wreck. Mr. Son, make

him behave and come talk to Cathleen.

SON: All right. You go on back to the kitchen and tell Cathleen I'll be right out. (*MILDRED goes.*) Come on, Doug. Let's go lie down and rest–you'll feel better.

DOUG: You know what they say to me? They say I talk ignorant. That I'm old timey.

SON: Don't worry about it. Now, come on.

DOUG: Cathleen think she so smart because she goes to the Junior College. I couldn't go to any Junior College. They didn't have no Junior College when I was coming along. They say I wouldn't have gone anyway, because I'm too ignorant. I said I would have gone. I can read and write and do the multiplication table, and they say that ain't nothing at all. Anybody can do that. Not when I was coming along, they couldn't.

SON: I know, I know, now don't get any more upset than you are—come on, now. Doug, it's not good for you to get upset. Come on. (*CATHLEEN and MILDRED come out.*)

CATHLEEN: I've been listening to every word you've said, old man. Nobody is making fun of you. You're the one making fun of people, saying I'm crazy, trying to go to college. Saying I'm forgetting my place—saying—

SON: All right, Cathleen. All right. (*She cries.*)

CATHLEEN: He talks so mean to me, Mr. Son. He talks so mean to me all the time.

MILDRED: You know what he told her? He told her her daddy is going to end up in the electric chair.

DOUG: No, I did not say that.

MILDRED: Yes you did.

DOUG: What I said is that they got him locked up over at the Retrieve Plantation, and if he cuts another man, they'll send him to Huntsville next time, and then the electric chair.

CATHLEEN: You see, you see, Mr. Son.

DOUG: (*He is yelling now.*) Your daddy is no good and you know he is no good. He beats you and your Mama. He cut that woman he was living with until she nearabout died. He cut three men, one of them white.

SON: All right, Doug. Just be quiet now. Cathleen, don't listen to him. Pay no attention to him.

CATHLEEN: Pay no attention to him? He follows me around all the time saying I'm trying to take his job.

DOUG: You're trying to get my job through conjure.

CATHLEEN: Shut up, you ignorant old man. Nobody believes in conjure anymore, except ignorant old fools like you. Just shut up. (*DOUG* *faints and falls to the floor.*)

MILDRED: (*Screams.*) Oh, Jesus—oh, Jesus.

CATHLEEN: (*Screams.*) God have mercy! (*SON goes to him.*)

SON: Doug, Doug . . . (*He turns to LUCY.*) Lucy, call Dr. Anderson.

LUCY: All right. (*She goes, CATHLEEN cries.*)

SON: Sh. Cathleen. Just take her into the kitchen, Mildred. (*LUCILLE is heard calling "Mildred, Mildred."*)

MILDRED: Yes'um.

LUCILLE: (*Offstage.*) Where are you?

MILDRED: In the living room.

LUCILLE: (*Offstage.*) Who's that crying? What's going on?

MILDRED: It's Cathleen— (*LUCILLE comes in.*)

LUCILLE: What on earth—what has happened?

SON: Cathleen had her feelings hurt by Doug.

LUCILLE: What's wrong with Doug?

SON: I don't know. He got excited and passed out. Lucy has called the doctor. (*LUCILLE goes to him.*)

LUCILLE: Doug—Doug.

DOUG: Yes'um, who's that? Oh, Miss Lucille. (*He sits up.*)

SON: Doug, lie down until the doctor gets here.

DOUG: What doctor?

SON: Dr. Anderson. Lucy has gone to call him.

DOUG: I don't need any doctor. I'm all right. Help me up, Son.

SON: Are you sure?

DOUG: Yes, I'm sure. (*SON helps him up. DOUG points to CATHLEEN.*) What's wrong with her?

MILDRED: You know what's wrong with her—your devilish ways is what's wrong with her. (*CATHLEEN cries.*)

LUCILLE: Now, Cathleen, Cathleen. (*She goes to her.*) Let's all keep calm —our company will be here soon.

CATHLEEN: Miss Lucille, I can't work no more today. I'm too nervous to work. I'm just too nervous.

LUCILLE: Well, all right. Son, will you drive her home?

SON: Come on, Cathleen. (*LUCY* enters.)

LUCY: The doctor says to bring him to the hospital right away.

SON: He doesn't need to go to the hospital now. He says he is feeling all right.

DOUG: Just get the conjure out of the house. I'll be all right. (*CATHLEEN begins to cry again.*)

LUCILLE: Cathleen . . .

MILDRED: Tell him to shut his mouth, Miss Lucille. He accuses Cathleen of conjuring him and that is a lie.

SON: Come on, Cathleen. Just don't pay any attention—he's an old man.

CATHLEEN: (*Wiping her eyes.*) Let me get my things. (*She goes out to the kitchen.*)

SON: Lucy and I will meet you out at the car. (*He and LUCY leave. MILDRED goes. DOUG has fallen asleep in his chair.*)

LUCILLE: Doug . . . Doug . . . (*He is asleep. She goes into the kitchen. LEWIS comes in.*)

LEWIS: (*Calling.*) Sister . . . Sister . . . (*LUCILLE comes back in.*)

LUCILLE: Sh—sh—Doug is asleep. He's not feeling well. Cathleen had to go home. I'm doing what I can do to help Mildred—we're having nine for dinner.

LEWIS: I have to have that money, Sister. Will you tell Son that?

LUCILLE: I can't interfere about that, Brother. (*DOUG wakes up.*)

DOUG: Who is here?

LUCILLE: Just me and Lewis, Doug. How do you feel?

DOUG: I feel fine. Who says I didn't?

LUCILLE: Why don't you go in the kitchen now and see if you can help Mildred? She's all alone out there.

DOUG: I'm serving the meal today?

LUCILLE: Yes, you are serving the meal today. (*DOUG closes his eyes and goes back to sleep. STELLA comes back in.*)

STELLA: Lucille.

LUCILLE: Yes, Mama.

STELLA: I wonder where Mary Jo and her family are? They're late.

LUCILLE: No, they're not late, Mama. (*LEWIS leaves the room.*)

STELLA: Doug is asleep. I don't want him asleep in here when Mary Jo and her family arrive.

LUCILLE: I'll wake him when I hear their car drive up.

STELLA: How long has Son's wife been dead?

LUCILLE: Let's see . . . (*A pause.*) A year. Is it possible?

STELLA: How long after she left Son was she killed?

LUCILLE: Let's see . . . (*A pause.*) Three months.

STELLA: Was she drunk when she had the accident?

LUCILLE: No, she was not drunk, Mother—heavens. The man she was with was drunk, they say. We don't know for sure.

STELLA: That was God's punishment to her for leaving Son and going out with other men.

LUCILLE: Now, Mama, you know God doesn't punish people for things like that by killing them.

STELLA: He certainly does.

LUCILLE: Well, then that's not a God I care to know about.

STELLA: He's a vengeful God, you know, punishing sinners.

LUCILLE: All right, Mama, if you say so. Was Charlie a sinner?

STELLA: No, Charlie wasn't a sinner.

LUCILLE: He certainly wasn't a sinner—all he did was slave for this family.

STELLA: That's right—morning, noon and night.

LUCILLE: Then why was he struck down, slaving away out at the farms for us?

STELLA: I don't know about that . . .

LUCILLE: Well, I can tell you, my husband was not a sinner. He was a good, kind man.

STELLA: Your father was a sinner—he fathered children all up and down this county, black and white. I warned him he'd be struck down right in a bed of iniquity, but he never was. He died just as peaceful . . .

LUCILLE: He didn't die peaceful, Mama. He was in great pain when he died.

STELLA: Well, he was in his own bed being cared for by his family. I despised him, you know.

LUCILLE: Mama, don't say that.

STELLA: I did. I despised him. I would've left him, too, except for you children.

LUCILLE: Why did you marry him, Mama? Didn't you know his ways?

STELLA: I was worried about them, but I was young and innocent and he was handsome, and I was flattered by his attention because he was known as such a good catch. I felt surely I could reform him. But I couldn't . . . (*A pause. LEWIS comes in.*)

LEWIS: Mama . . .

STELLA: Yes.

LEWIS: I have to borrow some money from the estate.

STELLA: My god, Lewis. You have asked me that four times today. And I have told you four times that I will not give you any more money.

LEWIS: Mama . . .

STELLA: Lewis . . .

LEWIS: It's life or death, Mama.

STELLA: Life or death?

LEWIS: Yes.

STELLA: Did you hear that, Lucille?

LUCILLE: Yes.

STELLA: You're not lying to me, Lewis?

LEWIS: No, Mama.

STELLA: Tell me why it is life or death—

LEWIS: I can't, Mama.

STELLA: Can you tell Lucille?

LEWIS: No.
STELLA: Can you tell Son?
LEWIS: Yes.
STELLA: Why can't you tell me?
LEWIS: Because I am ashamed to, Mama.
STELLA: Ashamed?
LEWIS: Yes. (*SON comes in with LUCY.*)
SON: Hello.
STELLA: Son, give Lewis the money he needs.
SON: Ten thousand dollars?
STELLA: Yes, if that's what he needs.
SON: But grandmother, we can't spare that money right now—I was explaining to Uncle Lewis . . .
STELLA: Well, you'll sell something then, Son. He says it's life or death—
SON: What do you want me to sell?
STELLA: Use your own judgment.
LEWIS: I need the money now, Son.
SON: Right now?
LEWIS: Yes, right now.
SON: All right—come on down to the bank and I'll see what I can arrange.
STELLA: He's going to tell you why he needs it, Son.
SON: That is really no concern of mine.
STELLA: I want him to tell you.
SON: All right. (*They leave.*)
STELLA: Lucille . . .
LUCILLE: Yes, Mama.
STELLA: Do you believe it's life or death?
LUCILLE: I don't know, Mama. (*DOUG wakes up.*)
DOUG: (*Singing.*) Rock of Ages, Cleft for me . . .
STELLA: Why are you singing that hymn, Doug? Son was singing it this morning, too. I don't care for that hymn, you know I never have.
LUCILLE: They sang it at Papa's funeral.
STELLA: Did they? Well, I forbid them to sing it at mine.
DOUG: You won't know what they're singing at your funeral.
STELLA: If either of you are around, tell them not to.
DOUG: I want it sung at my funeral. (*He sings.*) Rock of Ages, Cleft for me . . .
STELLA: Hush up, Doug, it's not your funeral now.
DOUG: I want you to promise me one thing: that they will sing "Rock of Ages" as they're lowering my coffin into the grave and that you'll buy

me a nice tombstone.

STELLA: I have already promised you that a million times—so has Lucille and so has Son. (*MILDRED comes to the door.*)

MILDRED: I need some help out in the kitchen. I can't do all the work myself.

LUCILLE: I'm going to help you, Mildred. (*She gets up.*)

STELLA: You go help her too, Doug.

DOUG: No, thank you. I'm tired. I'm going to set here and rest until it's time to serve your dinner. (*He closes his eyes.*)

STELLA: (*Singing half to herself.*) Rock of Ages, cleft for me . . . (*A pause.*) I hate that damn hymn. (*She closes her eyes.*)

DOUG: Fine tombstone and a fine coffin.

STELLA: We've promised you that, too, so be quiet. You know why Mary Jo and her husband are coming to pay me a visit?

DOUG: Because they're lonesome for you.

STELLA: No, indeed. Because they need money—and I bet you anything I have they won't be here for five minutes before Mary Jo will be nagging me about dividing the estate. (*A pause.*) I'm never going to divide it, Doug.

DOUG: Yes'm.

STELLA: She can beg and beg and Lewis can beg and beg. I'm never in this world going to divide it.

DOUG: If you divide it, who gets the house out back I live in?

STELLA: I'm never going to divide it—never.

DOUG: Well, I'm glad to hear that. I'm too old now to move from my house. (*A pause.*) Miss Stella—

STELLA: Yes?

DOUG: I want you to promise me one more thing.

STELLA: What's that?

DOUG: When I die . . .

STELLA: Yes, I know you want a tombstone.

DOUG: Something more—when I die I want you to bury me next to my mama's grave.

STELLA: I forget, does she have a tombstone?

DOUG: No, she don't.

STELLA: How will I find her grave?

DOUG: I'll go out there tomorrow and show it to you. I keeps red flowers in a Mason jar on it.

STELLA: What kind of red flowers are they, Doug?

DOUG: No kind. They're paper.

STELLA: I see. (*She closes her eyes.*)

DOUG: You'll go out there with me tomorrow?

STELLA: I will. (*DOUG closes his eyes. They are soon asleep as the lights fade.*)

SCENE II

Later the same day. SISSIE and EMILY, elegantly dressed, are in the living room. SISSIE is reading Cosmopolitan, *and EMILY is reading* People *magazine. Their mother, MARY JO, comes into the room.*

MARY JO: Oh, I had such a good time growing up here, girls, such a good time. We always had so much fun. I love this old house so. Don't you think it's beautiful?
SISSIE: It's O.K.
MARY JO: O.K.? Don't you think it's attractive, Emily?
EMILY: It's all right.
MARY JO: Well, thank you very much. I happen to think it's beautiful.
EMILY: Would you ever want to come here again to live?
MARY JO: Oh, my God, no. What would I do here, in heaven's name? I would die if I ever had to leave Houston. I would just die. (*LUCILLE comes in.*)
LUCILLE: Where is Bob?
MARY JO: He'll be along. When we were driving through town on our way home he saw Carson Davis and stopped off to visit with him.
LUCILLE: We have a plastic factory here now, you know.
MARY JO: A plastic factory?
LUCILLE: Yes. We had a washboard factory about six years ago, but it didn't seem to prosper.
MARY JO: Who owns the plastic factory? Anyone we know?
LUCILLE: No. It's owned by a man from Taiwan.
MARY JO: Taiwan? My God, how did he ever get here?
LUCILLE: I don't know. They're all over the coast fishing.
MARY JO: They're not from Taiwan, Sister—they're from Vietnam.
LUCILLE: Oh.
MARY JO: Excuse me, I'm going to check on Mama. (*She goes.*)
LUCILLE: Your mama tells me you have serious beaux.
EMILY: Sissie has. I did have one for about two weeks.
LUCILLE: What happened?
EMILY: He turned out to be obnoxious.
SISSIE: Mama says Son is going with a school teacher.
LUCILLE: Yes.

EMILY: Do you approve?
LUCILLE: I certainly would like to see him marry again, if she's the right girl.
EMILY: Sometimes I don't think I'll ever marry again, all I went through with my husband. Mama gets furious when I say that. She says, "Look at Son, all he went through, and he's not bitter at all." You know, she talked terribly about you all in Houston.
LUCILLE: Who did?
EMILY: Olive Louise. She said you all had broken up her marriage. She said you and Uncle Lewis were weak, and Grandmother was domineering and tight-fisted, and Son was no better than her slave. She said if she had to have another meal with you all in this house, she would have gone raving crazy.
LUCILLE: Who told you all this?
EMILY: Mama. She heard it some place.
LUCILLE: Why didn't she ever tell me this?
EMILY: I don't know. (*MARY JO enters.*)
LUCILLE: Mary Jo, why didn't you tell me about all these terrible things Olive Louise said about us in Houston before she died?
MARY JO: Who told you anything about that?
LUCILLE: Emily.
MARY JO: Emily, I told you not to repeat all that to your Aunt Lucille.
EMILY: No, you didn't.
MARY JO: I did, too. I most certainly did. I said I'm going to tell you something, but you must never repeat it to your Aunt Lucille.
LUCILLE: Why didn't you want it repeated to me?
MARY JO: Because I'm not even sure she said it.
LUCILLE: Who told you she said it?
MARY JO: Betty Grace Purcell.
LUCILLE: Who is that?
MARY JO: Someone I play bridge with once in a while in Houston.
LUCILLE: Did she say Olive Louise told that to her?
MARY JO: No.
LUCILLE: How did she hear it?
MARY JO: From Glen Eyrie Crawford.
LUCILLE: Who is that?
MARY JO: A third cousin of Olive Louise. (*STELLA enters.*)
STELLA: What's this about Olive Louise?
LUCILLE: Nothing, Mama.
STELLA: Well, don't tell me. I know all about it, anyway—Lewis told me when he was mad at me this morning. He said she wouldn't come back to Son until the estate was divided. Well, I said, "tell her that

she'll never come back, because this estate won't be divided until hell freezes over."

LUCILLE: Olive Louise is dead, Mama. Heavens . . .

STELLA: I know she is dead. She was on her way to the airport with a drunken man and they had a wreck. Where were they off to?

LUCILLE: Who?

STELLA: Olive Louise and the drunken man.

LUCILLE: I don't know, Mama. I never heard.

STELLA: I heard New York City to see some plays.

LUCILLE: Who told you that?

STELLA: I don't remember, but I heard it.

MARY JO: I think the estate should be divided. I agree with Olive Louise.

STELLA: Of course you do, Mary Jo, so you could throw it all away on trips to Europe and cars and expensive clothes. You wouldn't have a dime left after two months. Do you know how much you already borrowed from the estate.?

MARY JO: No, and I don't want to know.

STELLA: Three hundred thousand dollars.

MARY JO: How do you know?

STELLA: Because I look at the books. I know every penny that is spent and don't you forget it.

MARY JO: How much has Lewis borrowed?

STELLA: Two hundred thousand.

MARY JO: You mean I've borrowed three hundred thousand and Lewis has only borrowed two hundred thousand?

STELLA: Yes.

MARY JO: I find that hard to believe. All the money he's lost gambling, all the scrapes you've had to get him out of.

STELLA: Look at the books—it's all there. I told Doug not an hour ago you would begin on that the minute you got here. And I told Lucille the same thing . . .

LUCILLE: Now, Mama, you didn't say anything like that to me.

STELLA: I did, too. You said you absolutely agreed with me. You said she never came here unless she wanted something.

LUCILLE: Mama . . .

MARY JO: Thanks a lot, Lucille.

LUCILLE: Mary Jo, I did not say a single word of that.

MARY JO: How much has Lucille borrowed? And Son?

STELLA: Very little; two years for Son's college, and the money to bury Charlie.

MARY JO: What about them living here and eating here? I think they should be charged for that.

STELLA: Son works here, you know. Son takes care of all of this so you can borrow. If it weren't for Son . . .

MARY JO: Listen, I know all about Son—you don't have to tell me about Son. I appreciate Son just as much as you do. But do you mean to tell me that if Bob and Sissie and Emily and I come here to live that you wouldn't charge us for board and room?

STELLA: Certainly not. Not if you worked.

MARY JO: Well, I think we'll just move in this week. It would save us all a lot of money.

EMILY: Mama, let's change the subject.

MARY JO: All right, the subject's changed. (*BOB enters.*)

BOB: Hello Sister-in-Law.

LUCILLE: Hello, Bob.

BOB: You're looking well Mother-in-Law—nothing much has changed around here, pretty as ever, but I can't say as much for the town, it's dying on the vine. I must have counted twenty-five empty stores.

LUCILLE: We're having a hard time. Houston is too.

BOB: You can say that again. I know more people in Houston whose income was between seventy-five thousand and a hundred thousand dollars . . .

STELLA: How much?

BOB: Between seventy-five and a hundred thousand paying off homes of a hundred or a hundred fifty thousand dollars, with two kids in college, two cars, and suddenly the husband loses his job, and they lose everything, house, cars—now, this isn't just happening to one or two men but hundreds in the city of Houston. (*SON and LUCY enter.*)

SON: Hello. Lucy, this is my aunt and uncle, Mary Jo and Bob, and my cousins, Emily and Sissie.

LUCY: How do you do—

MARY JO: Hello.

BOB: Hi, young lady— (*MILDRED enters.*)

MILDRED: Can Doug serve your dinner now?

LUCILLE: We are waiting for Lewis.

SON: Uncle won't be here for dinner.

STELLA: Why?

SON: I don't know. When I left him at the bank he said to tell you not to wait dinner.

BOB: Then let's eat.

STELLA: I'm not hungry—I'm going to my room.

MARY JO: Now, Mama, why are you going to spoil it for us?

STELLA: I'm not hungry. And I'm going to my room. (*She leaves.*)

MARY JO: Oh, I could wring Brother's neck. Well, this is the last time

I'm coming fifty-five miles to eat a meal here, and have it spoiled because Brother gets on a drunk.

SON: Bob, Mary Jo, Mama . . . I think it's more than a drunk. He's in real trouble.

MARY JO: What in the name of God is it this time?

SON: He's been fooling around with a high school girl, and I don't know all the details. He was agitated when he told me about it. It seems her father has found out and threatened to kill him, and then he was told if he got money to him, the father would forget it. Uncle Lewis is scared to death of him, I know that. (*DOUG begins putting food on the table.*)

LUCILLE: Oh, Lord help us. Who is the girl?

SON: I don't know.

MARY JO: Mama is to blame for him, you know. She's spoiled him—all his life. Always making him think any woman he went with wasn't good enough for him. There is nobody in my opinion that he is too good for. I told Mama the last scrape he got into with a woman—let him get out of it himself—the best way that he can.

LUCILLE: Mama was thinking of the estate. If Lewis married, his wife would be entitled to half of what he has.

MARY JO: How much is it costing the estate to get him out of this one?

SON: It is not costing the estate anything. Whatever it costs is charged against his share.

BOB: Miss Lucy don't you teach in High School?

LUCY: Yes, I do, and I have some wonderful students, more like my chums than my students I'm happy to say. Of course I can't get more than two, a sweet little black girl and a darling little white girl from Davevang, interested in poetry but I refuse to get discouraged over that. (*LEWIS comes in. He seems quite subdued.*)

LUCILLE: Lewis, we thought you wouldn't be here for dinner.

LEWIS: I didn't think I would be able to be here, but everything has changed now. Hello, Mary Jo. Hello girls. Hello Bob.

MARY JO AND BOB: Hello.

SISSIE AND FAMILY: Hello Uncle Lewis.

BOB: Mary Jo, did you talk to your sister about what we were discussing on the way down here?

MARY JO: No. (*Pause.*) Bob has a friend . . .

BOB: Fraternity brother—I met him last week in Houston. He was there seeing some lawyer. He said he and his family were about to lose their minds worrying what the Government would take in taxes when his wife's father died, and so they all got together with father and had a good sensible talk and decided to put everything in his children's name then and there and keep the Government from taking them for four hundred thousand dollars. Now, I said to Mary Jo I thought we should all get together—Lucille, Mary Jo and Lewis and Son and me and take a real hard look at everything—the whole picture.

LUCILLE: Son, go tell Mama Lewis is here after all. Maybe she'll change her mind and join us. (*He goes.*) Let the rest of us take our seats. (*They go into the dining room.*)

MARY JO: Any special place?

LUCILLE: No. (*They seat themselves.*)

BOB: How are you Doug?

DOUG: I'm pretty well.

BOB: You look well.

DOUG: Thank you. You look well yourself. How is Houston coming along?

BOB: It's still there.

DOUG: There are fools that drive in every day to Houston to go to work. I say you wouldn't catch me driving sixty miles no place just to work.

BOB: Well, maybe they can't find work here.

DOUG: Hush.

BOB: When was the last time you were in Houston?

DOUG: Oh, God knows. It was before Mr. Charlie died.

BOB: Well, Sister-In-Law, what a great meal. You've done it again.

MARY JO: Sister-In-Law? Mildred cooked all this. Lucille can't boil water.

LUCILLE: You're crazy. I'm a good cook when I want to be.

MARY JO: When did you ever want to be?

BOB: How have you been Lewis? (*No answer from LEWIS.*)

MARY JO: Lewis, Bob asked you a question.

LEWIS: I heard him. (*A phone rings in another part of the house.*)

MILDRED: (*Calling.*) Phone call for Sissie. (*SISSIE gets up from the table.*)

SISSIE: Excuse me. (*She goes.*)

LUCY: Everything certainly looks good. Tastes good too. Sweet potatoes with marshmallows and pecans are my favorite.

LUCILLE: Lucy teaches school here.

BOB: Pass the biscuits please.

MARY JO: Now don't over do Bob.

LUCILLE: Here. (*She passes the biscuits.*) Butter?

BOB: Yes ma'am, butter. How long have you been teaching here Lucy?

LUCY: It's my second year.

LUCILLE: She loves it here, don't you Lucy?

LUCY: Oh yes, indeed I do.

BOB: That's nice. (*SON and STELLA enter.*)

STELLA: I have news for you all. Son and Miss Lucy are getting married.

LUCILLE: Son, why didn't you tell me?

SON: I had to ask for a raise, Mama, before I could think of marriage again, and Grandmother has just agreed to give me one, so . . .

BOB: How much will you be making now, Son?

SON: Six hundred a month.

BOB: What were you making before?

SON: Four hundred.

LUCILLE: Which was much too little.

MARY JO: And you get four hundred dollars a month, Lucille?

LUCILLE: Yes, same as you and Lewis.

MARY JO: My four hundred dollars is deducted from my share of the estate. Is yours, Lewis?

LEWIS: Yes.

MARY JO: Is yours, Lucille?

LUCILLE: No. I'm on salary.

MARY JO: So that makes a thousand dollars a month being paid to you and Son by the estate, plus room and board.

LUCILLE: Yes.

MARY JO: And we get nothing unless we have to borrow it, and we have to beg to do that.

LUCILLE: We're not on charity, you know. Son and I work for what we do.

MARY JO: I know what Son does, but what do you do?

LUCILLE: My God, Mary Jo, I can't believe you sometimes. What do I do?

MARY JO: Tell me one thing you do. You have three servants waiting on you hand and foot.

LUCILLE: Want to change places with me?

MARY JO: No, I don't.

LUCILLE: Well, then don't criticize. This house would fall apart if I weren't here to see to things.

MARY JO: My foot—

BOB: Now, come on, Mary Jo. (*MARY JO jumps up from the table.*)

MARY JO: I'm going home.

BOB: Now, Mama—

MARY JO: Now, don't Mama me, Bob. I'm sick of this house and this family. Everybody in this damn family gets everything they want but me. I have to get on my knees and beg to my Mama for every single cent I get. Lewis can borrow all he wants—Lucille and Son get money handed out to them right and left.

LUCILLE: No one hands out anything to me. I earn every penny I get.

MARY JO: In a pig's eye.

STELLA: What do you want, Mary Jo? Just tell me what in the name of God you want? Do you want to borrow money?

MARY JO: No, I do not want to borrow money—I am sick of borrowing money—I want the estate divided, so that me and my precious girls can have some peace for a change. Bob is too proud to tell you this, but I'm not. He's at his wit's end. He has not sold any real estate in the city of Houston for four months. He has not earned a red cent in four months.

STELLA: Well, why didn't you say so? The estate will loan you money.

MARY JO: I don't want the estate to loan me anything. I want us to divide the estate, so I can have a little dignity in my life.

STELLA: Isn't anybody going to congratulate Son and Miss Lucy on their engagement?

BOB: Congratulations, Son.

SON: Thank you.

EMILY: When do you plan on getting married?

SON: Ask my wife-to-be.

LUCY: I want to finish out this term at school at least.

BOB: Sissie is going with a lovely fellow who is in computers. He's begging her to marry him. That's who she's on the phone with right now.

LUCILLE: Son has just had a computer system installed here. It's very complicated.

LUCY: I read in the paper this morning that the Houston public schools are in real jeopardy—busing hasn't worked at all. One man interviewed was very upset. He said he had always been a liberal, and he had favored busing in the past, but now it had destroyed the concept of the old neighborhood school. He thought neither black or white benefitted by it. He said the whites were all going to private schools, leaving only blacks and Hispanics in the public schools.

EMILY: Who cares?

LUCY: Well, I happen to care very much about our public school system. In my opinion, it has been the backbone of our nation.

LUCILLE: Do you think busing is wrong?

LUCY: No, I didn't say it was wrong. I just said, in its present state it doesn't seem to be working . . . (*A pause.*) Our whole educational system is in jeopardy, it seems to me. The Japanese are surpassing us in every way because of their educational systems.

STELLA: We have a plastic factory here now, run by Japanese.

LUCILLE: Not Japanese, Mama—Taiwanese.

BOB: I fought the Japanese when I was eighteen. don't tell me anything about the Japanese.

LUCY: All I know is that their educational system far surpasses ours.

BOB: In what way, little lady?

LUCY: In terms of achievement.

BOB: How much would you say your estate's worth, Mother-in-Law?

STELLA: I don't know—ask Son.

BOB: Do you know, Son?

SON: Fluctuates. Of course, you know the basis is the land—five thousand acres.

BOB: That's easily five million right there.

SON: If you can get it. Two years ago you might have gotten it. I don't know about today.

BOB: Of course you can get it—maybe more.

SON: I don't know—land values are pretty depressed around here right now.

BOB: I could get you a thousand an acre tomorrow. I have at least five friends in Houston, maybe ten, maybe fifteen.

STELLA: I thought Houston was in a depression.

BOB: Not everybody in Houston, Mother-In-Law. There is still a lot of money in Houston, but what I am driving at, the point I wish clearly to make, is that God forbid anything happened to you, the old Government would slap the highest evaluation they could get by with on your land and your other assets, which I'm sure are not inconsiderable. I don't know what the house and ten acres is worth, for instance, but I could inquire if you ever want to sell it.

STELLA: This house is never going to be sold. I'm giving it to Son, if he promises never to sell it or let his children sell it, and Doug has to live out back during his lifetime.

MARY JO: Son?

STELLA: Yes, Son. S-0-N, Son.

MARY JO: When did you decide this?

STELLA: Just now.

BOB: Now, let's don't get sidetracked, Mama. For the time being, leave the house out of it. Figure, conservatively, your tax without the house would be easily a million dollars.

STELLA: A million dollars?

BOB: Yes, Ma'am.

STELLA: Oh, God Almighty.

BOB: Now, I don't know what your cash situation is.

STELLA: Well, we don't have a million dollars in all, do we, Son?

SON: No, Ma'am, no where near that.

BOB: Exactly, so you know what you have to do?

EMILY: Daddy, can't this wait until after dinner?
STELLA: Lewis has gone asleep. Wake him up, Sissie.
EMILY: I'm Emily.
STELLA: Well, where's Sissie?
EMILY: On the telephone.
MARY JO: Lewis, wake up.(*He opens his eyes and begins eating again.*)
BOB: Mother-in-Law, what you will have to do, or your heirs will, is sell off some of the land to pay the Government the inheritance tax—so that's a million dollars you are going to have to unnecessarily give to the Government, thus diminishing the estate's landholdings. There is, of course, a way to avoid all this . . .
EMILY: Excuse me. (*She gets up.*)
MARY JO: Don't you want dessert?
EMILY: No.
MARY JO: Where are you going?
EMILY: I'm going to read my *Cosmopolitan*. (*She leaves.*)
BOB: May I continue, Mary Jo?
MARY JO: I'm sorry, Bob.
BOB: Now the best and most sensible thing, in my opinion, is to go right away to a tax expert for advice. Now, I'm sure he will tell you the way to avoid all of this is to start each year giving a part of the estate to each of your children, so that in a given number of years you can legally give them their inheritance tax-free, or practically tax-free.
LEWIS: Sounds like a good idea to me, Bob.
LUCILLE: Have you and Brother been in cahoots over this, Mary Jo?
MARY JO: What are you talking about?
LUCILLE: He was begging Mama all morning before you came about dividing the estate. Did you and Bob put that idea in his head?
LEWIS: Nobody put any idea in my head, Sister.
LUCILLE: What will happen to Son, while this is all going on? What will happen to his job managing the estate?
MARY JO: What will happen to it when Mama dies?
LUCILLE: It's Mama's intention he'll go on managing it. At least, that's what she's always told me.
MARY JO: How is he going to do that when she dies and the estate is divided? He's certainly not going to manage my share, and I doubt if Lewis will let him manage his.
LUCILLE: Last time I talked to Mama she didn't ever want to divide the estate, she was thinking about turning the whole thing into a trust and having Son manage it—weren't you, Mama?
STELLA: That was one plan I had—
MARY JO: Seems to me you've had one too many plans. Lewis, I think

we're having our birthrights stolen right in front of our very eyes by Lucille and Son. (*DOUG comes in with a serving dish.*)

SON: Are you crazy, all of you? I bring my fiancee here to be introduced to you, and she must think I live with a bunch of lunatics.

LUCILLE: I will not sit here and let Bob and Mary Jo take your job away from you, after you and your father have served this family so unselfishly all these years.

SON: Let them take the job, Mama. I can always find something to do.

MARY JO: After all, he will always inherit your share of the money—

SON: I don't want her share of the money. I don't want anybody's share of the money. That's all I've heard all my life. Money, money, money— (*He gets up and leaves. DOUG changes the dish and it shatters, spilling the food.*)

LEWIS: My God, Doug—what are you doing? (*He calls.*) Mildred. Mildred.

MILDRED: (*Calling back.*) What?

LEWIS: Doug dropped a dish. (*MILDRED enters and picks it up.*)

DOUG: I'm going to lie down. I don't feel too good. (*DOUG goes into the living room and sits down.*)

STELLA: Come have your dessert, Son.

SON: I'm not hungry, thank you, Grandmother. I'm giving notice. You'll have to get someone else to take over here—it's really very impractical, my staying on.

STELLA: I won't give you the house if you leave.

SON: Then you won't give me the house.

LUCILLE: You won't give him the house anyway, Mama. He's no fool. You've been giving him that house and taking it back at least six times in the last year. (*A pause.*) Well, sit down at least, and let Lucy finish her dessert. (*He sits.*) Did you ever see a family like this, Lucy? (*LUCY smiles.*)

BOB: Do you come from a large family, Lucy?

LUCY: No. Just my mother and father. My father came here from North Carolina to work in the oil fields.

BOB: Well, I hope he's not dependent on the oil fields now. He's in a terrible mess if he is.

LUCY: No, he's retired.

BOB: Where do they live?

LUCY: Austin.

BOB: Certainly not as depressed as Houston, but it's getting there. (*LUCILLE gets up to leave. She is crying. SON goes to her.*)

SON: Come on, Mother.

LUCILLE: You are just like your father. You let everyone push you around and take advantage of you. Your father dropped over dead in the heat of summer while walking around those farms. That summer he had been up every day at five and never got home until dark. He fell over in the fields from exhaustion. He slaved every day for this family—not his family even, but mine, and what thanks did he get for it. What thanks did poor Charlie get for it? An early death is all he ever got. All they did was to take advantage of your father's good nature.

SON: No one's going to take advantage of me. Sit down and finish your dessert. (*She goes back to her place. He goes to his.*)

LUCY: Have you gotten V.C.R.'s yet?

MARY JO: We have.

LUCY: They are life savers here because we have no movie theater here now.

STELLA: What was that song you were humming this morning, Son?

SON: "Rock of Ages."

STELLA: Oh, yes. You remember, they sang that at your father's funeral, children.

LEWIS: No, they didn't.

STELLA: They certainly did.

LEWIS: They did not.

LUCILLE: I thought they did, too, Lewis.

LEWIS: Well, they didn't.

STELLA: What did they sing then?

LEWIS: "In Heavenly Love Abiding."

STELLA: How does that go?

LEWIS: I don't remember—

STELLA: Do you remember, Son?

SON: *(Singing.)* IN HEAVENLY LOVE ABIDING, MY HEART SHALL KNOW NO FEAR. AND SAFE IN GOD'S CONFIDING FOR NOTHING CHANGES HERE.

STELLA: Ever since he was a little boy, Son has always loved hymns—you should have been a preacher, Son.

SON: Maybe that wouldn't have been a bad idea.

BOB: If you leave now, do you have any prospects for a job, Son?

SON: No. I have thought about going back to college and getting a degree and then going to law school, if I can get in.

BOB: At thirty-five?

SON: You have to start sometime—

STELLA: Well, this is just all a lot of talk. You're going no place. You're going to put all our affairs on that computer system and I'm going to raise your salary . . .

MARY JO: By the way, Bob, Mama says we have borrowed three hundred thousand dollars from the estate. Do you believe that?

BOB: No.

STELLA: Well, you have.

BOB: You'll have to prove it to me.

STELLA: It's all there in black and white.

MARY JO: And she says that Lewis has borrowed two hundred thousand and I certainly don't believe that.

LEWIS: And neither do I.

MARY JO: Why don't you believe it?

LEWIS: Because I don't think I have.

MARY JO: Well, that's not why I don't believe it. I think if we've borrowed three hundred thousand, then you have borrowed four or five.

LUCILLE: Oh, my God. I find this all so depressing. Let's change the subject, please. (*A pause.*) Have you selected your silver pattern yet, Lucy?

LUCY: No. Not yet.

LUCILLE: Your china pattern?

LUCY: No.

MARY JO: My silver and china pattern are both out of stock.

LUCILLE: So are mine. (*DOUG enters.*)

DOUG: Good night, everybody.

STELLA: It's not night, Doug—we're having our dinner, and go out in the kitchen if you're feeling better and help Mildred.

DOUG: Yes'um. I was having the sweetest dream. I dreamt I was in glory and there was angels everywhere and they were singing. My God, you never heard such singing.

STELLA: That wasn't any angel, Doug, that was Son singing.

DOUG: Yes'um. I was out in the field and heard Mama hollering and come running across the fields to where she was and I said Mama what is it—what in the name of God is it?—and she says the bull killed your daddy—go yonder to the next place and get help. I ran across the fields as fast as I could to another family working on the place and I says come quick the bull has killed my daddy—and then there was the funeral and they buried my daddy and Mama says what's to become of us now you have no daddy and I have no husband and then Miss Stella's daddy came and then he says to Mama I'm going to take you and the boy to town so you can live on our place and we come here and Mama cooked for these good people until she went to her rest and we lived out yonder in the back in the house I still live in from that day on.

MARY JO: What do you pay him?

STELLA: I don't know. What do we pay him, Son?
SON: Two hundred a month.
DOUG: I'm tired, Miss Stella. I am so tired. (*DOUG lies down on the dining room floor.*)
STELLA: Doug, get up from there. Son, take him to his room.
SON: All right. (*MILDRED comes out.*)
MILDRED: Ready for your dessert?
STELLA: I am.
MILDRED: How many wants dessert? Raise your hand.
STELLA: Doug, get up off the floor. Mercy, Son, go to him. (*SON goes to him.*)
SON: Doug. Doug. (*He feels his forehead, he listens to his heartbeat.*) Poor old man, he's dead. (*SON holds him as the lights fade.*)

ACT II

SCENE 1

Two days later. LUCILLE is in the living room. LUCY and SON enter from outside.

SON: Where is everybody?
LUCILLE: Mary Jo and Bob are looking at the farms, Mama and Lewis are upstairs taking naps, Sissie and Emily are reading and listening to music. The funeral wore Mama and Lewis out, they said. I thought it was lovely, didn't you?
SON: Yes, I did.
LUCILLE: I don't know what I had expected. Something much more emotional, I suppose. I thought you spoke beautifully about Doug, Son. Didn't you, Lucy?
LUCY: Yes, I did. I thought he was very eloquent.
LUCILLE: That is the word—eloquent.
SON: Well, I was devoted to him.
LUCILLE: We all were. It has affected Mama very much. Brother, too. Son, I know in my heart Mary Jo and Bob are going to start in again with some kind of scheme or another to get Mama to divide the estate. Bob always has some kind of hare brained scheme to get everybody rich. Why if Mama had listened to him and the things he wanted her to invest in, we'd all be in the poor house. Houston this and Houston that. All his rich friends and their rich schemes. Well, I don't see how it's helped him one bit.

SON: Mama . . .

LUCILLE: I don't think the estate should be divided just because they need money. They always need money. They live way, way beyond their means.

SON: Mama . . .

LUCILLE: Now do not be foolish and filled with false pride. You must not give up your position here. You must not abandon all you've worked for.

SON: Mama, please—this is very difficult for me. It's not that I'm not attached to the farms, Mama—I am. Very. I mean, Spring and Fall, Summer and Winter, since I was a little boy I've gone out there part of every day.

LUCILLE: And he has, too. First with Papa, and then with his father. When his father died, Son was eighteen and just beginning college, and Mama and I tried to manage the farms ourselves, but we didn't know how and things just went from bad to worse, and so when he was at the beginning of his junior year in college, Mama and I wrote him and asked if he would come back here and take over for the family, and he did. And his coming back saved us.

SON: Maybe it is wisdom, Mother, to work out some plan now to avoid unreasonable inheritance taxes. Some day it will have to be divided—the day Grandmother dies. Every year the income from the estate gets less and less—the taxes increase. Every year it gets more difficult to make any kind of a profit.

LUCILLE: Some farms are making profits.

SON: I don't know how. There is only one thing that can finally save us and that is to get an oil or gas lease.

LUCILLE: Well, we never have in all these years . . .

SON: I know, and I don't really think we will now, but there is interest in land out that way now. I have been called on twice about a prospective lease.

LUCILLE: Oh, Son, wouldn't that be wonderful!

SON: Yes, I suppose it would. Wonderful and sad. Sad because it means we no longer know how to make a living out of our land unless we find oil and gas there.

LUCILLE: How much do you think an oil or gas lease would bring the estate?

SON: Oh, I don't know. That would have to be negotiated, but Mama, don't in any way get your hopes up about that. In all these years, we have never had one, and we likely won't get one now.

LUCILLE: But I hear with the new technology, they are finding oil and gas in places they never could find it before.

SON: That's true.

LUCILLE: Well, I'm certainly not going to lose any sleep worrying about it. (*A pause.*) But if they make an offer for an oil or gas lease, how much do you think we could expect?

SON: Enough to pay our taxes this year.

LUCILLE: Is that all? (*MARY JO and BOB enter.*)

MARY JO: What's this about oil and gas?

SON: I was just telling Mother that in the last few days I had two inquiries about a lease on our land by an oil and gas company.

MARY JO: Why weren't we informed?

SON: Because there was nothing to inform you about. A scout called me twice and asked about the location of the land, and was it leased, and had it ever been leased . . .

BOB: I was talking just now up town to Damon Jackson. He made a fortune in oil, you know—many years ago when they first . . .

MARY JO: (*Interrupting.*) I wish in the future to be informed if there is oil interest in our estate.

SON: It was only two phone calls.

MARY JO: I don't care if it is only one phone call. I want to be informed.

SON: All right I'll inform you. I am supposed to call him back this afternoon and if there is anything to report I'll tell you.

LUCILLE: Son says you don't get a lot from an oil lease.

BOB: That is true. The big money starts if you strike oil!

MARY JO: How much would we get from an oil lease?

SON: Depends how bad they want the lease.

MARY JO: Well, how much?

SON: I hear lately some people are getting twenty thousand dollars for a year.

MARY JO: Twenty thousand dollars, is that all?

SON: That's all! And that's tops around here, but you have to first get a lease so they'll drill and of course if they strike oil . . .

MARY JO: Well, how much would we get if they strike oil?

SON: Not as much now with the price of oil so low, but still plenty.

LUCILLE: Of course in the old days those that had the land over by Boling and New Gulf were the one's that really got rich. That's where they found sulphur, you know.

LUCY: Have you heard the horrible things they are trying to do out there? Some French company has bought the sulphur company from Texas Gulf and they are trying to lease the pockets left underground when the sulphur was removed to some other French company for the storage of chemical wastes.

SON: When did you hear about this?

LUCY: I just heard about it. Do you know what that can mean to us if it happens? If there is a leak of any kind, or an accident, the water supply of this part of the Gulf Coast could be poisoned.

LUCILLE: No.

LUCY: It certainly could. (*LEWIS comes in.*)

LEWIS: I thought I heard someone down here. (*A pause.*) Son, I want to apologize to you and Lucy for the way I've been acting. I was drunk, and I'm truly sorry.

SON: That's all right, Uncle Lewis.

LEWIS: I'm fond of you, Son.

SON: I know that, Uncle Lewis, and I'm fond of you, too.

LEWIS: And I appreciate all you have done for this family.

SON: Thank you.

LEWIS: Lucy, when his father died, I said to myself I'll try to be the father to him that death had so cruelly taken away. As a matter of fact, that first night sitting here by Charlie's coffin, I said to Son, "Son, I'm going to make up to you in all ways, the father you have lost." Do you remember my saying that to you, Son?

SON: Yes, I do.

LEWIS: And I wanted to, you know, but then my weakness would get the best of me, that terrible weakness that almost wrecked my life; and I apologize profusely to you.

SON: Now, now, Uncle Lewis.

LEWIS: I thought you spoke eloquently at Doug's funeral.

SON: Thank you.

LEWIS: I wanted to speak, but I was too emotional—I didn't dare try.

BOB: I called a fine tax lawyer in Houston and asked him if he could recommend a tax lawyer here that we could consult, but he said he thought we'd be wasting our time talking to a lawyer here when I told him the size of the estate.

LEWIS: What do you want a tax lawyer for?

BOB: Don't you remember our conversation at dinner the day Doug died?

LEWIS: No.

MARY JO: Oh, come on, Lewis. You weren't that drunk.

LEWIS: I don't remember it. I'm sorry.

MARY JO: You don't remember Bob explaining to us all in front of Mama about these friends of his getting their father's . . .

LUCILLE: Well, don't anyone mention death to Mama today. I warn you, she's very depressed.

MARY JO: No one wants to talk to Mama about anything. It's just that since Son said he was leaving his job here, Bob and I talked it over and I thought he should at least start investigating the tax options, in case Mama . . .

LUCILLE: Son is not leaving his job here.

MARY JO: Well, he said he was, right in there, unless I'm losing my mind entirely.

LUCILLE: It is certainly not definite.

LEWIS: Son, you can't leave here. Who would take care of the estate? This estate is very complicated, you know. (*SISSIE and EMILY come in.*)

BOB: Why don't you girls go back and read? We're talking over some business.

EMILY: I've read until my eyes are about ready to fall out.

BOB: Watch a little television then.

SISSIE: I don't want to.

EMILY: I don't either.

BOB: Well, if you stay here, don't interrupt us. Like the lawyer says, "strategy is everything."

LUCILLE: I flat out don't want to divide the estate.

LEWIS: I don't either.

MARY JO: You don't? Are you crazy? You were demanding we do it two days ago.

LEWIS: I was drunk. I don't want to divide the estate. And I certainly want Son to stay to see to it.

BOB: You don't have to divide anything at present. This will take a year maybe, to work out with your Mama.

LEWIS: I don't want to divide the estate. Not now, not a year from now . . .

MARY JO: (*Interrupting.*) Lucy would you mind if I give you a little advice?

LUCY: No. Not at all.

MARY JO: Don't live on here after you and Son marry. It will drive you absolutely crazy if you do. That is what happened to his first marriage, you know. His wife, Olive Louise, said that one more meal here with this family and she would go screaming mad out of this house.

LUCILLE: Son, do you believe she said that?

SON: I don't know, Mother.

LUCILLE: Did she ever say that to you?

SON: Not in so many words.

MARY JO: She loved Son, you know. She loved him until the day she died.

LUCILLE: How do you know that?

MARY JO: Because a cousin of hers was a friend of a friend.

LUCILLE: Oh, yes—you told us that.

MARY JO: And she said she loved Son until the day she died.

LUCILLE: You've already told us that.

MARY JO: Olive Louise was always getting her cousin to call my friend to call me to see if Son was interested in any other girls. She said when she heard Son was seeing Lucy, she cried her eyes out.

LUCILLE: Oh, I don't believe that for one minute. Do you believe that, Son?

SON: How would I know, Mama?

LUCILLE: Did she ever tell you she was still in love with you?

SON: No.

BOB: Folks, let's get back on track. What I'm trying to explain to you . . . (*STELLA comes in.*)

STELLA: I've been thinking all afternoon about putting Doug to rest. Oh my—poor old fellow.

LUCILLE: Now, he had a good life, Mama. (*LEWIS starts to cry.*)

MARY JO: Brother, what on earth is the matter?

LEWIS: I'm sorry. I'm just very emotional.

STELLA: Oh, I was thinking all afternoon of Doug and my father and my grandfather—and God knows, all kinds of things crossed my mind. I was thinking of the time you came into my room after school, Son. You asked me if we were Yankees. Why did you do that, Son? I remember your doing it, but I can't remember why.

EMILY: Are we part Yankee, Mama?

STELLA: Why did you ask me that, Son?

SON: Because Robert Daley had hollered out during history class that my grandfather was a Yankee soldier and a carpetbagger.

STELLA: It wasn't your grandfather, it was your great-grandfather.

SON: Whomever—and I came home very upset, and I asked you if it was true my grandfather was a Yankee.

STELLA: Great-grandfather.

EMILY: Was he, Mother?

MARY JO: Yes, he was.

SISSIE: How did he get here?

STELLA: I don't remember.

MARY JO: Oh, you do too remember, Mama.

STELLA: No, I don't.

MARY JO: Well, I certainly don't remember. What's more, I don't care.

SISSIE: Do you remember, Uncle Lewis?

LEWIS: No, I don't.

SON: I remember. At least, I remember what Grandfather told me: that grandmother's father came down here as a Union soldier during the occupation and then went back north to someplace . . .

STELLA: Illinois.

MARY JO: I thought you didn't remember.

STELLA: I remember that much.

MARY JO: You remember what you want to.

SISSIE: Well, what happened when he got back to Illinois?

SON: Well, he liked it here so much that he decided to come on back, and he was here during the Reconstruction.

STELLA: And my daddy told me that his daddy told him that you could buy land here for a dollar-fifty an acre, and people were abandoning their plantations because they couldn't make a living on them without their slaves, and he saved his money and bought as much land as he could, and that makes up our estate.

SON: That's not what that boy told me in front of the class that day. He said my grandfather . . .

STELLA: Great-grandfather.

SON: Great-grandfather stole everything we have. He said he was elected to a county office at the courthouse.

STELLA: County Clerk.

MARY JO: You see? —she remembers everything.

SON: And that he stole land right and left by destroying legal records in the courthouse.

STELLA: Which is not true, of course.

SON: And this boy said "I bet you have a blue belly just like your Yankee grandfather."

STELLA: Great-grandfather.

SISSIE: Well, I never knew that before.

EMILY: Who did he steal the land from?

STELLA: He didn't steal the land. He didn't steal anything.

MARY JO: Well, let's change the subject. Who cares about all that? When are you going to talk to the man about . . .

STELLA: Son, I want you to take me for a ride in the car.

LUCILLE: Lewis can take you, Mama.

STELLA: I don't want to ride with him. His hands shake worse than Doug's. I'm afraid to ride with him.

LUCILLE: I'll take you, Mama.

STELLA: I don't want you to. I want Son to take me.

LUCILLE: Where in the world do you want to go, Mama?

STELLA: Well, I'll tell you. As I was lying in my bed thinking of Douglas, I thought, "Well, we've done everything for him we promised—a lovely funeral, a handsome coffin, a fine, big tombstone." But then I remembered that just before he died, he said he had one more thing to ask me: that after he died, to find his mama's grave and bury him next to her. He said he would take me out to the colored cemetery and show me her grave. Well, he died before he could, and so I want to go out there now to the colored cemetery and find her grave.

LUCILLE: What on earth for, Mama?

STELLA: To keep my promise to Doug.

LUCILLE: He's already buried, Mama. How can you possibly keep that promise to him now?

STELLA: Well, I'll dig him up and bury him again, or dig her up and bury her beside him.

LUCILLE: Dig her up? What will be left, Mama, after all these years? I bet she only had a pine-board coffin.

MARY JO: Before anybody digs anybody up, Son, for God's sake call the man about the oil lease.

STELLA: What oil lease?

MARY JO: An oil lease on the estate. Hasn't Son told you?

STELLA: No. Not on my estate. I want no oil wells or no gas wells cluttering up my land. They poison the land. Ruin it forever.

MARY JO: That is so foolish, Mama.

STELLA: When my father was alive, they tried to drill for oil on our land and he took a shotgun and he went out there and he said, "Get off this land of mine or I'll blow your brains out."

LEWIS: Mama, that's not true. You used to say you prayed every night we would get an oil lease.

STELLA: Say again the eulogy you spoke at Doug's funeral.

LUCILLE: Not now, Mama.

STELLA: Yes, now. I want to hear it now. Say it, Son.

SON: All right. (*A pause.*) Ever since I can remember Doug Alexander has been a great part of my life. He was always in our house and yard when I was growing up—never too tired or too busy to talk to me or to show me . . .

MARY JO: I think I am losing my mind. Do you mean to tell me, Mama . . .

STELLA: Be quiet, Mary Jo. Son is saying Doug's eulogy.

MARY JO: I don't want to hear Doug's eulogy.

STELLA: Then leave the room.

MARY JO: I will not leave the room. I think this whole family has gone crazy. Are you going to calmly sit here and let an oil lease slip through our hands?

LEWIS: Why are you getting so excited, Mary Jo? If Mama doesn't want an oil lease, she doesn't want one. I, for one, have everything I need.

MARY JO: Well, I don't have all I need. Nor does my husband or my daughters. We are in a desperate condition—on the verge of bankruptcy. Do you understand? We owe money to everybody. We can lose our cars, our house . . .

STELLA: Is that true, Bob, or is that just some more of Mary Jo's tales.

BOB: I'm afraid it's true. I have to tell you good people I'm on the ropes as they say.

MARY JO: Mama, will you please let Son call about that oil lease?

STELLA: All right. God help me, I will. If you swear to me that you will never again mention about dividing the estate.

LEWIS: I don't want to divide the estate. I am happy the way things are.

BOB: What none of you understand . . .

MARY JO: Be quiet, Bob . . .

STELLA: Son, go call that oil man about the lease.

SON: You're sure now?

STELLA: Yes, I'm sure. (*SON goes.*) I remember the eulogy I gave at Henrietta's funeral.

BOB: Who in the world is Henrietta, Mother-in-Law?

STELLA: Doug's mother.

BOB: Oh.

STELLA: I said Henrietta and her son, Doug, came to live on our place when I was a girl of six. She and her husband and her son had been tenants on one of our farms and her husband was killed tragically by one of our bulls. I remember the day Papa brought Henrietta and her son to live in the house in our back yard. Often, after she cooked our dinner and was in her house resting, I would go and visit with her and we would talk. She was always kind and patient with me. (*A pause.*)

BOB: Can we just take a second to clarify . . .

STELLA: (*She gets up.*) Lewis . . .

LEWIS: Yes, Mama.

STELLA: Help me upstairs. I'm tired. I want to rest.

LEWIS: All right, Mama.

STELLA: All this talk about dividing the estate has worn me out.

LUCILLE: Nobody has been talking about dividing the estate, Mama. We were talking about an oil lease. (*STELLA rises. She and LEWIS start upstairs.*)

LUCILLE: Well, thank God, she forgot about going out to the colored cemetery and traipsing around.

MARY JO: I'm worn out. I'm exhausted. Mama just exhausts me.

LUCY: Hasn't it been dry? I heard last night on TV that everyone's worrying about a new dust bowl, only maybe this time it's being caused by the ozone. Do you all remember the dust bowl?

MARY JO: The what?

LUCY: The dust bowl.

MARY JO: No.

BOB: We never had a dust bowl here Lucy, not on the coast.

LUCY: I'm having my class read *The Grapes of Wrath*. That's all about the dust bowl.

MARY JO: Is that so.

LUCILLE: Who wrote *The Grapes of Wrath*?

LUCY: John Steinbeck.

LUCILLE: Oh, yes. I think I read that. What is it about?

MARY JO: Didn't you hear her? The dust bowl.

LUCY: And the Okies.

LUCILLE: Oh, yes, I think I do remember that.

LUCY: Remember, this family from Oklahoma are trying to get to California.

LUCILLE: Oh yes, I have a vague memory of it. (*SON enters*.)

MARY JO: Did you reach the oil man?

SON: Yes, he'll come tomorrow afternoon.

MARY JO: Tomorrow. I think you should see him today.

SON: He didn't want to see me today. He wants to see me tomorrow.

MARY JO: It is always tomorrow in this family. Tomorrow we'll see about the oil lease. Tomorrow . . . (*LEWIS enters*.)

LEWIS: Son, Mama wants to see you.

MARY JO: What does she want to see him about?

LEWIS: I don't know. I didn't ask her, Sister. (*SON leaves*.)

LUCILLE: Yes, Yes, *The Grapes of Wrath*, I did read that, it's a great story.

LUCY: Yes.

MARY JO: The last book I read was— (*A pause*.) I can't remember.

BOB: *Gone with the Wind*?

MARY JO: Yes, I read that, but that wasn't the last book I read.

BOB: You can get that on video cassette now, you know. Play it on your VCR whenever you want to.

LUCILLE: *Gone with the Wind*?

BOB: Yes, ma'am.

LUCILLE: Isn't that wonderful.

LUCY: They're talking about making a sequel to it you know.

MARY JO: I wouldn't care for that. I think it's perfect just as it is, just perfect.

SON: (*Calling offstage*.) Mama, Aunt Mary Jo, Uncle Lewis, can you come up here, please.

MARY JO: Oh, I knew it was too good to be true. (*LUCILLE, LEWIS, and MARY JO leave*.)

BOB: How long have you been teaching?

LUCY: Twelve years.

BOB: That so . . . I hope you will help me talk sense to this family about inheritance taxes, and hiring a lawyer. You see, it just makes common sense. It's for everybody's benefit. (*A pause.*) I want to go on record as saying I think Son is mighty lucky to get you.

LUCY: Thank you.

BOB: I mean no disrespect to the dead, but Olive Louise never fit in. Never tried to. She always had a chip on her shoulder, it seemed to me. Did you ever meet her?

LUCY: No.

BOB: She was nice-looking, but never smiled. Always seemed to have a sour expression. (*MARY JO enters.*) I was trying to explain to Lucy, who seems to me a very sensible girl, about my feelings about the inheritance tax, like I said . . . (*MARY JO cries.*)

BOB: What is it, honey?

MARY JO: Mama has left us, Bob. She has gone to her rest.

BOB: My God! My God Almighty! (*A pause.*) Well, the estate is going to be divided now, after all these years. (*A pause.*) Well, she had a good full life, didn't she?

MARY JO: Yes.

BOB: (*Singing half to himself.*) In heavenly love abiding . . .

MARY JO: Yes, she had a good, full life. Son would like to see you upstairs, Lucy.

LUCY: Thank you. (*She goes.*)

MARY JO: Will you go call the funeral parlor, Bob? Ask them please to come get Mama?

BOB: I will. And then I'm going to call the bank and tell them we will have some money soon. I'm sure tomorrow or the next day I can borrow on our share of the estate.

MARY JO: I'm sure you can. (*He starts out.*) Bob, how much do you think our share will be?

BOB: Oh, I'd just be guessing until I see some actual figures. But enough. And it's come just in time let me tell you. (*She goes to him.*) Now, now. It's going to be all right. But I was scared to death there for awhile.

MARY JO: I know you were. I was too.

BOB: I had no one to talk to. I didn't want to worry you anymore than I had to, my friends were all so depressed, out of work, needing money. Well, it's going to be all right now. The estate is going to be divided. Of course, I could have saved the family thousands if they'd only listened to me. (*He starts away.*)

MARY JO: Bob, just take a guess at what you think our share will be?

BOB: All right, just let me call the funeral parlor and then I'll do some figuring. (*He goes. LUCILLE enters.*)

LUCILLE: Sister, she's at peace. Mama's at peace.

MARY JO: I know. Bless her sweet heart.

LUCILLE: Let's make a list of pall bearers.

MARY JO: All right.

LUCILLE: She said she always wanted Doug as an honorary pall bearer but he died first.

MARY JO: Who else did she want?

LUCILLE: Son.

MARY JO: And Lewis?

LUCILLE: I asked him. He can't. He's too upset. Bob.

MARY JO: Certainly Bob.

LUCILLE: Sister, can you believe it? Mama's gone.

MARY JO: It's hard to realize.

LUCILLE: Mama's gone. (*BOB comes in.*)

BOB: I got the funeral director. He'll be right over. He said had you discussed how much you want to spend on her coffin.

LUCILLE: I want the best. Doug had the best coffin you know.

MARY JO: What did it cost?

LUCILLE: I don't know. You'll have to ask Son, I just knew it was the best they had. (*LEWIS comes into the room.*)

LUCILLE: Can you believe it, Brother? Mama's gone. (*LEWIS begins to cry. She goes to him.*) Oh, Brother—Brother—Brother.

LEWIS: Everything will be different now.

LUCILLE: Yes, it will.

LEWIS: Everything will be different now. Everything—everything. (*The lights fade.*)

ACT II

SCENE 2

A week later. EMILY, SISSIE and MARY JO are there. MARY JO has a piece of paper on which she is writing.

MARY JO: Now look around, and anything you want I'll write down and put your initial after it, and we'll ask for it. Of course, you understand you may not get it if Son or Lewis or Lucille ask for it, too. In that case, we will have to have a drawing. Mama always said that the china belonged to me, and the silver to Lucille and Lewis. I hope that's in the will.

EMILY: Who gets her jewelry?

MARY JO: She said that was divided three ways, between Lucille, Lewis and me. I have asked for the diamond brooch, but that doesn't mean I'll get it, because the minute I asked for it, Lucille said she had always wanted it. Now, let's carefully go through all the rooms and we'll write down whatever it is you'd like. We'll start in here. What would you like in here? Sissie?

SISSIE: Nothing.

MARY JO: Nothing?

SISSIE: Not a single, solitary thing. I don't want a lot of junk like this around me. I want something new and modern.

MARY JO: Well, maybe your fiancé would like something. Did you ever think of that?

SISSIE: What? It's just a lot of old junk.

MARY JO: You do not have an ounce of sentiment, do you? Not an ounce. Emily?

EMILY: Could you sell any of this?

MARY JO: Sell it? Why in the world would you want to sell what belonged to your grandmother and your great-grandmother?

EMILY: To get money.

MARY JO: Well, I don't think we're going to have to worry about money for a while now.

EMILY: How much are we going to get when the estate is divided?

MARY JO: I don't know exactly. We'll know better when Daddy and Son come back from the lawyers.

EMILY: How much do you think it will be?

MARY JO: Oh, I don't think we should speculate, girls. I really . . .

SISSIE: I heard you and Daddy speculating last night. Daddy said he thought you might clear at least seven hundred and fifty thousand dollars if you can get them to sell this house.

MARY JO: Well, we'll soon know.

EMILY: I tell you right now, the first money you get, I want another trip to Europe.

MARY JO: If you girls don't want anything here, what about in the dining room and the bedrooms?

EMILY: There is not a thing in a single room in this house that I want, thank you.

SISSIE: Ditto.

MARY JO: Ditto?

SISSIE: Ditto.

MARY JO: What a way to talk. Well, if you don't want anything, I'm still going to pretend you do and put down things I want in your names. That way Lucille won't end up with everything. Now, I want the sofa and these chairs, and . . . (*LUCILLE enters.*)

LUCILLE: Mary Jo, I went through the house early this morning and I made a list of what I would like. Have you made your list?

MARY JO: Partly.

LUCILLE: Do you want to hear mine?

MARY JO: What about Lewis? Is he making a list?

LUCILLE: No. If we live on in the house, he said just to include him in my list, as he will live on here with us. Of course, I still think if Mama left the house to Son, she certainly meant for the furnishings to stay with the house.

MARY JO: Well, we don't know that she left the house to Son, do we?

LUCILLE: Well, you heard her say in this very room she was going to.

MARY JO: I also heard her say she wasn't going to.

LUCILLE: If he quit working here, which he didn't.

MARY JO: Well, Mama said a lot of things she didn't mean. You know that as well as I do. If she put in writing somewhere she left the house to Son, that is fine with me. If she didn't, I'm not about to agree to giving him the house. Let me hear your list.

LUCILLE: All right. I'll start in this room. I would like the sofa and the two chairs. Lewis would like . . .

MARY JO: The sofa and the two chairs?

LUCILLE: Yes.

MARY JO: I want them, too.

LUCILLE: Well, if I know you, I'm sure you're going to want everything. You always have.

MARY JO: I want everything—what about you? (*MILDRED comes in with CATHLEEN.*)

MILDRED: What you want for supper?

LUCILLE: I'll be out in a minute, Mildred.

MILDRED: Cathleen and I wants to know if you're going to keep us on here.

LUCILLE: We really are not able to make plans just yet. We'll know soon now.

CATHLEEN: Doug told me the day before he died that Miss Stella left us something in her will.

LUCILLE: She never told me that. Did she you, Mary Jo?

MARY JO: No, she didn't.

LUCILLE: But if it's in the will, you will certainly get it.

MILDRED: When will we know?

LUCILLE: Sometime this afternoon. Son and Mr. Bob are with the lawyers now.

MILDRED: Thank you. (*She and CATHLEEN leave.*)

LUCILLE: Shall I continue with my list?

MARY JO: Please.

LUCILLE: I would like the two library lamps, and Lewis wants the floor lamp.

MARY JO: I want the lamps, too.

LUCILLE: You can't have everything, Mary Jo.

MARY JO: Neither can you. (*LEWIS comes in.*) Are you all through at the lawyers?

LEWIS: No. It all gave me a headache. I don't understand any of it, anyway.

LUCILLE: Did you look at the will?

LEWIS: Yes.

LUCILLE: Did it say she left the house to Son?

LEWIS: No.

LUCILLE: Did you tell the lawyer that she said she wanted to give the house to Son?

LEWIS: Yes. But he said that would mean nothing in a court of law unless we all agreed to give him the house. I said I agreed.

LUCILLE: And I certainly agree.

MARY JO: Well, I don't. And I don't think I'm being unreasonable. We owe the estate three hundred thousand dollars. Bob thinks this house and ten acres would bring half a million or more.

LUCILLE: And Bob is crazy.

MARY JO: Thank you, but I don't think so. Now, Bob says, and I agree, if you want to cancel our three hundred thousand dollar debt, you may keep the house.

LUCILLE: What!

MARY JO: I said . . .

LEWIS: Be careful, Sister. Don't agree to anything without legal counsel. That is what the lawyer said. He warned the estate is a very complicated one since we have so little cash, and so much of our assets are in land. He said each of us might want to retain a lawyer. I've retained one for myself.

LUCILLE: Why?

LEWIS: To protect my interests.

LUCILLE: Oh, I think it is a shame for brothers and sisters to need lawyers.

LEWIS: It may be a shame, but you'd better get one. Bob has one.

LUCILLE: How do you know?

LEWIS: I saw him. He's over there with Bob right now, going over the will.

LUCILLE: Did you know that Bob had hired a lawyer, Mary Jo?

MARY JO: Yes, I did.

LUCILLE: My God— (*She leaves.*)

MARY JO: I hope, Lewis, you'll remember the girls in your will and not leave everything to Son and Lucille. I don't care about myself, but they are your nieces, you know.

LEWIS: I know, but I don't plan on dying just yet. (*He leaves.*)

EMILY: Mama, heavens . . .

MARY JO: You have to be practical about these things, honey. If we end up with seven hundred and fifty thousand dollars, which it looks like we will, now that the house does not belong to Son, that means that Lewis will have that, too, and there is no reason when he dies that you shouldn't have half of that, which will be . . . (*A pause.*) What is half of seven hundred and fifty thousand dollars?

EMILY: I don't know.

MARY JO: Sissie, do you know?

SISSIE: No. (*Mary Jo writes figures on her pad.*)

MARY JO: Two into seven goes three times and carry one, and two into fifteen goes seven times and carry one, and two into ten goes five. Three hundred and seventy-five thousand dollars. Now add that to seven hundred and fifty thousand and you will have . . . (*A pause.*) just a moment. One million, one hundred twenty-five thousand dollars. (*LUCILLE enters.*)

LUCILLE: What is this about a million, one hundred and twenty-five thousand dollars?

MARY JO: Nothing.

LUCILLE: Well, I hope you are not counting on anything like that from this estate. Son says after you pay back your three hundred thousand dollars, and the inheritance taxes are paid, and the lawyer gets his percentage . . .

MARY JO: What percentage does the lawyer get?

LUCILLE: He told Son his fee was ten percent of the value of the estate.

MARY JO: For what?

LUCILLE: For settling the estate.

MARY JO: That's highway robbery! Get another lawyer.

LUCILLE: We can't, Son says. Mama put it in her will that he was to settle the estate for us.

MARY JO: My God. (*LUCILLE goes out to the kitchen.*) I am so depressed. Lucille always paints a black picture of everything. She takes the joy out of everything. Always has. (*LUCY enters carrying a flowering plant.*) Hello, Lucy. How pretty.

LUCY: I thought you all might enjoy it.
MARY JO: Thank you. The flowers were beautiful at Mother's funeral, weren't they?
LUCY: Yes, they were. Son not back yet?
MARY JO: No. Still with the lawyer.
LUCY: Emily and Sissie, when Son and I marry, I would like you to be in the wedding party.
EMILY: Thank you.
MARY JO: You're having a big wedding, then?
LUCY: I plan to. Why?
MARY JO: Nothing. It's just that I thought since Son had been married before . . .
LUCY: I haven't been married before.
MARY JO: Of course, you haven't. You plan on marrying as soon as school is out?
LUCY: Yes.
MARY JO: Sissie may beat you to the alter then. She plans on marrying in early Spring.
LUCY: Will you have a big wedding, Sissie?
SISSIE: As big as we can afford. Can I have my reception at the Houston Country Club?
EMILY: You'll have to join first.
SISSIE: Well, can we join now, Mama?
MARY JO: We'll see.
SISSIE: I'd rather join the Houston Country Club than go to Europe.
EMILY: Well, I hadn't . . .
SISSIE: Well, you go to Europe and I'll join the Houston Country Club.
EMILY: Do you know how much that would cost to get in? Plus the yearly dues. Have you any idea?
SISSIE: Don't worry about that—let Mama and Daddy worry about that. It is Mama's money.
MARY JO: And Daddy's. What is mine is his. (*LEWIS enters*.)
LEWIS: Not back yet?
MARY JO: No.
LEWIS: Hello, Lucy.
LUCY: Hello. (*LUCILLE enters*.)
LUCILLE: Well, I've hired me a lawyer, too.
LEWIS: Who did you hire?
LUCILLE: Mervin Bay.
LEWIS: I hired Ted Malone.
LUCILLE: I wouldn't trust Ted Malone as far as I could throw him, Lewis. He'll end up with everything you have. (*SON and BOB enter*.) Lucy,

how lovely. (*Taking flowering plant.*)

MARY JO: Here they are.—Bob.

LUCILLE: Well,

SON: (*A pause.*) It's very complicated, Mama.

LUCILLE: What is?

SON: The estate. There is so little cash, you see.

LUCILLE: Well, we've known that all along.

BOB: I have a splitting headache.

MARY JO: I don't want to hear how complicated it is. Did the lawyer estimate how much we would get when it is divided?

BOB: No.

MARY JO: Why?

BOB: Well, if you'll be quiet for a minute and stop snapping questions at me, I'll try and explain. All he can do now is try to make us understand the alternatives.

MARY JO: What alternatives?

BOB: There are a couple of possible scenarios: One is a rough estimate of the value the Government will put on the estate . . .

MARY JO: Which is?

BOB: Between five and six million, and given that figure, he made a rough estimate of what we could expect the inheritance tax to be.

MARY JO: Which is?

BOB: Well over a million dollars.

MARY JO: God Almighty.

BOB: God knows I tried to warn you all about it. Didn't I plead with you and try to get around this?

MARY JO: You certainly did, Bob.

BOB: And let me give you the bad news all at once. The lawyer figures if the estate is valued at between five and six million dollars, his fee for settling it could be between five hundred and six hundred thousand. So that's almost two million we owe already. Plus Miss Stella left a cash gift of five thousand to Mildred and five thousand to Cathleen, and twenty thousand each to two cousins out in West Texas that I never heard of.

MARY JO: You have too heard of them—Cousin Irene and Cousin Julia.

BOB: Well, if I have, I've forgotten it.

LEWIS: What is the other scenario?

BOB: The other is that since land is so devalued around here now, we can make a claim that the estate is worth about half its former value, which would make us only owe a million, if the Government will accept our evaluation, which we have no assurance it will, and we could spend four of five years in appeals. No matter what, we have to raise at least a million—plus the money for the cash bequests. How much cash is there on hand now, Son?

SON: Well, we've the taxes to pay, and we have the cash for that because of the oil lease, and we have some stocks and a few bonds of about a hundred thousand that we could dispose of in a hurry, but the rest we would have to raise by selling some of the land.

MARY JO: Or this house and ten acres.

SON: Selling this house and ten acres wouldn't anywhere near cover it—it would have to be the house and some farm land.

BOB: And even if the Government doesn't challenge us, it could be a year and a half before it is finally settled.

MARY JO: A year and a half?

BOB: Maybe two.

MARY JO: My God, Bob.

EMILY: You mean we won't see any of the money for two years?

BOB: Who knows if there will be any money at all? It's a terrible time now to have to sell land—unless you want to give it away. A year ago . . .

MARY JO: A year ago . . . a year ago . . . I don't want to hear about a year ago. What about now?

BOB: Nobody knows for sure about now, Mama. He says houses that were getting a hundred thousand a year ago can't find buyers at half that price. What was his estimate for this house and acreage, Son?

SON: A hundred and fifty thousand dollars, if we can find a buyer.

MARY JO: A hundred and fifty thousand dollars for this lovely old house and ten acres?

BOB: Nobody wants this big old house, Mama. If they want anything, it would be the land. They will just tear the house down.

MARY JO: It's all so depressing. What are we going to do?

BOB: What can we do?

MARY JO: Stop going around in circles. Just tell me how much will I get.

BOB: If the Government insists on valuing the land at what it was once worth—say, six million, and they would get a million and a half in inheritance taxes, and the lawyer would get another six hundred thousand that would come to over two million, and to pay those taxes and the lawyer's fee, we would have to sell land in a hurry at very low prices.

MARY JO: I don't want to hear all of that. I just want to know how much will I get.

BOB: Very little.

MARY JO: Very little. How much is very little?

BOB: After we pay off what we owe the estate, maybe a hundred thousand dollars, we could end up with as little as sixty thousand.

MARY JO: I am sick. Of course, Son and Lucille will both come out very well. You'll have three hundred thousand from us, two hundred thousand from Lewis . . .

SON: Only if we sell the house and some of the farms. So what I suggest is this: let's not divide the estate, let's keep it intact and borrow what we have to pay off the taxes and the lawyer. We can all live here together, form a corporation, tighten our belts until we pay off the bank loan.

BOB: And like Son says, we have an oil lease now, and they can always find oil or gas out there.

MARY JO: If we're lucky, but we're not lucky.

BOB: But we could be. Look on the bright side, Mama.

MARY JO: I will never, never come back here to live.

EMILY: And I certainly won't.

SISSIE: You wouldn't catch me dead here.

MARY JO: Never, Bob. Let's go home. (*She starts out.*) When can we get whatever is coming to us from the estate?

SON: Not for a year at the earliest, the lawyer says.

MARY JO: Can we borrow against what we're to get in the meantime?

SON: No. It's in probate. We can't touch it without special permission from the administrator.

MARY JO: Who is the administrator?

BOB: The lawyer.

MARY JO: Well, let's ask him.

BOB: I did—he said he can't do it.

MARY JO: Why?

BOB: It's against his principles.

MARY JO: I'm going home before I lose my mind. Come on . . .

BOB: We can't go there anymore, Mama.

MARY JO: Why?

BOB: They foreclosed on our house in Houston today, Mama.

MARY JO: Bob . . .

BOB: I'm sorry, Mama, that's how it is. I didn't want to tell you before hoping there would be a way out once we saw the will. (*A pause.*)

MARY JO: Well, I guess we can stay here. This house belongs to me too, now.

BOB: I'll have to go into Houston and pack our clothes. Will you come with me, Mary Jo?

MARY JO: No. I never want to see that house again.

BOB: Will you girls come with me?

EMILY: Do we have to?

BOB: Yes, you have to. Somebody has to.
SISSIE: Come on, Emily. It won't kill us.
EMILY: This means we're going to have to live here.
SISSIE: We have to live someplace. When shall we go, Daddy?
BOB: As soon as we've eaten.
SON: I love this land, you know. I've thought of all the times I've walked over it. In good times and bad. With my father and my grandfather. Watched the crops grow. My heart was very sad at the thought of parting with any of it.
MARY JO: How are we all going to live here together until the estate is settled without killing each other? Can you tell me that?
LUCY: I think it can be exciting, and a real challenge to us all. We can be like the Korean and Vietnamese families moving into Houston, and all over the coast—they live together, they work together.
MARY JO: Well, I'm neither Korean or Taiwanese, thank you.
LUCY: I find the way they all work together very inspiring.
MARY JO: Please, please, Lucy. You're sweet and I know you mean well, but please . . . (*MILDRED and CATHLEEN enter.*)
MILDRED: Did you all read the will?
BOB: Yes. You and Cathleen are both left five thousand dollars.
MILDRED: Good God Almighty. Did you hear that, Cathleen?
CATHLEEN: Yes, I did.
MILDRED: Didn't I tell you she was going to generously remember us? I felt it.
CATHLEEN: You sure did.
MILDRED: Excuse me for asking, but when do we get our money?
SON: Not until the estate is settled.
MILDRED: When will that be?
SON: It could be a year.
MILDRED: A year?
SON: Yes—even longer.
LUCILLE: In the meantime, Mildred, you and Cathleen will have to look for work someplace else. We are going to start doing our own work.
MILDRED: You don't mean that?
LUCILLE: Yes, I do.
MILDRED: Why?
LUCILLE: So we can pay off our debts.
MILDRED: Debts? I thought the estate was left to you.
LUCILLE: I know. It is very complicated, Mildred.
CATHLEEN: The will is in probate Miss Mildred.
MILDRED: Probate, how do you know that?
CATHLEEN: We studied it last semester.

MILDRED: Good lord, probate, it's always something. (*MILDRED and CATHLEEN go back into the kitchen.*)
MARY JO: Well . . . (*A pause.*) Lucy . . .
LUCY: Yes.
MARY JO: What about the Korean and the Vietnamese that live together. Do they get along?
LUCY: I think so. They seem to.
LUCILLE: They have to.
MARY JO: What if they don't?
LUCILLE: Then they don't, I guess.
LEWIS: Will someone tell me one thing; why doesn't that Taiwanese man put a sign on his plastic factory? Does anyone know the answer to that?
LUCY: I do. I heard just the other day from Priscilla Knight that works at the Chamber of Commerce—she said she went out and asked him, and he said in Taiwan you didn't advertise because everyone knew by the look of your building, what your business was.
LUCILLE: Is that so . . .
LEWIS: That doesn't make sense to me. His building is made of cinder blocks and shaped like a million others I have seen.
LUCILLE: Do they go to church?
LEWIS: Who?
LUCILLE: The Taiwanese.
LEWIS: I don't know.
LUCILLE: They certainly don't go to the Baptist Church. Do they go to the Methodist Church, Lucy?
LUCY: I have never seen them there.
BOB: Maybe they're not Christians.
LUCY: The Vietnamese fishermen on the Coast are Catholics.
LUCILLE: Is that so?
BOB: Just like Mexicans.
LUCILLE: There are plenty of Mexican Baptists, you know.
MARY JO: Is that so? Here?
LUCILLE: I mean here.
MARY JO: Do they go to our church?
LUCILLE: No, they go to their own church.
MARY JO: Do they preach in Mexican or English?
LUCILLE: I don't know. I've never been.
LUCY: How do you feel about bilingual education?
MARY JO: What's that?
LUCY: It means having two languages in the school system.
MARY JO: Two what kind of languages?

LUCY: Well, here in Texas, because of the large Spanish speaking population, it would mean Spanish and English.

MARY JO: I think it is absolutely insane. If you are in America, you learn American period. What do you think about it?

LUCY: I haven't made up my mind. There are pros and cons, like there are about everything.

LUCILLE: Maybe we should make out a schedule.

MARY JO: For what?

LUCILLE: For when Mildred and Cathleen leave.

MARY JO: When will they leave?

LUCILLE: As soon as they find other jobs. We just can't turn them out.

MARY JO: No.

LUCILLE: I thought one week you would cook and I would clean house, and the next week, I'd cook and you'd clean. (*LEWIS gets up.*)

LEWIS: I'm going out to the cemetery and say goodnight to Mama. (*He goes.*)

MARY JO: Son, what was the name of the girl whose father Lewis gave the ten thousand dollars to?

SON: I don't know.

MARY JO: Did you ask him her name?

SON: Yes, but he wouldn't tell me.

BOB: I know her name—Vaughn Evans told me up town today: Irene Ratliff. And to tell you the truth, Vaughn thinks he's still seeing her. I don't think he's going out to the graveyard to say goodnight to anyone—I think he's going out to see her. She works just down the street at that hamburger place.

LUCILLE: McDonalds?

BOB: No, the other one.

LUCILLE: Sonic?

BOB: No. No. The other one.

LUCILLE: Whataburger?

BOB: That's right.

MARY JO: Oh, my God. The next thing is he'll be marrying her and bringing her here to live. Then there will be nine of us when Lucy moves in.

LUCY: Let's try to look on the bright side.

MARY JO: What's the bright side?

LUCY: I know Irene Ratliff. I taught her in high school. She is very nice.

MARY JO: Is that the bright side?

LUCY: Yes.

MARY JO: God help us all, then. God help us all. (*A pause.*) I know what I'm praying for, every night down on my knees—that we strike oil If we strike oil, then can we divide the estate?

SON: I suppose so, if everyone wants to.

MARY JO: I want to go on record right now as saying I want to. Every night on bended knees. I'm not good at this communal living. I'm not Vietnamese and I'm not Korean.

LUCILLE: I thought the girl's father said he was going to kill Lewis if he didn't stay away from her?

SON: That's what Uncle Lewis told me. He had to give him ten thousand dollars to keep him from killing him.

BOB: That's before your Mama died. Now the father thinks he's going to be rich and he's welcoming him.

MARY JO: How do you know that?

BOB: Vaughn Evans told me. He said she and her father and her mother came to your Mama's funeral.

LUCILLE: Oh, my God.

MARY JO: Did you see them at the funeral, Lucille?

LUCILLE: No.

LUCY: I did. She waved at me.

LUCILLE: Who did?

LUCY: Irene Ratliff.

LUCILLE: Oh, my God. (*A pause.*) Of all things. Do you know what I was just thinking of just now? (*No one asks to be told. She continues on as if they had.*) The night Papa died. It was a cold December night. Bitter cold. The day before it was warm, so warm we were almost prostrated with the heat. Then early the next morning this fierce blue norther blew up and we were freezing. We had fires in every fireplace in the house. Papa wouldn't let anybody near him but Dr. Dailey you remember and when we saw he was sinking fast brother went over to get Dr. Dailey but the Doctor was drunk and couldn't be roused and by the time brother came back Papa was dead.

EMILY: When did he die?

LUCILLE: Let's see—1960—Is it possible? (*A pause.*) Papa's dead, Doug is dead, Mama, Charlie— (*A pause.*) Who will be next?

MARY JO: Good Lord, Lucille. (*A pause.*) Who were papa's pall bearers?

LUCILLE: Mr. Scott Jordan, Elmo Douglas.

MARY JO: Mr. Leslie Crockett.

LUCILLE: Yes. All of them are dead now.

MARY JO: All of them?

LUCILLE: Every last one of them.

MARY JO: Mr. Leslie Crockett?

LUCILLE: Oh, yes. He's been dead a number of years. At least five isn't it son?

SON: I think so.

MARY JO: Brother, of course was always Mama's favorite, but I always felt I was Papa's.

LUCILLE: I didn't think so at all. I thought I was Papa's favorite. (*SISSIE begins to cry.*)

EMILY: What's the matter with you?

SISSIE: What kind of wedding can I have now if we're so poor? (*BOB goes to her.*)

BOB: Come on, honey.

SISSIE: Couldn't we just borrow money for the wedding daddy?

BOB: I don't see how if we follow Son's plan—if we borrow money from the bank for our taxes, we can take nothing from the estate again until the bank is paid off. Isn't that right, Son?

SON: Yes. I won't be able to have my salary any longer. I will have to get me another job now.

LUCILLE: Then who is going to keep the accounts and see to the farms?

SON: I'll have to do that in my spare time Mama.

BOB: I can help him.

SON: And Uncle Lewis can no longer expect his four hundred dollars each month, or you Mama or you Aunt Mary Jo.

MARY JO: What will we do?

SON: You'll have to try and get jobs too until the bank loan is paid off.

MARY JO: Get a job? Are you crazy? I've never worked a day in my life.

BOB: You're not going to have to work, Mary Jo. I'll get a job.

MARY JO: Where?

BOB: Here.

MARY JO: Doin' what?

BOB: Somethin'. There's bound to be a job somewhere. The girls can get jobs.

EMILY: Doin' what?

BOB: I don't know. Somethin'.

MARY JO: And you expect Lewis to get a job?

BOB: He'll have to. (*A pause.*)

MARY JO: My God. It has all changed. Hasn't it? So quickly. (*A pause.*) What about Mama's jewelry? Did she say in the will who is to get what?

SON: Yes. You get the diamond brooch and her diamond bar pin, a string of her pearls, a cameo, and Mama is to get the ruby ring and the diamond earrings, a string of pearls, and cameo brooch, and Uncle Lewis is to get—

MARY JO: (*Interrupting.*) And I suppose we'll have to wait for the estate to be divided before we get them—

SON: No, the executor said as soon as he can have them appraised you may have them.

LUCILLE: But we mustn't ever sell Mama's jewelry. No matter how badly we need money, she wouldn't like that.

MARY JO: No, she wouldn't like that. When will they start drilling on our land, Son?

SON: An oil company will never tell you that. Maybe tomorrow, maybe next week, maybe next month. The lease says they have a year.

LUCILLE: I can get a job I suppose if I have to.

MARY JO: What can you do? You've never worked a day in your life.

LUCILLE: Well, Grace Ann Davis had never worked a day in her life either, but when Mr. Davis died and left no money and she was penniless she went to Austin and got a job working in a cafeteria.

MARY JO: Well, there's no cafeteria here. Maybe we could get a job at Whataburger with brother's girlfriend. I can just see the four of us: Lucille, Sissy, Emily and me all working at Whataburger with brother's girlfriend.

SISSIE: Don't be funny, Mama.

LUCY: That's what they say America is becoming you know, a service economy.

LUCILLE: Who says it?

LUCY: I'm always reading it somewhere—*Time* or *Newsweek*. One or the other is always saying it. (*LEWIS and IRENE RATLIFF come in.*)

LEWIS: Folks, I want you to meet a dear friend of mine, Irene Ratliff.

LUCY: Hello, Irene.

IRENE: Hello, Miss Lucy.

LEWIS: This is my sister Lucille, my sister Mary Jo, my nephew Son.

IRENE: Howdy.

OTHERS: Hello.

LEWIS: Irene works at the Whataburger. I stopped off to get a bite to eat and she was just finishing work, so I asked her to come over here with me to meet you all.

IRENE: I am so sorry about your mother. I went to the funeral with my mama and daddy. I thought it was a very nice funeral. A big crowd too. My daddy said there are not many people in this town could fill a church like she done. Did anybody count how many came?

LUCILLE: No, I don't believe we have.

IRENE: My daddy said if he was guessing he'd guess near two hundred. Mama said she thought nearer three hundred and my daddy said, of course you'd say that, you exaggerate everything and mama got mad at him then, the least thing he says can get her mad and she said, you'll be lucky if we can get five people to come to your funeral mean as you are.

MARY JO: Every night I'm going to pray. On bended knee—pray.

IRENE: What are you praying for, Mrs. . . .?

MARY JO: That we strike oil, so we can divide the estate.

IRENE: Oh. My Mama told me that her Mama told her that her granddaddy struck oil out on his farm a long time ago. He couldn't read or write and he went crazy with all the money from oil, and had a lot of kids, twelve, I think. And he went down and bought them all cars—big expensive cars, Reos and Packards and Buicks—and they moved into town here from the country and parked all the cars out under the Chinaberry trees and everybody in town used to ride by their house to see all them new cars parked in the yard, and one day a man from the Valley came to town and knew my great-granddaddy couldn't read or write and he took advantage of him and sold him some land . . .

MARY JO: On bended knees. On bended knees.

LUCILLE: What happened to the land?

IRENE: Well, Mama says when her granddaddy went out to the Valley to look at the land he bought, it was all under water and worthless. And all that was left to show for all of his oil money was them cars he bought his kids. She said people in town used to ride by all the time to see all those cars sitting under the Chinaberry trees.

LUCILLE: Under the Chinaberry trees. My.

LEWIS: You remember Irene's grandfather. He ended up as the town night watchman. John Moon.

LUCILLE: Oh, yes.

LEWIS: We had this joke—John Moon only comes out at night.

MARY JO: I'm praying every night on bended knees.

IRENE: Ma'am.

MARY JO: Praying every night for my deliverance on bended knees. Praying for an oil lease.

IRENE: Yes, Ma'am.

LUCILLE: John Moon. Yes, I remember him.

IRENE: All I say is, if you strike oil watch out for crooks from the Valley. They will sell your land under water every time. Every time.

LUCILLE: John Moon. My I hadn't thought about him for the longest kind of time.

MARY JO: I'm praying . . . I'm praying . . . (*Curtain.*)

TALKING PICTURES

TALKING PICTURES's premier stage production was at the Asolo Theatre Center for the Performing Arts and was directed by John Ulmer with the following cast:

KATIE BELL JACKSON: Meghan Cary
VESTA JACKSON: Jamie Martin
MYRA TOLLIVER: Kathryn Grant
MR. JACKSON: Donald Christopher
WILLIS: Michael James Laird
MRS. JACKSON: Barbara Bates Smith
ESTAQUIO: Jack Boslet
PETE ANDERSON: Rafael Petlock
GLADYS: Carol Hanpeter
ASHENBACK: Eric Tavares
GERARD ANDERSON: Jack Conley

Characters

KATIE BELL JACKSON
VESTA JACKSON
MYRA TOLLIVER
MR. JACKSON
MRS. JACKSON
WILLIS
ESTAQUIO TREVINO
PETE
GLADYS
ASHENBACK
GERARD ANDERSON

Setting

Place: Harrison, Texas. Time: 1929.

TALKING PICTURES

ACT I

A living room, bedroom, porch and a portion of the yard of the JACKSON house in Harrison, Texas. It has very small rooms, a small parlour and yard. KATIE BELL JACKSON, 16, is reading a book in the living room. Her sister, VESTA, 18, is eating popcorn.

KATIE BELL: Sister, come give me some popcorn.
VESTA: No. Go out in the kitchen and get your own.
KATIE BELL: Selfish!
VESTA: Selfish, yourself. (*MYRA TOLLIVER, 34, comes into the house looking down at a run in her stockings.*) What's the matter?
MYRA: I've got a run in my stocking. Brand new, too. (*MYRA goes into her room and takes off the stocking.*)
KATIE BELL: How was the picture show this afternoon?
MYRA: Pretty fair.
VESTA: (*Calling to her.*) Was it hot walking from town?
MYRA: Yes. And dusty.
KATIE BELL: Who was in that picture show?
MYRA: Bessie Love. (*She has changed stockings and begins to darn stockings.*)
VESTA: Who?
MYRA: Bessie Love. What are you reading, Katie Bell?
KATIE BELL: *Ben Hur*.
MYRA: Oh, that was a wonderful movie.
KATIE BELL: It looks like it. There are scenes from the movie in the book. Were you playing the piano for the picture show when you saw it?
MYRA: Yes, I was.
KATIE BELL: Ramon Navarro was in the movie, wasn't he?
MYRA: Yes, and Frances X. Bushman.
KATIE BELL: Was the movie like the book?
MYRA: I don't know. I never read the book.
KATIE BELL: Is Ramon Navarro very handsome?
MYRA: I think so.
VESTA: He's a Mexican.
KATIE BELL: No, he's not.

VESTA: Yes, he is too.
KATIE BELL: Is he, Miss Myra?
MYRA: Yes, he is. And he's very worried, I read.
KATIE BELL: Why?
MYRA: What will happen to his career when the movies are all talkies.
KATIE BELL: Why does that worry him?
VESTA: Because he talks Mexican, goose. Once people hear him talk Mexican they'll all knows he's not American.
KATIE BELL: Can't he learn to speak English? I saw a Mexican boy up town the other day and I asked him his name and he said it was Estaquio Trevino and he spoke English just as plain as anybody.
VESTA: Katie Bell Jackson, were you talking to a Mexican? Mama would have a fit if she knew.
KATIE BELL: I wasn't talking to him. I just asked him his name.
VESTA: You mean you walked right up to a strange Mexican and asked him his name?
KATIE BELL: No, I didn't go right up to anybody. Sally Meyers and I were walking down the street and he came up to us and asked us if there were any other Mexicans here and Sally said yes, there were some across the track and I said yes that was true and he said enough to start a church?
VESTA: Enough to start a church?
KATIE BELL: That's what he said.
VESTA: Why did he say that?
KATIE BELL: I don't know. I didn't ask him and then he asked us our name and we told him.
VESTA: You told him? You told a Mexican boy your name?
KATIE BELL: Yes.
VESTA: Sister, I am shocked. Then what happened . . .
KATIE BELL: And then we asked him his name, and a colored boy walked by and he asked if there were many colored people here and I said as many as there are white, and Sally said she thought more, and then we bid him goodbye and walked on.
VESTA: Myra, Mama says in exchange for part of your rent you are going to give Katie Bell and me music lessons—
MYRA: Yes.
VESTA: Mama says after I learn to play the piano, I can take organ lessons so I can play for the church on Sunday. (*KATIE BELL makes a face.*) Why are you making a face?
KATIE BELL: Because I don't ever want to play an organ in church or anywhere, I want to play the piano for picture shows like Myra.
VESTA: I'd like to hear you tell Mama that.

KATIE BELL: I'm not about to tell Mama that.

MYRA: Well, honey, don't ever think about playing piano in picture shows. Those days are about over, I fear. I think the Queen here is about one of the last of the silent theaters. Mr. Santos says he will keep it that way as long as he can, as he doesn't care for the talkies, but I don't think he can hold out much longer. The theaters in El Campo, Bay City and Richmond have all gone talkie, and I hear Eagle Lake and Columbus are about to. Why, I read the other day in some movie magazine or other where they may stop making silent pictures all together. (*She goes into the bedroom which she rents from the JACKSONS.*)

KATIE BELL: Miss Myra has seen a talking picture. She saw it in Houston when she took Pete in to stay with his daddy. I wish I could see a talking picture.

VESTA: Well, you're never going to get to so just get over wishing that. You've never seen a silent movie.

KATIE BELL: Well, neither have you—Anyway, Miss Myra tells me the stories of all the movies she sees and she tells them so wonderfully I feel like I've seen them.

VESTA: Does Mama know she tells you the stories of all those pictures?

KATIE BELL: No.

VESTA: Well, I bet she would have a fit if she knew. (*A pause.*) Did she tell you the story of that talking picture she saw in Houston?

KATIE BELL: Yes. She did.

VESTA: Was it a love story?

KATIE BELL: Miss Myra, was that talking picture you saw in Houston a love story?

MYRA: No, not really. Well, now I don't know. It was a love story, I suppose, but an unconventional one. It was the story of the love of a father for his son.

VESTA: What was the name of it?

MYRA: *The Singing Fool.*

KATIE BELL: Would you tell the story to Vesta? She's never heard you tell the story of a picture show and I told her . . .

MYRA: You tell the story to Vesta—

KATIE BELL: Oh, I can't.

MYRA: Sure, you can. Tell it like I told it to you.

KATIE BELL: I can't remember it all.

MYRA: Sure you can.

KATIE BELL: I remember there was this man and he was a famous singer and he was married. Is that right?

MYRA: Yes, that's right.

KATIE BELL: And they had a little boy and he loved his little boy very much, but then he and his wife were separated and one night when he was to sing his little boy got sick and died. But he had to go on stage and sing anyway, even though his heart was breaking.

VESTA: That's sad.

KATIE BELL: Of course, it's sad. Miss Myra said everybody in the picture show was crying. Didn't you?

MYRA: Yes.

VESTA: Were you crying?

MYRA: Oh, yes. Like a baby.

KATIE BELL: Sing that song for Vesta.

MYRA: (*Singing.*) FRIENDS MAY FORSAKE US
LET THEM ALL FORSAKE US
I STILL HAVE YOU, SONNY BOY.
YOU CAME FROM HEAVEN
AND I KNOW YOUR WORTH,
YOU MADE A HEAVEN FOR ME RIGHT HERE ON EARTH.
BUT THE ANGELS THEY GOT LONELY
AND THEY TOOK YOU BECAUSE THEY WERE LONELY
NOW I'M LONELY, TOO, SONNY BOY.

VESTA: Did the little boy die?

MYRA: Yes.

KATIE BELL: And the father had to go and sing that song even though his heart was breaking.

VESTA: Oh, that's so sad. It's like the story Brother Meyers told in church the other night about this poor widow who had no money and no job.

KATIE BELL: Didn't she have a husband?

VESTA: No, goose. Didn't you hear me say she was a widow? Widows don't have husbands. If you're a widow your husband is dead. And if you're a grass widow your husband is alive and you're divorced. Myra is a grass widow.

KATIE BELL: Are you?

MYRA: Yes.

KATIE BELL: What did that woman's husband die of?

VESTA: What woman?

KATIE BELL: The one Brother Meyers told you about.

VESTA: Good heavens, I don't know that. Ask Brother Meyers.

KATIE BELL: Is that the whole story?

VESTA: No, there's more to it.

KATIE BELL: Well, what's the rest of it?

VESTA: Well, she was desperate because she had starving children and everything . . .

KATIE BELL: And what happened?

VESTA: Well, if you'll be quiet for five minutes I'll tell you.

KATIE BELL: I know what happened. She prayed to God and he saved them.

VESTA: How did you know that?

KATIE BELL: Because that's what always happens when Brother Meyers tells a story.

VESTA: What was the name of that talking picture you saw?

MYRA: *The Singing Fool.* (*MR. JACKSON, 45, in overalls, carrying a lunchpail comes in. A soft spoken, sad man.*)

MR. JACKSON: Hello.

VESTA: Hello, Daddy.

KATIE BELL: Hello, Daddy.

MYRA: Hello, Mr. Jackson.

KATIE BELL: Daddy got bumped.

MYRA: I know I heard, I'm so sorry.

MR. JACKSON: Well, it's not the end of the world. I still have a job.

VESTA: Who bumped you Daddy?

MR. JACKSON: Someone with more seniority than I have that wanted my job here.

KATIE BELL: Now Daddy's going to have to bump somebody—We're going over to Cuero on his day off to look it over and if he likes it, he'll bump the man that works there, and we'll all go live in Cuero. When are we going to Cuero, Daddy, if we go?

MR. JACKSON: Well, we have to try and sell our house, see if we can't find a place to live there.

KATIE BELL: Have you ever been to Cuero, Miss Myra?

MYRA: Yes, I've played in the picture house there.

KATIE BELL: Is it a nice town?

MYRA: I think so.

VESTA: As nice as here?

MYRA: I like it here better—

VESTA: Oh, Daddy, if we move to Cuero in six weeks I better start my piano lessons with Myra right away, if she's going to teach me.

MR. JACKSON: Well, that's up to you and your Mama.

VESTA: Can you start teaching me right away?

MYRA: Why, yes, I don't see why not.

VESTA: Oh, grand.

MR. JACKSON: Where is your Mama?

VESTA: She's at the Missionary Society.

MR. JACKSON: I'm going to work in my garden while it's still light. (*He* *starts out. He pauses.*) Your boy coming here today, Myra?

MYRA: Yes, I'm waiting for him now.

MR. JACKSON: How long has he been in Houston?

MYRA: Two weeks.

MR. JACKSON: Two weeks? Doesn't seem possible. Staying with his father?

MYRA: Yes.

MR. JACKSON: Is he married again?

MYRA: Yes.

MR. JACKSON: Does he have any other children?

MYRA: Yes, two. Both boys.

MR. JACKSON: Where did you come from Myra?

MYRA: I was born and raised in Nacogdoches.

MR. JACKSON: Oh yes. I remember now. Mrs. Jackson told me that. I used to have a run through Nacogdoches.

MYRA: Did you?

MR. JACKSON: That was the run I had before I came to Harrison. (*MRS. JACKSON enters through the front door.*)

MRS. JACKSON: Well, Daddy, you beat me home.

MR. JACKSON: Yes, I did. How was the Missionary Society?

MRS. JACKSON: Oh, I tell you the sorrow in this world. You don't know when you are blessed. Mrs. Davis was with us today telling us about the missionaries among the leper colonies. Oh, the tales of those lepers are harrowing. Brother Meyers is going to preach a whole sermon about the lepers on Sunday, he says.

MR. JACKSON: I thought Mrs. Davis was a Presbyterian.

MRS. JACKSON: She is.

MR. JACKSON: Then why was she at the Methodist Missionary Society?

MRS. JACKSON: To get us all interested in the leper work. She says it's interdenominational. Brother Meyers agrees. He prayed so beautifully about it. I just love to hear Brother Meyers pray—Well, I'd better get supper started.

MR. JACKSON: And I'm going out to my garden.

MRS. JACKSON: Your boy not home yet, Myra?

MYRA: No, I'm expecting him any second now.

VESTA: Mama, may I start my piano lessons right away with Myra. Daddy says we may be moving to Cuero pretty soon.

MRS. JACKSON: We'll discuss that later. (*She starts out.*)

VESTA: I'll help you, Mama. (*They leave.*)

KATIE BELL: If I tell you a secret will you swear not to tell anybody?

MYRA: Yes, I swear.

KATIE BELL: Two years ago when I was in El Campo visiting Sarah

Lundy we slipped into the picture show over there. We saw Clara Bow in *Rough House Rosie*. Did you see that?

MYRA: Yes, I did.

KATIE BELL: How many picture shows have you seen?

MYRA: Oh, hundreds—

KATIE BELL: How long have you been playing the piano at picture shows?

MYRA: Let's see. About eight years.

KATIE BELL: What made you come here?

MYRA: Because they were looking for someone to play the piano at the Queen.

KATIE BELL: What was the best picture show you ever saw?

MYRA: Oh, heavens . . . I'll have to think about that.

KATIE BELL: Who is your favorite actor?

MYRA: I'll have to think about that, too. (*A pause.*) I think *Romona* with Dolores Del Rio was one of my favorite pictures.

KATIE BELL: She's Mexican, too, isn't she?

MYRA: Yes—

KATIE BELL: Are there any other Mexican movie stars?

MYRA: Yes. Lupe Velez, Antonio Moreno.

KATIE BELL: They're movie stars?

MYRA: Yes.

KATIE BELL: How do you get to be a movie star?

MYRA: Oh, I don't know.

KATIE BELL: Are there only Mexican and American movie stars?

MYRA: No. There are Russian and German and Italian and English and Polish—

KATIE BELL: Movie stars?

MYRA: Yes.

KATIE BELL: How much money does a movie star make?

MYRA: Depends on the movie star.

KATIE BELL: They're all rich aren't they?

MYRA: Pretty rich. Richer than I am certainly. (*She goes outside to the porch, sits on the steps. WILLIS enters.*)

WILLIS: Hi—

MYRA: Hello.

WILLIS: Pete home yet?

MYRA: No. How was work?

WILLIS: Hot. I'm tired. Laying bricks in the hot sun is not my idea of a classy job. (*A pause.*) Well, beggars can't be choosers.

MYRA: Is your room over the garage hot?

WILLIS: Like an oven. How is your room?

MYRA: It gets pretty hot.

WILLIS: A little breeze now.

MYRA: Yes.

WILLIS: How about a date Sunday night after the picture show?

MYRA: Don't you have to get up early Monday morning?

WILLIS: Five o'clock. Same as usual.

MYRA: Willis, you'll be dead if we go on having dates at night and your having to get up for work so early. Anyway, where can we go at ten o'clock at night, but the ice cream parlour and it closes at eleven and they just sigh when we come in at ten as if to say I hope you won't loiter.

WILLIS: When else can I see you? You work at the picture show every afternoon and every night, seven days a week. I wanted a date tonight, but you said you thought you should come back since it was Pete's first night home. (*KATIE BELL comes to the door.*)

KATIE BELL: Phone, Myra—

MYRA: Excuse me— (*She goes into the house. KATIE BELL comes outside.*)

KATIE BELL: Did you ever see a talking picture?

WILLIS: I saw one in Houston that was partly talking.

KATIE BELL: How do they get those pictures to talk?

WILLIS: Beats me.

KATIE BELL: Are you a Baptist?

WILLIS: Born and bred.

KATIE BELL: Someone said you were. We're Methodists. Myra is Methodist, too. Can Baptists and Methodists marry?

WILLIS: They can if they want to.

KATIE BELL: Vesta was about to date a Baptist boy, but Mama discouraged it. She says mixed marriages are not a very good idea. It's very confusing to the children. With the father going to one church and the mother to another. Now my father doesn't go to any church and that worries my mother considerable. Of course, like Mama says, he is the best man that ever walked this earth, but still. (*A pause.*) Do you think people that attend picture shows are going to Hell?

WILLIS: No, I don't.

KATIE BELL: I don't either. Brother Meyers says if they go on weekdays they are liable to go and if they go on Sundays they are bound to. I certainly don't think Myra is going to Hell, do you?

WILLIS: No.

KATIE BELL: Anyway, she has to go. It's her job. (*MYRA comes back out.*)

KATIE BELL: Willis says you're not going to Hell if you go to the picture shows.

MYRA: I wasn't worried. Thank you anyway, Willis, for telling me. That was Pete's daddy on the phone. He said Pete wanted to know if he could stay another day—I said, yes. Well, it's time for me to go to work. See you all later. (*She goes.*)

KATIE BELL: She had been crying. Couldn't you tell?

WILLIS: No.

KATIE BELL: Well, she had. I can tell. She cries all the time, too, in her room when Pete isn't there. I guess she doesn't think we can hear her, but we can. Papa says she's worried over losing her job. She says she has lots to worry her, says it's hard having to raise a boy by herself. I think she's pretty, don't you?

WILLIS: Yes, I do. (*MRS. JACKSON comes to the door.*)

MRS. JACKSON: Katie Bell, come here, please.

KATIE BELL: Yes, Ma'am. (*She goes to her mother.*)

MRS. JACKSON: What's all this about some little boy dying at the picture show. Vesta's all upset about it.

KATIE BELL: He didn't die at the picture show, Mama. He died in the picture show.

MRS. JACKSON: Oh, is that how it was. I thought some little boy died at the picture show here.

KATIE BELL: No, he died in a picture show in Houston.

MRS. JACKSON: It seems to me you are awfully interested in picture shows all of a sudden.

KATIE BELL: No, Ma'am. Just interested in the stories, Mama. (*A pause.*) Mama—

MRS. JACKSON: What?

KATIE BELL: Do you think that people that go to picture shows will go to Hell, especially if they go on Sundays?

MRS. JACKSON: No, I don't. Not that I would go myself and I don't want you or your sister ever going. (*A pause.*) I went to a tent show once.

KATIE BELL: You did?

MRS. JACKSON: Yes, and a medicine show, too. I didn't care too much for either of them, but I don't think I'm going to Hell, because I went. That's just Brother Meyers talking. He's a good man, but extreme in his views. How are you, Willis?

WILLIS: Pretty fair, thank you.

MRS. JACKSON: Hot enough for you?

WILLIS: Oh, yes. (*He starts out.*) See you all later. (*He goes.*)

KATIE BELL: Mama?

MRS. JACKSON: Yes.

KATIE BELL: I think he is courting Miss Myra, don't you?

MRS. JACKSON: It seems. He's over here a lot.
KATIE BELL: I think he's nice, don't you?
MRS. JACKSON: Yes, I do. And I think Myra is nice, too.
KATIE BELL: Pete isn't coming home today.
MRS. JACKSON: Oh.
KATIE BELL: When she came out to tell us that I think she'd been crying.
MRS. JACKSON: She's very emotional. I think it's seeing all those picture shows.
KATIE BELL: Papa says it's not, he says—
MRS. JACKSON: (*Interrupting.*) I know what he says, but your Papa isn't the final authority on everything. Just think how hearing the story of one of those picture shows upset your sister, what if you watched as many as she does—why I think you'd be upset all the time.
KATIE BELL: Mama, do you know any Mexicans?
MRS. JACKSON: Good Lord, no. Why would I know any Mexicans? You're the strangest child I ever saw. Never know what you're going to worry me with next. Moving picture shows and now Mexicans. (*She goes in the house. KATIE BELL sits on the steps as the light fades. The lights are brought up—later that evening. WILLIS is sitting on the JACKSON steps. MYRA comes in.*)
WILLIS: Good evening.
MYRA: Sh. Mr. Jackson's asleep. He goes to bed by eight–thirty or nine. He's up at four. He takes his train at five.
WILLIS: I know. There are lights on in the house though.
MYRA: That's the girls in the living room listening to the radio.
WILLIS: They let them listen to the radio, but not go to the picture show?
MYRA: They can only listen to programs of classical music. Jessica Dragonette, the Firestone Hour, Lawrence Tibbett. Once Mrs. Jackson caught Katie Bell listening to Rudy Vallee and she threatened to throw the radio out the window.
WILLIS: The Joplins have a radio. They invited me over the other night to listen to a boxing match.
MYRA: Did you go?
WILLIS: Oh, yes.
MYRA: Why aren't you in bed asleep?
WILLIS: It's very close in my room tonight.
MYRA: You should have a fan.
WILLIS: I know, I'm going to get one. Do you have a fan?
MYRA: No.
WILLIS: I bet your room is hot too?

MYRA: Terrible.

WILLIS: I'd say let's walk back to town and get some ice cream but I think the drug store would be closed by the time we got there.

MYRA: Yes, it would. Anyway, I'm too tired tonight to walk another step.

WILLIS: Why were you so late getting home tonight?

MYRA: Sue Jessie had to leave early because of some kind of going on at the Eastern Star, so I told her I would total up the ticket sales for her. She sells the tickets, you see, and she's always worrying she'll come out short. Anyway, it took me longer than I thought to get it all straight so Sue Jessie wouldn't have a breakdown when she comes tomorrow. And then I went for a walk.

WILLIS: By yourself?

MYRA: Yes, sir—

WILLIS: Myra, don't be walking around by yourself this time of night. (*Inside, KATIE BELL changes the radio station.*) It's not safe.

VESTA: Katie Bell Jackson, what are you doing? That's dance music! Mama would have a fit if she knew you were listening to dance music! Turn that off and come to bed! (*They exit.*)

WILLIS: Myra—

MYRA: What?

WILLIS: Were you crying today?

MYRA: When?

WILLIS: Right after you talked to your husband.

MYRA: My ex-husband. I was crying. (*A pause.*) My ex-husband can be so insensitive sometimes. After I gave my permission for Pete to stay he said right out that Pete didn't want to live with me any longer. He said he wanted to stay in Houston with him and his wife and his boys all the time.

WILLIS: What is his name?

MYRA: Whose?

WILLIS: Your ex-husband's?

MYRA: Gerard. Gerard Anderson. His new wife's name is Jacqueline Kate. They call her Jackie Kate.

WILLIS: Would you let Pete live permanently in Houston?

MYRA: No, he's just making the whole thing up to get at me. I said to him why don't you leave me alone, stop tormenting me. The courts have given Pete to me except for two weeks in the summertime. He said, it wasn't his doing, Pete doesn't want to come back, well, I said, put Pete on the phone and let him tell me that. He's in the pool swimming, he says, in our swimming pool. Do you have even a public swimming pool in Harrison, he said? No, I said we don't, we do have the River which Pete is not allowed to go in because of snakes, alligators, and suckholes. That's what you think, he says. He goes into that river all the time, sneaking, he said, while you're busy playing the piano at the picture show. Well, listen, I said, that's the way I put a roof over our head and food on the table by playing at the picture show. Then he said, in a very sarcastic way, I hear you may lose your job at the picture show to the talking pictures. How are you going to support a fourteen year old boy if that happens, he said, don't you worry about me, I said, I'll get a job. I always have. And I have, too. When we divorced I didn't have a dime and he was working in construction then and barely making anything and so I knew I couldn't count on him for any kind of support, and I didn't want to take anything from him even if I could—And so it was up to me to always take care of Pete and myself from then on. Oh, he sent Pete five dollars at Christmas and on his birthday, but that's all. He'd been drinking, you know.

WILLIS: Does he drink?

MYRA: He sure does, all the time these days.

WILLIS: I don't drink.

MYRA: I know you don't.

WILLIS: My daddy drank something fierce. The sight of him cured me once and for all. Is that why you left him because he drank?

MYRA: No, he didn't drink then.

WILLIS: Why did you separate?

MYRA: Oh, Lord. I don't know really. I've asked myself that a million times, to tell you the truth. We started going together back in High School.

WILLIS: Nacogdoches?

MYRA: Yes. (*A pause.*) I guess you might say we just outgrew each other. My daddy said if I left him he'd never speak to me again and he didn't until the day he died and then he just barely nodded to me when I went into his room. But Gerard and I thought it was the best thing to do at the time. A year after the divorce he came over where I was living with Pete and asked me to marry him again. But by then I had my first job at a picture show and was supporting myself and Pete. (*A pause.*) Gerard's a contractor now. He's a rich man, he tells me and Pete says he thinks he is. He has a car and a truck and a swimming pool and a two story house and a new wife and two more sons—(*A pause.*) Of course, I've never regretted leaving him. He wasn't mean to me, he never hit me or yelled at me—but he never stayed home except to eat and sleep. I don't think he was running around with other women and he wasn't drinking then, but he just never stayed home. I had Pete the first year we were married, and he'd say, come on and bring the baby, where to, I'd say, the Domino Parlour or the pool hall? I can't bring a baby to a Domino Parlour or a pool hall, I'd tell him. Do you mind if I go, he'd say, no, I would always say, go on, I don't mind. I got lonesome, of course. (*A pause. She sings half to herself.*) When there are grey skies. I don't mind the grey skies.

WILLIS: I hope to be rich one day.

MYRA: Well, I hope you are for your sake. If that's what you want. And if it brings you happiness—(*She sings again to herself.*) The angels, they grew lonely—

WILLIS: What's that song? I never heard it before.

MYRA: It's a song they sang in that picture show I saw in Houston.

WILLIS: Was it a talking picture?

MYRA: Yes.

WILLIS: What was it called?

MYRA: *The Singing Fool*, with Al Jolson.

WILLIS: Oh, yes. I saw him in *The Jazz Singer*. Did you see that?

MYRA: No.

WILLIS: That wasn't all talking. That was part talking and part silent. He sang "*Mammy*" in that one. He wore black face when he sang it.

MYRA: He wore black face in this one, too.

WILLIS: When he sang?

MYRA: Yes.

WILLIS: I wonder why he does that?

MYRA: I don't know.

WILLIS: You've been here a year, Myra?

MYRA: Yes, and before that Flatonia and before that—

WILLIS: Were you always playing the piano in picture shows?

MYRA: Yes.

WILLIS: Did you ever think of marrying again?

MYRA: Once. A man in Lufkin, Harold Menefee. I almost married him, but Pete didn't like him and I don't think he liked Pete, though he swore he did and I was afraid he might not be good to Pete after we married, so I said no.

WILLIS: I like Pete.

MYRA: I'm glad.

WILLIS: Does he like me?

MYRA: I don't know, I've never asked him.

WILLIS: We played catch together the night before he went to visit his daddy.

MYRA: I know you did.

WILLIS: I bought a glove just so I could play with him—I want to play with him a lot when he gets back. My youngest brother is sixteen and

I play catch a lot with him when I go back home.

MYRA: It's not easy, you know living in a rented room in somebody else's house with a fourteen year old boy. I dream some day of having my own house with a room for myself and a room for Pete. (*A pause.*) It's a pretty night, isn't it?

WILLIS: Yes. (*A pause.*) I had some good news tonight.

MYRA: What?

WILLIS: Mr. Charlie called me into his house tonight after supper and he said his business had improved a lot and that he was very pleased with my work and that he has had contracts for four more houses and I could count on steady work and a raise in pay. I told him that was certainly good news because I was trying to make some plans of my own, what kind of plans he asked, and I said, personal plans. (*A pause.*) I don't know what you think about me exactly, but I think you're a mighty fine person. I have my eye on a small lot and now that I know I'll have a steady job and a raise in pay I can see my way clear on making an offer on the lot and if I can get it at a price I can afford, I could start building a house. Mr. Charlie said he would help me every Sunday after church. It would be a small house, of course, and it wouldn't have a swimming pool. Anyway, like I said, I don't know what you think about me, but I think highly of you. (*A pause.*) Of course, I don't know if you remembered my telling you I was married before, too.

MYRA: Yes, I remember you telling me that.

WILLIS: We had no children, my wife left me for another man two years after we were married. That hurt a lot, of course, because I won't lie to you, I was sure crazy about her. And I thought the sun rose and set on her. And I swore to myself at the time I would never marry again, it shook me up so. That was five years ago, of course, and I only think of her once in a while now, like when she sends me a postcard from New Orleans or Galveston—we're still married because I could never get the money together for a divorce, but now—

MYRA: (*Interrupting.*) What's your wife's name?

WILLIS: Gladys.

MYRA: Gladys what?

WILLIS: Gladys Mayfield was her girlhood name, then Gladys Toome when she married me—

MYRA: Is it Ashenback now?

WILLIS: Well, that's the name of the man she left me for.

MYRA: Well, I never.

WILLIS: That's if they're still together and they were last I heard—

MYRA: I got a postcard from her a week ago—

WILLIS: You did? Do you know her?

MYRA: Never heard of her before in my life.

WILLIS: What did the postcard say?

MYRA: "Keep away from my husband. I warn you." Gladys Ashenback. I said to Pete this must be a crazy woman. I don't know anybody named Gladys Ashenback.

WILLIS: Well, I'll be switched.

MYRA: So will you please tell her for me the next time you see her I'm not interested in her husband.

WILLIS: Maybe she meant me—You see, like I said, we've never divorced.

MYRA: Well, then, maybe she did.

WILLIS: Well, she can just send all the postcards she wants, she will never get me back—(*A pause.*) I've told you what I think about you, Myra. What do you think about me?

MYRA: I think you're very nice, too, Willis.

WILLIS: If I get a divorce now, would you ever consider marrying me?

MYRA: I might.

WILLIS: Would I have to get my house built first? I know a nice two bed-room apartment over at Mrs. Carver—

MYRA: Well, Willis—

WILLIS: Marry me, Myra, please. Please marry me. I'm very lonesome, Myra. I know I'm a Baptist and you're a Methodist, but I'll join the Methodist church if you wanted me to.

MYRA: Oh, I don't care about that at all, Willis. But I think you have to get a divorce first and then we'll talk of marriage—and, of course, I'll have to see how Pete feels about my marrying. (*MRS. JACKSON comes out of the house.*)

MRS. JACKSON: Oh, excuse me, Myra. I didn't realize you had company. Hello, Willis.

WILLIS: Hello, Mrs. Jackson.

MRS. JACKSON: Mr. Jackson is snoring so it woke me up. Did you hear him snoring?

MYRA: No.

WILLIS: I didn't either.

MRS. JACKSON: I'm surprised, he was snoring loud enough, I thought, to wake the dead—listen. (*A pause, we can hear snoring.*) I swear, Gabriel won't need a trumpet on resurrection morning, I tell him, they'll just have to get you to snore. (*A pause.*) It's so warm in the house—cool out here. (*A pause.*) What time is it?

WILLIS: Eleven.

MRS. JACKSON: Is it? I'll be dead tomorrow. You're a Baptist, Willis?

WILLIS: Yes.

MRS. JACKSON: We're all Methodists in this house. Except Mr. Jackson, I'm sorry to say. He belongs to no church, of course, he's the finest man I know—good and steady, no bad habits. Myra?

MYRA: Yes, Ma'am.

MRS. JACKSON: I have to speak with you about the girls' piano lessons. I know we talked of their studying with you in exchange for part of your rent, but with all the expenses facing us in moving after Mr. Jackson bumps another man, we can't afford to give up even part of the rent. I hope you don't mind and you haven't counted too much on it. Vesta's very disappointed and upset. She had her heart set on studying with you. (*A pause.*) Oh, I almost forgot to tell you there is a note for you by the phone, Myra. It's from Pete. He said to tell you he's spending the rest of the summer in Houston. He'll go to summer school there if he can. (*A pause.*)

MYRA: Well, I'm going to say good night.

MRS. JACKSON: Good night.

WILLIS: Good night. (*She goes into her room.*)

MRS. JACKSON: She's a very nice person. We often hear her crying in her room at night these last two weeks, but she's nice. That worries Mr. Jackson so. I think she gets upset from watching all those picture shows. A lot of them are sad, you know. Mr. Jackson says it is not picture shows worrying her, he says it's having to raise a boy alone on little money and now having to worry about maybe losing her job. That's why we were all hoping Pete would come home soon—he's comforting for her. He's a nice boy—

WILLIS: Yes, he is.

MRS. JACKSON: Well, I think I'm going to bed and try to get to sleep. Good night.

WILLIS: Good night. (*He starts out of the yard as the light fades. The lights are brought up. It is the next day. VESTA is sitting on the porch doing her nails, her hair is in curlers. ESTAQUIO TREVINO, 17, a Mexican, comes into the yard.*)

ESTAQUIO: Buenos dias.

VESTA: What did you say?

ESTAQUIO: Buenos dias. Good day—Buenos dias. That's Spanish for good day.

VESTA: Well, you couldn't prove it by me.

ESTAQUIO: Buenos noches is good night. Don't you study Spanish in school?

VESTA: No.

ESTAQUIO: I would think you would study Spanish being so close to Mexico and all. Texas used to belong to Mexico. It was called Tejas then.

VESTA: Any fool knows that.

ESTAQUIO: I just a met a colored boy who didn't. He said I was making the whole thing up. I'm a preacher's son.

VESTA: My foot—

ESTAQUIO: I certainly am. We came here hoping to start a church. A Spanish speaking church. We hoped with the Mexicans in New Gulf and the Mexicans here there would be some interest. But we got discouraged very soon. There are plenty of Mexicans in New Gulf, but they are all Catholic.

VESTA: I thought all Mexicans were Catholic.

ESTAQUIO: No. Definitely not. There are plenty of Mexican Baptists and we're spreading the word. Do you have a sister?

VESTA: Yes. What's it to you?

ESTAQUIO: And her name is Katie Bell.

VESTA: Why?

ESTAQUIO: I've come to tell her goodbye.

VESTA: How do you know my sister?

ESTAQUIO: We exchanged greetings downtown the other day. (*KATIE BELL comes in.*) Hello.

KATIE BELL: Hello. (*VESTA goes into the house.*) What are you doing here?

ESTAQUIO: I've come to say goodbye. I'm going back to Mexico.

KATIE BELL: Oh, well. Goodbye.

ESTAQUIO: And I've come to invite you to visit me in Mexico one day.

KATIE BELL: Thank you, but I wouldn't dare go there.

ESTAQUIO: Why?

KATIE BELL: It's too far away and besides, I wouldn't know a word anybody was saying.

ESTAQUIO: You could learn to speak Spanish—

KATIE BELL: I guess I could. I almost took it in school. I took Latin instead because Vesta did. Did you and your Papa get your church started?

ESTAQUIO: No.

KATIE BELL: I didn't ask the other day what kind of church it was.

ESTAQUIO: Baptist.

KATIE BELL: We are all Methodists.

ESTAQUIO: Are you? We Baptists believe in total immersion and we have no crosses in our church—

KATIE BELL: Is that so?

ESTAQUIO: I hope to be a preacher one day—

KATIE BELL: Baptist?

ESTAQUIO: Certainly—Jesus was a Baptist, you know—
KATIE BELL: Was he?
ESTAQUIO: Yes.
KATIE BELL: I never knew that. When you preach are you going to preach in English or Spanish?
ESTAQUIO: In Spanish. Jehova es mi salvador, nada me faltara.
KATIE BELL: What does that mean?
ESTAQUIO: The Lord is my Shepherd, I shall not want.
KATIE BELL: Oh, go on—(*PETE comes into the yard. He is 14. He has a suitcase.*)
PETE: Hello, Katie Bell.
KATIE BELL: Hi.
PETE: Is my Mom here?
KATIE BELL: She's still at the picture show. (*He puts the suitcase on the porch. He starts out.*)
PETE: I'm going to find my mom. (*He leaves.*)
KATIE BELL: (*Whispering.*) His Mom and Daddy are divorced. She's a grass widow. Do you know what that means?
ESTAQUIO: No.
KATIE BELL: Well, if you're a widow your husband is dead, but if you're a grass widow he's still alive.
ESTAQUIO: I'm going to be a Baptist preacher, too. My papa may let me start preaching soon. I'm practicing now. My first sermon is going to be about sin. That's a terrible thing, you know, sin is.
KATIE BELL: Yes, I expect so—
ESTAQUIO: Sin makes you drink and makes you gamble and go wrong. I wrestle with the devil all the time.
KATIE BELL: Do you?
ESTAQUIO: All the time. I talk rough to him. I tell him to go away and leave me alone. The devil got hold of my Mama, you know.
KATIE BELL: Did he?
ESTAQUIO: Oh, yes. Got hold of her and wouldn't let her go. My Papa prayed and I prayed but he won out. She ran off and left Papa and me. She hated church. Hated the Bible. Hated hymns. Hated Jesus. That was just the devil making her say that. I'm going to pray. Bow your head. Dious, dame valor para testificar a esta muchacha y su familia la palabra de dious. Y que sean vendicidos. Tambien por medio de tu vendicion, ellos logren sus metas. Te pido SENOR, que con ternura ella se fije en mi. AMEN. Don't I pray good? Papa taught me to do that. What does your Papa do?
KATIE BELL: He's an engineer. He's been bumped.
ESTAQUIO: What does that mean?

KATIE BELL: It means when you work for the railroad when someone who has more seniority than you do wants your job they can have it.

ESTAQUIO: Is he out of a job?

KATIE BELL: No, but now he has to bump someone and take their job.

ESTAQUIO: Maybe he'll bump someone in Mexico.

KATIE BELL: Oh, I don't think so.

ESTAQUIO: We don't know where my Mama is. We saw her on the street one day in Mexico City, but when we went up to her she said she didn't even know who we were. She told us to go away and mind our own business. But we didn't listen to her. We stayed right there beside her on the street corner praying, and then we went on. She never was a true Baptist, Papa said. Not in her heart. She used to slip off and go to confession all the time. (*MRS. JACKSON comes out followed by VESTA.*)

MRS. JACKSON: Come in the house now, Katie Bell.

KATIE BELL: He's a preacher's son.

MRS. JACKSON: Who is?

KATIE BELL: That boy there. He and his daddy came here to start a Mexican Baptist church.

MRS. JACKSON: What kind of a Baptist church?

KATIE BELL: Mexican. They do everything in Mexican. Preach and all. (*She turns to ESTAQUIO.*) Is your Bible in Mexican, too?

ESTAQUIO: Yes.

MRS. JACKSON: Why, I never heard of such a thing.

VESTA: We have colored Methodist and Baptist churches—how many, Mama?

MRS. JACKSON: Oh, Lord. More than I can count.

KATIE BELL: Say to her what you said to me.

ESTAQUIO: Jehova es mi salvador, nada me faltara.

KATIE BELL: You know what that says?

VESTA: No, and you don't either.

KATIE BELL: I do, too. The Lord is my Shepherd and I shall not want—

MRS. JACKSON: Is that so? Mercy. Why, that's remarkable. (*ESTAQUIO begins to sing "Rock of Ages."*)

ESTAQUIO: (*Singing.*) ROCA DE LA ETERNIDAD, FUISTE ABIERTA TU POR MI, SEMIESCONDEDERO FIEL, SO LO ENCUENTRO PAZ EN TI, RICO LIMPIO MANANTIAL, EN EL CUAL LAVADO FUI. (*MR. JACKSON comes in.*)

MRS. JACKSON: Daddy, that was "*Rock of Ages*" in Mexican.

MR. JACKSON: Is that so. I thought I recognized the tune. You from Mexico?

ESTAQUIO: Yes.

MRS. JACKSON: His daddy is a preacher.

ESTAQUIO: There are plenty of Mexicans across the tracks over there. They told my daddy they're going to start a Mexican school.

MRS. JACKSON: Is that so? Have you heard that, daddy?

MR. JACKSON: No.

MRS. JACKSON: We have a nice white school here, of course, and a colored school and now we'll have a Mexican school. Well—(*MYRA comes in.*)

MR. JACKSON: I wonder if there are any Mexican Methodists—(*MYRA and PETE come in.*) Well, look who's home. When did you get here?

MYRA: He came in on the four o'clock bus. He wanted to take the train, Mr. Jackson, but it would have gotten him home too late.

MR. JACKSON: Oh, don't worry about hurting my feelings. I don't own the railroads. I just work for them.

MRS. JACKSON: But I worry a lot about it, Daddy. Now more people seem to me ride the bus—what'll happen to the trains if everybody starts riding the bus?

MR. JACKSON: I don't know. I got enough to worry about without worrying about that. (*He goes inside.*)

MRS. JACKSON: He does worry about it. He worries about it all the time. Only he says one day we could wake up and find there are no trains at all. But that's foolishness, of course. There will always be trains.

KATIE BELL: Myra, Estaquio is Mexican. Estaquio, Myra plays the piano at the picture show and she says that Ramon Navarro, Lupe Velez, Antonio Moreno and Dolores Del Rio are Mexican. Do you know them?

ESTAQUIO: Oh, yes. Very well. They're all Baptists.

MRS. JACKSON: Is that so?

ESTAQUIO: Just like Jesus.

MRS. JACKSON: Oh—

ESTAQUIO: Well, so very nice to have met you all. (*He leaves. WILLIS comes in.*)

WILLIS: Well, look who's home. Get your glove and let's play a game of catch.

PETE: I don't want to play catch— (*He goes inside the house.*)

MYRA: He's mad because he had to come home. Well, he'll get over it. (*She goes inside.*)

VESTA: His daddy has a swimming pool in Houston, I guess he misses that— (*MRS. JACKSON goes into the house.*)

KATIE BELL: Did you know Jesus was a Baptist?

VESTA: That's a big lie—who told you that?

KATIE BELL: That Mexican boy.

VESTA: My foot. That's a big lie. (*Calling into the house.*) Mama, was Jesus a Baptist? (*MRS. JACKSON comes out on the porch.*)

MRS. JACKSON: What?

VESTA: You heard that Mexican boy tell her Jesus was a Baptist. Was he?

MRS. JACKSON: Well, that don't make it so—

VESTA: What was he, Mama?

MRS. JACKSON: What was who?

VESTA: Jesus—was he a Methodist?

MRS. JACKSON: Well, now. I'm not sure—he could have been, of course. I don't know if it says in the Bible, do you Willis?

WILLIS: What?

MRS. JACKSON: What denomination Jesus was.

WILLIS: I don't believe so. He was born a Jew.

VESTA: Well, he's certainly not any Mexican Baptist. I know that. Tell that to your Mexican friend next time you see him— (*She goes into the house.*)

WILLIS: I'm going to wash up. (He *goes, KATIE BELL goes inside. The lights are brought up in the bedroom MYRA and PETE share. PETE is there with his glove and baseball. He is angrily throwing the ball into the glove over and over. MYRA comes in. She gets a newspaper and tries to read, ignoring the noise of the ball as it hits the glove.*)

MYRA: If you want to do that, Son, go outside.

PETE: I don't want to go outside.

MYRA: Let's both go outside, it's cooler out there.

PETE: I don't want to go outside.

MYRA: Come on.

PETE: How many times do I have to tell you, Lady, I don't want to go outside.

MYRA: All right, then. (*A pause.*) Your daddy told me you'd been swimming in the river here. (*PETE doesn't answer. He continues to smack the ball into the glove.*) Did you hear my question, Pete?

PETE: I heard it.

MYRA: Is what your daddy said true?

PETE: I guess so.

MYRA: You guess? Don't you know? Did you go swimming in that river?

PETE: Yes.

MYRA: How many times?

PETE: Six or seven.

MYRA: Pete, I told you not to do that, you promised me you wouldn't.

PETE: What do you expect me to do—just sit around here in this room and rot.

MYRA: I don't want you to go into a river that's dangerous and that has suckholes and alligators and poisonous snakes and where you could be drowned—

PETE: A lot of boys go in the river.

MYRA: I don't care what a lot of boys do. I don't want you to go. (*A pause.*) You hear me? (*A pause.*) Pete?

PETE: What?

MYRA: How do you like Willis?

PETE: He's o.k.

MYRA: He likes you.

PETE: So?

MYRA: He likes you a lot. (*He goes back to the ball and glove.*) Put the ball down, Son, it's making me very nervous. (*He does so.*) Pete . . .

PETE: Yes?

MYRA: He's asked me to marry him when he gets a divorce from his wife. (*A pause.*) How would you feel about that? (*He shrugs his shoulders, but says nothing.*) I told him I couldn't say I'd marry him until I talked it over with you first, I told him I couldn't marry anyone you didn't like. (*A pause.*) Do you like him? (*Again he shrugs his shoulders.*) Maybe if you could get to know him better you would get to like him. (*A pause.*) Pete, I'm at my wits end, Son. I promised you we would never move again and I am going to keep my promise if it's humanly possible, but so far I've found no other job if the picture show goes talkie, but if I married Willis we would live on here, he has money to buy a lot and build a house where you can have your own room. He's a nice man, Son, kind, he doesn't drink, he works hard and could support us—(*A pause.*)

PETE: Mama?

MYRA: Yes, Son.

PETE: I feel terrible about this, Mama—

MYRA: What about, Son?

PETE: What I'm about to tell you.

MYRA: What is it, Son?

PETE: Well, you go ahead and marry Willis, if you want to Mama, but I don't want to live here anymore—

MYRA: You don't?

PETE: No.

MYRA: Well, that makes everything different, then.

PETE: Mama—

MYRA: Yes, Son.

PETE: This sure is hard for me to say, because it's not that I don't love you, because I do, but I don't want to live here with you anymore,

Mama, or any place—

MYRA: Now that's just your daddy poisoning your mind. He has no right to—

PETE: It's not daddy, Mama. It's me. I almost ran off just now and hitch hiked back to Houston without saying anything, but I just couldn't do that, Mama. So please let me go back.

MYRA: When?

PETE: Tomorrow.

MYRA: Tomorrow?

PETE: Yes, Ma'am. (*A pause.*) You see, Mama, there's nothing for me to do here—

MYRA: I know that.

PETE: Dad said he will teach me to drive his truck and I can start to work for him in my spare time. They have a swimming pool and a car and a nice house and he's married to a nice lady.

MYRA: Is she?

PETE: Oh, very nice and I like my brothers. We all have a lot of fun together. (*A pause. She cries.*) Mama, please don't cry. I don't mean to make you cry. (*A pause. She wipes her eyes.*)

MYRA: I know that. If I let you go will you come and spend your holidays with me?

PETE: Sure. Are you gonna marry Willis?

MYRA: I don't know.

PETE: Dad said the other night he hoped you would get married again. He said you sure couldn't make a living any longer playing the picture shows.

MYRA: When do you want to leave, Son?

PETE: Tomorrow.

MYRA: Tomorrow?

PETE: Yes, Ma'am, if you don't mind. Dad is driving everybody to Colorado for a two week vacation and they all want me to go with them.

MYRA: What about summer school?

PETE: I'll catch up next summer.

MYRA: Pete.

PETE: Please, Mama. I want to go.

MYRA: All right, then. (*She looks at her watch.*) I have to go to work. Here's some money. Go on uptown and get something to eat later on.

PETE: Yes, Ma'am.

MYRA: I'll see you later, Son.

PETE: All right.

MYRA: And when you go to Houston tomorrow take the train instead of the bus, it would please Mr. Jackson.

PETE: I don't have to take either, Dad is coming for me.

MYRA: Oh, bye, Son. (*She leaves him.*)

PETE: Mama. (*She goes out of her room, into the living room and outside. He takes his glove and baseball and follows after her. When he gets to the yard he stops.*)

MYRA: So long—

PETE: So long—(*She continues. He throws the ball up in the air and catches it as the lights fade. The lights are brought up an hour later. PETE is still in the yard. KATIE BELL comes to the door.*)

KATIE BELL: Mama says if you'd like to have supper with us there's plenty.

PETE: Thanks, I'd like to.

KATIE BELL: We'll eat in about a half hour.

PETE: Thanks. (*She goes as WILLIS comes over with his glove.*)

WILLIS: Feel like a game of catch now?

PETE: Sure. (*They start to play catch. GLADYS, WILLIS' wife comes in.*)

GLADYS: Well, Willis—(*WILLIS looks up.*) Aren't you going to say hello?

WILLIS: Hello.

GLADYS: How have you been?

WILLIS: All right. How have you been, Gladys?

GLADYS: Tolerable. Who's your friend?

WILLIS: He's Pete.

PETE: Hello.

GLADYS: You're Myra's boy, aren't you?

PETE: Yes, Ma'am.

GLADYS: I just bought a ticket to the picture show so I could get a look at her, but it was too dark in there and her back was turned so I couldn't see a thing. She plays the piano nicely though. Where do you live, Willis?

WILLIS: Up there over that garage.

GLADYS: Are you working?

WILLIS: Yes.

GLADYS: I'm miserable, Willis. Just miserable.

WILLIS: I'm sorry to hear that, Gladys.

GLADYS: Has Ashenback been around here?

WILLIS: Not that I know of.

GLADYS: Well, I'm warning you. He's liable to come with a gun, too. He's very jealous hearted, he's very jealous of you ever since I told him I made a mistake in leaving you. I walked up to your girlfriend at the picture show, tapped her on the back and told her her game was up. She didn't even turn around and look at me if she heard me. She didn't miss a note on that piano. I'm very tired, Willis. I've come a long way. Aren't you going to invite me up to your room?

WILLIS: It's just a small room, Gladys.

GLADYS: I don't care how small it is. Nothing could be smaller then the room we had when we first married. Do you remember that room, Willis?

WILLIS: Yes.

GLADYS: A regular closet. Ashenback is a four flusher, Willis. He talks big but it never comes to nothing.

WILLIS: Is that so?

GLADYS: Oh, my God, Willis. I made a mistake running off with him.

WILLIS: Did you?

GLADYS: Yes, I did. You know what he's doing now? He's a vendor for cigarette machines. That's how I heard about you and Myra. He said he looked you up the last time he was in Harrison and you proceeded to tell him about your girlfriend, Myra.

WILLIS: He never looked me up.

GLADYS: Ashenback is such a liar. He's lied since the first day I met him. Told me the first time I met him that he had a bank account of a hundred thousand dollars. And I believed him, too. And that's not the only lie of his I believed. We'd be here all night if I told you all the lies Ashenback has told me since we were together. (*ASHENBACK comes in.*) Ashenback, you are the biggest liar God ever made. Willis never told you nothing about a girlfriend. Did you, Willis?

WILLIS: No.

ASHENBACK: Never mind about that. His having a girlfriend wasn't a lie, was it? You don't always tell the truth yourself—You told me you were going to visit your mama and when I called your mama to see if you had gotten there, she said she hadn't heard a word from you in a month. But I wasn't born yesterday, I figured exactly where you had done. (*He draws a gun.*) Keep away from Gladys, Mister.

WILLIS: Are you crazy? I don't know what you are talking about. This is the first time I've seen Gladys in I don't know when.

GLADYS: Willis, don't let him intimidate you, he's all bluff. (*KATIE BELL appears.*)

KATIE BELL: Supper, Pete.

PETE: I'll be along in a minute.

KATIE BELL: Who's your company?

GLADYS: I'm Willis' wife.

KATIE BELL: How do you do?

ASHENBACK: Come on home, Gladys. Don't cause me to commit murder.

GLADYS: You're all bluff.

ASHENBACK: Am I?

GLADYS: You sure are. (*MRS. JACKSON comes out.*)

MRS. JACKSON: Children, supper's on the table and getting cold. Who are these nice people, Willis?

GLADYS: I'm Willis' wife— (*ESTAQUIO comes in with a Bible.*)

ESTAQUIO: Evening, everybody. (*He goes to KATIE BELL and MRS. JACKSON.*) I have brought you a Spanish Bible.

MRS. JACKSON: Isn't that nice. I called Brother Meyers and told him about "Rock of Ages" being sung in Spanish. He was thrilled. He says there are Methodist Mexicans.

ESTAQUIO: Yes, Ma'am. Glad to hear it. (*VESTA comes out.*)

VESTA: Mama, the food is getting stone cold. (*She sees ESTAQUIO.*)

MRS. JACKSON: Vesta, the Mexican boy brought us a Spanish Bible.

ESTAQUIO: Estaquio.

MRS. JACKSON: Est—

ESTAQUIO: Estaquio.

MRS. JACKSON: (*Slowly.*) Estaquio. Would you read something to us from the Bible?

ESTAQUIO: Sure. (*He takes the Bible.*)

VESTA: Mama, our supper is getting cold.

MRS. JACKSON: Be quiet, Vesta, this is a chance of a lifetime.

ASHENBACK: Well, I'm not standing around here listening to any Mexican read the Bible. Come on Gladys. (*He grabs her.*)

GLADYS: (*Pulling away.*) I don't love you anymore. Leave me alone.

ASHENBACK: Gladys—

GLADYS: I don't love you and I never have. I love Willis and I always have and he loves me and I'm leaving you and going back to him.

WILLIS: Now look here—

ASHENBACK: Do you mean that, Gladys? Do you really mean you don't love me?

GLADYS: From the bottom of my heart, I mean that. You and Willis fight it out. I'm going up to his room. (*She walks out.*)

ASHENBACK: Gladys, wait. Please. Don't leave me. I'll kill myself if you do. (*He runs after her.*)

MRS. JACKSON: They're very upset, aren't they?

ESTAQUIO: Shall I read some—

MRS. JACKSON: If you will.

ESTAQUIO: (*Reading in Spanish.*) En el principio creo Dios los cielos y la tierra. Y la tierra estaba desordenada y vacia, y las tinieblas estaban sobre la faz del abismo, ye le Espiritu de Dios se movia sobre la faz de las aguas.

MRS. JACKSON: Isn't that interesting. What does all that mean?

ESTAQUIO: That's the first few verses of Genesis.
MRS. JACKSON: Is that right?
ESTAQUIO: (*Reading*.)
In the beginning God created the heaven and the earth.
En el principio creo Dios los cielos y la tierra.
And the earth was without form and void.
Y la tierra estaba desordenada y vacia,
And darkness was upon the face of the deep.
Y las tinieblas estaban sobre la faz del abismo,
And the spriit of God moved upon the face of the waters.
Ye le Espiritu de Dios se movia sobre la faz de las aguas.
MRS. JACKSON: Spirit of God? Do you know any other hymns in Spanish?
ESTAQUIO: Oh, yes.
MRS. JACKSON: "*Blessed Assurance*?"
ESTAQUIO: Oh, yes.
MRS. JACKSON: Would you sing that, please?
VESTA: Mama—
MRS. JACKSON: Oh, Vesta—
ESTAQUIO: (*Sings.*) BENEDITA CONFIANZA, JESUS ESTA' EU MI. OH, QUE' MANIFESTACION DE LA DIVINA GLORIA. AIRE DE SALVACION' AD QUIRIDO DE DIOS, NACIDO EN SU ESPIRITU Y LAVADO CON SU SANGRE. *(A gun is fired offstage. A woman screams. GLADYS comes running in.)*
GLADYS: Oh, Willis. Come quick. Ashenback has shot himself. Somebody call a Doctor. (*VESTA and KATIE BELL scream. WILLIS goes running off to get to ASHENBACK.*)
MRS. JACKSON: Now keep calm girls. (*To GLADYS.*) I'll call a doctor.
GLADYS: Thank you. (*MRS. JACKSON goes into the house. (GLADYS goes off as the lights fade. The lights are brought up. Later that night: MYRA sits on the steps. MRS. JACKSON comes out in her robe.*)
MRS. JACKSON: Willis not back from the hospital yet?
MYRA: No.
MRS. JACKSON: Oh, my heavens. I almost died myself when I heard that gun go off. Do you know what Mr. Ashenback's religious affiliation is?
MYRA: No.
MRS. JACKSON: I don't either, but I called Brother Meyers to stand by in case he's a Methodist and he's needed. Brother Meyers said he would go right over to the hospital in case he wanted someone to pray for him. (*KATIE BELL and VESTA come out.*) Why in the world aren't you girls in bed asleep?

VESTA: Who can sleep with all that has been going on?
KATIE BELL: Where's that Bible Estaquio left, Mama?
MRS. JACKSON: In my room.
VESTA: I hope he doesn't make a practice of coming by here.
KATIE BELL: How is he going to make a practice of coming by here if he is leaving for Mexico in the morning? (*PETE and WILLIS come in.*)
PETE: He's going to live. He just shot his foot is all.
VESTA: That can be dangerous—Cal Burton shot his foot to keep from going into the Army—
MRS. JACKSON: Sister—
VESTA: Well, he did. Everybody knows that and he developed gangrene and they had to amputate his leg. He had to use a wooden leg which swells when you get it wet and when he went to college and was taking a bath in his fraternity house, one of his fraternity brothers, a practical joker, used to come into the bathroom and say it's Saturday night and you're supposed to wash all over and throw that wooden leg in the tub with him.
MRS. JACKSON: Sister—
VESTA: It's the truth, Mama, Thomas told me so.
MRS. JACKSON: Well, don't be talking about such unladylike things, it's not refined.
PETE: I'm going to bed, good night. (*He starts in.*)
MRS. JACKSON: In all the excitement you never did get your supper did you, Son?
PETE: No, Ma'am.
MRS. JACKSON: There's some cold chicken in the ice box.
PETE: Thank you.
MRS. JACKSON: I hear you're leaving in the morning, Son?
PETE: Yes, Ma'am.
MRS. JACKSON: We'll sure miss you.
PETE: Yes, Ma'am.
VESTA: Who do you look more like. Your daddy or your mama?
PETE: I don't know.
VESTA: Miss Myra. Who does he look more like? You or your ex-husband?
MYRA: I don't know, Vesta. I'm not a good judge of things like that.
KATIE BELL: Myra, tell her the story of that talking picture you saw in Houston with that colored man—
MYRA: He wasn't colored, honey. He just put on black face when he sings—
KATIE BELL: Why does he do that?
MYRA: I don't know.

KATIE BELL: Anyway, tell her the story. I tried to today and I got it all mixed up.

MRS. JACKSON: You better not start. We might get Vesta all upset again.

KATIE BELL: Let her go in the house if it upsets her.

VESTA: You go in the house. I'm not about to go into the house.

KATIE BELL: Will it upset you if she sings the song?

VESTA: No.

KATIE BELL: Sing the song to Mama, Myra, that the man sang in the picture show after his son died.

MRS. JACKSON: Was this a little colored boy?

KATIE BELL: No, Mama.

MRS. JACKSON: Oh, I thought you said the man was colored.

MYRA: No, Ma'am. He is a white man, but he puts on black face when he sings.

MRS. JACKSON: I wonder why he does that.

KATIE BELL: Nobody knows that, Mama, didn't you just hear Myra? Will you sing it for us, Myra?

MYRA: I'm sorry, honey. I just don't feel like singing now. (*She goes into the house.*)

MRS. JACKSON: Oh, heaven, she's so emotional isn't she? I think it's from watching all those picture shows.

KATIE BELL: Mama, if I tell you something will you not get mad at me?

MRS. JACKSON: Depends on what it is.

KATIE BELL: No. I'm not going to tell you.

MRS. JACKSON: Tell me. I won't get mad.

KATIE BELL: No matter what it is?

MRS. JACKSON: No.

KATIE BELL: Swear.

MRS. JACKSON: No, I won't swear. I promise, but I won't swear. What kind of language is that?

KATIE BELL: I went to a picture show once.

MRS. JACKSON: When?

KATIE BELL: Two years ago when I was visiting in El Campo.

VESTA: What did you see?

KATIE BELL: Clara Bow in *Rough House Rosie*.

VESTA: No, you didn't. You're just telling Mama that to get attention.

KATIE BELL: I did too. Are you mad at me, Mama?

MRS. JACKSON: No, not as long as you don't ever go again.

KATIE BELL: My conscience hurt me something terrible.

MRS. JACKSON: Of course, it did. Mine did, too, when I went to the medicine show and the tent show. Did you ask God to forgive you?

KATIE BELL: Yes, Ma'am. Every night for a month.
VESTA: Oh, rot.
KATIE BELL: I did, too.
VESTA: You don't even say your prayers at night.
KATIE BELL: I do, too.
VESTA: You do not. I hear you snoring as soon as the lights are turned off. (*GLADYS comes in.*)
GLADYS: Willis?
WILLIS: Yes?
GLADYS: One of the nice doctors from the hospital drove me over here. I got me a room at the hotel but I left my suitcase here. I said you could drive me over to the hotel.
WILLIS: All right.
MRS. JACKSON: How's your husband?
GLADYS: He's not my husband. An ex-boyfriend.
VESTA: Is he going to lose his foot?
GLADYS: No, I don't think so. You know what he said to me, Willis, just before I left. He said he loved me as much as he did his God.
MRS. JACKSON: What is his religious affiliation?
GLADYS: Good Lord, Lady, I don't know. We never discussed religion.
MRS. JACKSON: Our Methodist minister, Brother Meyers, went over to see him in case he wanted prayer.
GLADYS: And you know what else he said to me, Willis? He said I love you too much to stand in the way of your happiness. I want you to do what you want. Tell Willis he has my blessing. Wasn't that sweet? Of course, like I told Ashenback, I said, Willis may not want me back.
WILLIS: Gladys?
GLADYS: Yes?
WILLIS: I don't want you back.
GLADYS: You don't?
WILLIS: No. I want a divorce now. I am going to marry someone else.
GLADYS: Myra?
WILLIS: If she'll have me.
GLADYS: Oh, I thought so. What a sneak she is. Moving next door to you taking advantage of you because you're lonely and missing me. Didn't you tell me when I left you you would never get over it? Never look at another woman as long as you lived!
WILLIS: Yes, I did, but—
GLADYS: Don't give me any buts, please. You men are all alike. Philanderers . . .
MRS. JACKSON: Vesta, you and Katie Bell come on in the house now. (*She and the girls go in.*)

GLADYS: I have no money, I'm tired and I want to go to the hotel, but I have no money.

WILLIS: Here's fifteen dollars—

GLADYS: I can't walk into town with my suitcase.

WILLIS: Come on, I'll take you. (*He picks up the suitcase. They start out. MRS. JACKSON comes to the door and watches. VESTA and KATIE BELL join her at the door.*)

VESTA: She's gone.

KATIE BELL: And I hope she never comes back (*They come outside. MYRA comes outside.*)

MRS. JACKSON: We'll miss Pete. He's been a lot of company.

KATIE BELL: I finished *Ben Hur*—I'm starting *The Four Horsemen* now. It says in the book it was a movie with Rudolph Valentino. Did you see that movie?

MYRA: Yes, I did.

KATIE BELL: Did you play for it?

MYRA: No, I hadn't begun to play the movie houses then. (*ASHENBACK comes in. His foot's bandaged.*)

ASHENBACK: Ladies. Do you know where Gladys went to?

MRS. JACKSON: She went to the Riverside Hotel, I think.

ASHENBACK: Thank you. I want to apologize for the scene I caused. Jealousy is a terrible thing and I'm infected with it. I can tell by your kind faces you've never been infected by jealousy. You should thank your Maker for that blessing. (*MR. JACKSON comes out.*)

MR. JACKSON: How do you do? I'm Ray Jackson.

ASHENBACK: Delbert Ashenback.

MR. JACKSON: You the fellow shot his foot?

ASHENBACK: Yes.

MR. JACKSON: Mama was telling me about it. You're lucky to be alive. Well, I hope you have that out of your system now.

ASHENBACK: I hope so.

MR. JACKSON: You certainly got everything fired up in this house. I'm usually asleep way before this, but I haven't been able to sleep. What doctor treated your foot, Vails or White?

ASHENBACK: White.

MR. JACKSON: Then your foot is going to be all right. Not that Dr. Vails isn't a perfectly competent doctor, but I have great faith in Doctor White.

ASHENBACK: Does Willis live up there over the garage?

MR. JACKSON: Yes, he does.

MRS. JACKSON: He's not there now, he drove that lady to the hotel.

ASHENBACK: I see, when you see him tell him I'm sorry for all the trouble I caused him. (*He starts out.*)

MR. JACKSON: Will you be getting a room at the hotel too?

ASHENBACK: No, I'm driving on home tonight, alone.

MR. JACKSON: I see. (*He goes.*) I'm turning in. I think I'll sleep now. You coming, Mama?

MRS. JACKSON: I think so. (*She goes in too.*)

KATIE BELL: Rudolph Valentino died with appendicitis, didn't he?

MYRA: Yes, he did. There were headlines in all the Houston papers when he died.

VESTA: Was he a Mexican?

MYRA: No, Italian. He was 31 when he died. On the anniversary of his death, there appeared at his grave a mysterious lady with a long black veil. She told the reporters, she's coming back every year. Some say it's Pola Negri, but I don't think so.

KATIE BELL: Who do you think it is?

MYRA: I don't know.

KATIE BELL: Guess.

MYRA: I just don't know—Wouldn't do me any good to guess— (*WILLIS comes in.*)

VESTA: The man that shot his foot was here looking for you. He said he was sorry for all that had happened.

WILLIS: Where is he now?

VESTA: He said he was going back to his home.

KATIE BELL: Without that lady.

VESTA: I'm going to bed.You better come too, Katie Bell. (*They go in.*)

WILLIS: I told Gladys I wanted a divorce so I could marry you. She said she'll fight me in every court in the land to keep me from getting a divorce. I said go ahead I don't care how long it takes I'm getting a divorce so I can marry Myra, if she'll have me. What time is Pete leaving?

MYRA: Around noon.

WILLIS: Has he gone to bed?

MYRA: I think so.

WILLIS: I didn't get to tell him goodbye. Will you tell him I'm sorry I didn't get to tell him goodbye.

MYRA: I will. (*PETE comes out of the bedroom and goes outside.*) I thought you were asleep.

PETE: I'm too excited to sleep.

WILLIS: You're journey proud Pete.

PETE: I guess. Have you ever been to Colorado, Willis?

WILLIS: No.

MYRA: Ever since you've told me about Colorado I've been thinking about my Mama. She always said there were two places she wanted to go before she died—Colorado and California. Colorado in the summer time and California in the winter.

WILLIS: Did she ever get there?

MYRA: No, she never got out of Nacogdoches. If Mr. Santos puts in talking pictures I've decided I'll stay on here and look for another kind of job. I'll see if I can get a job clerking in one of the stores here and I can teach music on the side. (*A pause.*) I'm tired. I think I'm ready for bed. I bet I'll sleep sound tonight. Goodnight, Willis.

WILLIS: Goodnight.

MYRA: You better come to bed too, son.

PETE: I can't get to sleep Mama, I'm too excited.

MYRA: You'll get to sleep—come on.

PETE: All right, goodnight. (*He goes into the house. MYRA starts in.*)

WILLIS: Myra, what was your Mama's name? I never heard you say.

MYRA: Corinne.

WILLIS: Corinne?

MYRA: Yes, like Corinne Griffith, the movie star. My Mama died when I was sixteen.

WILLIS: Is Myra the name of a movie star?

MYRA: Not that I ever heard of.

WILLIS: I don't think Willis is either.

MYRA: No, I don't believe so. There is a Wallace, a Wallace Berry, and there was a Wallace Reed.

WILLIS: He's dead?

MYRA: Yes. He died a dope fiend.

WILLIS: My Mother's name was Lena.

MYRA: That's the name of a movie star—Lena Basquette.

WILLIS: Is that so? I never heard of her. My Father's name was Arnold. (*PETE appears.*)

PETE: Mama—I thought you were going to bed?

MYRA: I am.

WILLIS: (*Starting out.*) Well, goodnight.

MYRA: Goodnight. (*WILLIS leaves.*) Warm in our room?

PETE: Like an oven.

MYRA: Well, you'll be out of it soon. It's cool in Colorado. You sleep under blankets at night I'm told. (*They go inside as the lights fade. Next day: The lights are brought up. In MYRA'S room. PETE'S bags are packed and waiting to be put into his father's car. PETE is in front of the house with his glove and ball. The JACKSONS, dressed for a trip, come into the living room. MRS. JACKSON knocks on MYRA'S door.*) Yes.

MRS. JACKSON: We're leaving for the day, Myra. We won't be back until late tonight.

MYRA: You're going to look over Cuero?

MRS. JACKSON: Yes, to see if we like it.

VESTA: Mama and I think it's terrible of the railroad pulling something like this. Daddy has been an engineer for twenty-five years.

MR. JACKSON: That's the System, Sister. I knew it when I started with the railroad. Seniority is everything. I always knew every time I went to a town I could be bumped and my job taken by someone who had been longer with the railroad. Mama knew that when she married me. I bumped somebody to get here.

MRS. JACKSON: Only because you were bumped by somebody in the last town we lived in.

MR. JACKSON: And I can be bumped again, I guess, if someone with seniority wants my job there. Mama wants me to quit the railroad, but like I explained to her I've given twenty-five years of my life working there, I have benefits. Not every place gives you benefits.

MRS. JACKSON: That's true. He has a pension when he retires, and health insurance.

KATIE BELL: (*Cries.*) I don't want to leave Harrison. All my friends are here. Sally Doris said I could live with her until I finished school.

VESTA: Oh, that would be just fine. Sally Doris! You'd be ruined forever living here with her.

KATIE BELL: Shut up, Vesta.

VESTA: Shut up, yourself. You'd be sneaking out to the picture show all the time just like you did in El Campo.

KATIE BELL: Vesta, you are mean. I told Mama I was sorry I did that.

MRS. JACKSON: Yes, she did, Vesta—

KATIE BELL: Can I stay on here, Mama?

MRS. JACKSON: No, you can't do that. We have to be together as a family. Where's Pete?

MYRA: He's outside.

MRS. JACKSON: We want to tell him goodbye. (*They all go out. MYRA follows after them.*) I expect you'll be gone by the time we get back, Pete. So we want to say goodbye to you.

PETE: Goodbye.

MRS. JACKSON: So long, Son. When's your daddy coming for you?

PETE: He was supposed to be here at twelve o'clock.

VESTA: It's two now.

PETE: I know that.

VESTA: Maybe he's not coming today.

PETE: No, he's coming. We're all going to Colorado tomorrow on a two week vacation.

VESTA: That's up in the mountains. Have you ever been on a mountain?

PETE: No, have you?

VESTA: No, and I don't care to. Laurie La Belle and her family drove out to Colorado and when they got there they took one look at those mountains standing up ahead and they scared them so, the very thought of taking a car up them things, that they turned right around and came home. Her Mama said, "no mountains" for me. I was born where it was flat and I intend to die where it's flat.

KATIE BELL: I'd like to see the mountains. I'm going to take Spanish in school next year so I can visit Mexico one day.

VESTA: Is she, Mama?

MRS. JACKSON: If she wants to.

VESTA: Are you going to let her go to Mexico?

MRS. JACKSON: Well, that's a long way down the road. We'll see about that when the time comes.

VESTA: If she goes to Mexico, are you going to let her see that Mexican Baptist man preach?

MRS. JACKSON: No, if she goes to Mexico or anywhere, she'll go to the Methodist church just like she does here.

KATIE BELL: What if they don't have a Methodist church in Mexico? Can't I go to the Baptist church then?

MRS. JACKSON: We'll talk about that when the time comes.

MR. JACKSON: I'll talk about that right now. No child of mine is going to Mexico to be carried off by bandits and white slavers.

KATIE BELL: Papa.

MR. JACKSON: No and that settles that.

MRS. JACKSON: Well, let's don't stand here arguing about Mexico. Let's go if we're going. Goodbye, Pete.

PETE: Goodbye.

OTHERS: Goodbye, Pete. Have a good time in Colorado . . . etc. . . . (*They go off. MYRA sits in a chair.*)

PETE: I wonder where Daddy is, Mama?

MYRA: I don't know, Son. Something delayed him, I'm sure. He'll be along. Now I've all your things packed. I put some paper, a pencil, some stamps and envelopes in the small bag which is the one I expect you'll take to Colorado, and be sure and drop me a line when you get there. I'll be anxious to hear. (*The phone rings. PETE goes to answer it. She goes into the house and to the piano. She plays a Chopin etude. PETE comes back in.*)

MYRA: Was that your daddy?

PETE: No. His wife. (*A pause.*) The trip's off. (*MYRA stops playing.*)

MYRA: Why?

PETE: He's on a drunk and they had a fight and she says she won't go any place with him now or ever. She's mad.

MYRA: Oh, I expect she'll calm down. They'll probably call you tomorrow and say they're coming for you.

PETE: No, Mama I don't think so. She asked me if he had invited me to live with them and I said yes he had, and she said she can't have me living there. That she has two boys of her own to see to. She said daddy is always saying things he shouldn't and putting his foot in it.

MYRA: I thought she knew you were going there to live?

PETE: I thought so, too, but I guess she didn't.

MYRA: I'm awfully sorry.

PETE: That's o.k. I'll go and unpack my clothes.

MYRA: I'll unpack them. (*He goes out. She goes into their room and begins to unpack the clothes. ESTAQUIO comes in.*)

ESTAQUIO: Hi.

PETE: Hi.

ESTAQUIO: Is Katie Bell in?

PETE: No, she's gone for the day.

ESTAQUIO: Oh, well give her this will you? (*He hands him a sheet of paper.*) Tell her my papa has decided not to go back to Mexico. He will stay and do missionary work trying to convert the Mexican Catholics to Baptists. He is preaching his first sermon this Sunday. All are invited, you too.

PETE: Thank you.

ESTAQUIO: Do you speak Spanish?

PETE: No.

ESTAQUIO: Then you probably won't enjoy it. It will be in Spanish. Tell Katie Bell I will be going to the Mexican school here next year.

PETE: All right.

ESTAQUIO: Are you a Baptist?

PETE: No, Methodist.

ESTAQUIO: Explain to me about the Methodists.

PETE: What do you want to know about them?

ESTAQUIO: Their creed, what exactly do they believe?

PETE: Oh, I don't know a whole lot about things like that.

ESTAQUIO: Do you go to church?

PETE: Not too often, Christmas, Easter . . .

ESTAQUIO: Then how do you know you're a Methodist?

PETE: Because my mother told me I was. John Wesley was Methodist. I remember hearing that.

ESTAQUIO: Who is John Wesley?

PETE: I don't know exactly. I just remember hearing he was a famous Methodist. (*A man very drunk comes in. He is GERARD ANDERSON, PETE'S father.*)

GERARD: Pete?

PETE: Yessir.

GERARD: Who is your Mexican friend?

ESTAQUIO: Estaquio. Estaquio Trevino.

GERARD: Run on. I have to discuss personal matters with my son. (*ESTAQUIO leaves.*) Did that old witch I'm married to call you?

PETE: Yessir.

GERARD: The Colorado trip is off because of that old witch. I said, all right. We won't go to Colorado, and I'm going to see my boy and tell him why. Tell him I'm married to the meanest white woman God ever created. Nag, nag, nag, all the time. Where's Myra?

PETE: She's inside. (*He goes to the door and calls.*) Mama, Daddy is here.

GERARD: How is your Mama?

PETE: She's all right—she may lose her job in the picture show.

GERARD: My God. I've told and told her. There's no future in picture shows. Where are your suitcases, I've come to take you to Houston.

PETE: Well, I don't know. Your wife says I can't come.

GERARD: Did she? Well, hell, she'll get over that. Well, maybe I better not take you back today while she's still on the warpath. (*MYRA comes out.*)

MYRA: Hello, Gerard.

GERARD: Hello, Myra. How are you today?

MYRA: Pretty well.

GERARD: I'm in trouble myself. I tied one on last night and Jackie Kate pitched a fit. Called our trip to Colorado off. Did Pete tell you that?

MYRA: Yes.

GERARD: Well, hell, who was that Mexican boy I just saw here?

MYRA: He's a Baptist preacher's son.

PETE: A Mexican Baptist preacher.

GERARD: Well, hell, I don't care whose son he is. I don't want my boy associating with Mexicans. That's one reason I'm determined to have him live with me so I can teach him right from wrong. Pete says you may lose your job playing in the picture show. God Almighty—where are picture shows going to get you? I have a truck, a car, a beautiful house in a lovely part of Houston, a swimming pool, a wife and two lovely children and I didn't get that playing in no picture show. I got it by being practical in a practical world. (*A pause. He sways. He sits on the steps.*) Excuse me. I'm drunk. I'm very drunk. I beg your pardon. I have lots of troubles. I have to lie down for a while.

MYRA: Take him into our room, Pete. He can lie down on your bed.

PETE: Come on, Daddy. (*He takes him into the house and into the bedroom and helps him onto the bed. The phone rings. MYRA goes to answer it. WILLIS comes in with his glove. PETE comes out.*)

WILLIS: I thought you were going to Houston today?

PETE: No, sir, not now. Our plans have changed.

WILLIS: I see. Want to play a game of catch?

PETE: I don't mind. (*They begin their game.*) My daddy is in there.

WILLIS: Is he?

PETE: Under the weather. That's why we're not going on our trip to Colorado. (*MYRA comes out.*)

MYRA: Pete, your father's wanted on the phone, see if you can rouse him.

PETE: Yes'm. (*He goes inside and into the bedroom and begins to try and rouse his father.*)

WILLIS: Hello, Myra.

MYRA: Hello, Willis.

WILLIS: Been warm today. A little cooler now.

MYRA: Yes. (*A pause.*) Don't tell Pete, because I don't want to worry him. But Mr. Santos called me up this morning and said they decided they are not going to hold out any longer. They're going to put in a sound system right away.

WILLIS: I'm sorry, what will you do now?

MYRA: I don't know. I want to try to find a job here.

WILLIS: Don't despair—I learned that from my mama. She used to say no matter how bad things look, Willis, we musn't despair. My mama was a blessed woman. She had more than her share of troubles, God knows, but she never despaired. Never, never—as God is my witness she never despaired. (*PETE comes out.*)

MYRA: Did you rouse him?

PETE: Yes, Ma'am. Who wanted to talk to him?

MYRA: His wife. She sounded very agitated.

WILLIS: I'm moving out tonight. I'm staying with a friend I work with. Gladys is moving into my room. She spent the fifteen dollars I loaned her on clothes. The hotel won't let her stay on and I can't pay her bills there. (*He and PETE start to play catch. GERARD comes outside.*)

GERARD: Myra, I went to see that talking picture *The Singing Fool* because you recommended it. I thought it was awful. I don't go to the motion pictures to be depressed. I like happy picture shows. Pete, who is your friend?

PETE: This is Willis. Willis, this is my dad.

WILLIS: How do you do? (*They shake hands.*)

GERARD: I have to go back to Houston or there'll be no living with her whatsoever—she's on a real tear now. Accusing me now of being unfaithful with you, Myra. I guess the trip is really off now, Son.

PETE: Yessir.

GERARD: And I guess, too, I spoke too soon about your living with us. She said I had dreamed the whole thing up. I thought you liked the boy, I said. I do like him, she said, he's nice and polite, but our boys get jealous when I pay attention to him. She's just making all that up, of course, they are not jealous of anybody, she just changed her mind because she knew I wanted you there. Well, she may change her mind again. (*A pause.*) If you lose your job, Myra, at the picture show, what will you do?

MYRA: Well—

GERARD: Not many silent picture theaters left, I guess.

MYRA: No.

GERARD: I know you don't want my advice, but you're still an attractive woman. You should get married and have somebody take care of you. You're not getting any younger, you know. (*To WILLIS.*) Did you see that picture *The Singing Fool*?

WILLIS: No, I sure didn't.

GERARD: Don't waste your money. Unless you like being depressed. What was that song he sang after his boy died?

MYRA: *Sonny Boy.*

GERARD: Oh, yes. How did it go?

MYRA: I don't remember.

GERARD: Jackie Kate said there ought to be a law against having picture shows like that that did nothing but get you upset and depressed. (*GLADYS comes in. She carries a suitcase.*)

GLADYS: I thought you were coming for me in your car?

WILLIS: I said after supper, Gladys.

GLADYS: After whose supper—I ate mine an hour ago, not that I had much. A tuna fish sandwich and a coke was all I could afford.

GERARD: How do you do? I'm Gerard Anderson. I'm Pete's father.

GLADYS: I'm Willis' wife. In name only it seems. He's smitten with somebody else.

GERARD: Well, those things happen, unfortunately.

GLADYS: Unfortunately. You still want a divorce, Willis?

WILLIS: Yes.

GLADYS: Well, you give me a thousand dollars and I'll give you one.

WILLIS: I can't do that, Gladys. You know I can't afford that kind of money.

GLADYS: You can't?
WILLIS: No way in the world.
GLADYS: Hell, I knew that before I asked you, what can you afford?
WILLIS: Let me think about it?
GERARD: Well, I'm going to have to go, folks. I have a long ride ahead of me.
GLADYS: Where are you going?
GERARD: Houston.
GLADYS: Houston, oh, you lucky thing. Do you live there?
GERARD: Yes, I do. I have a lovely new brick house and swimming pool. Right in a lovely section of Houston.
GLADYS: Oh, you lucky thing. How much can you afford, Willis?
WILLIS: I'm thinking.
GLADYS: Seven fifty.
WILLIS: Well . . .
GLADYS: Five hundred, two–fifty—
WILLIS: I could afford a hundred—
GERARD: Well, I'll be seeing you, goodbye now. If you get to Houston look me up. Gerard Anderson, I'm in the phone book.
GLADYS: Oh, I will.
GERARD: So long everybody.
PETE: Goodbye, Papa.
GERARD: So long, Son. (*He leaves.*)
GLADYS: When can you get me the hundred dollars, Willis?
WILLIS: By the end of next week—
GLADYS: All right. You sure you can't make it a hundred and fifty?
WILLIS: No, I can't, Gladys.
GLADYS: All right, will you take my suitcase up to your room for me?
WILLIS: I will.
GLADYS: Where are you staying?
WILLIS: With a friend. (*WILLIS goes out. GLADYS follows after him.*)
PETE: If the Jacksons move and sell their house where will we live, Mama?
MYRA: We'll find some place.
PETE: Mama—
MYRA: Yes, Son.
PETE: What if you can't get a job?
MYRA: I'll find something.
PETE: Mama—
MYRA: Yes, Son.
PETE: I'm scared.
MYRA: You musn't be, Son, we're going to be all right. (*She holds him.*)

You're awfully disappointed about your daddy, aren't you?

PETE: Well. I knew it wouldn't work out. Nothing ever does.

MYRA: Don't say that, Son.

PETE: Does it?

MYRA: Sometimes—

PETE: What—

MYRA: Well—

PETE: What—

MYRA: Some things have worked out.

PETE: Name me one. (*WILLIS comes in.*)

WILLIS: I'll be staying here tonight after all. Mr. Joplin loaned me twenty five dollars to give Gladys on that hundred I promised her. She doesn't want to stay here. She wants to take the bus on into Houston. She says she wants to start divorce proceedings in the morning. Well, I said, Gladys, I don't know if I can afford to give you your hundred dollars and start divorce proceedings at that same time. I may have to wait on that and save a little more money. Don't wait, she said, get the divorce first. You can pay me later. (*GLADYS appears.*)

GLADYS: Let's go.

WILLIS: All right.

GLADYS: So long, you all. (*She goes out—WILLIS follows as the lights fade. The lights are brought up a week later. KATIE BELL is in the yard. She has the paper ESTAQUIO left. It is "Rock of Ages" in Spanish. She is trying to learn the words. MYRA comes in. She sits on the steps.*)

KATIE BELL: Any luck?

MYRA: No, not yet. Mr. Jordon said if he had a vacancy any time soon he would gladly take me on, but he hasn't had a salesgirl leave in five years.

KATIE BELL: We've had some good news.

MYRA: What's that?

KATIE BELL: The man that bumped Daddy to get his job, has changed his mind and he wants to stay where he is and so we can stay on here.

MYRA: Oh, that is wonderful, Katie Bell. I am so happy for you. (*VESTA and MRS. JACKSON come out.*)

MRS. JACKSON: Did Katie Bell tell you our news?

MYRA: Yes, she did. I'm very happy for you.

VESTA: And now Mama says I can take music lessons from you if you stay on here.

MYRA: That's nice. I would like that.

VESTA: Are you going to stay on?

MYRA: If I can find work. I've no luck so far.

VESTA: When may I start my lessons?
MYRA: As soon as you want.
VESTA: Oh, grand.
KATIE BELL: Are you going to the opening of the talking pictures tonight?
MYRA: Yes, Willis is taking me.
KATIE BELL: I bet it will seem funny going there and not playing the piano.
MYRA: I expect it will.
MRS. JACKSON: What will happen if you don't find a job here?
MYRA: Then I will have to look for a job somewhere else. (*PETE comes in with books*.)
KATIE BELL: How is school?
PETE: It's all right. I'm only taking one course. I wouldn't have to take that, if we hadn't had to change schools so many times.
MYRA: It'll be behind you soon.
PETE: Did you find a job?
MYRA: No, not today—
KATIE BELL: We don't have to leave. Papa is not bumped any longer.
PETE: That's good. I have to study—(*He goes into his room*.)
VESTA: Could I have a lesson on the piano now?
MYRA: All right. Come on.
MRS. JACKSON: We'd better make some business arrangements first—will you still be willing to teach in exchange for your room rent?
MYRA: Yes. Thank you.
MRS. JACKSON: May Katie Bell and I watch the lessons?
MYRA: Oh, yes. (*VESTA: and MYRA go to the house and to the piano*.)
KATIE BELL: Mama, do you know what this is? (*She looks at the paper*.)
MRS. JACKSON: It doesn't look like anything I've ever seen.
KATIE BELL: It's "Rock of Ages" in Spanish. Estaquio gave me the words and I've learned to sing it. Want to hear me? (*Starts to sing*.)
VESTA: (*Calling from living room*.) Mama, are you coming?
MRS. JACKSON: Maybe later. (*She goes inside. KATIE BELL steps in the yard*.)
VESTA: I am so nervous.
MYRA: Now, don't be nervous. Now, you sit on the piano stool and I'll sit beside you. We'll start with some scales—now—let me explain the keyboard—This is middle C. (*WILLIS comes in*.)
WILLIS: Hi.
KATIE BELL: Hi, Myra is giving Vesta a music lesson.
WILLIS: I hear—
KATIE BELL: And I'm learning to sing "Rock of Ages" in Spanish. We

don't have to leave Harrison after all.

WILLIS: You don't?

KATIE BELL: No.

WILLIS: Well, that's good news. (*GLADYS and GERARD come in.*)

GLADYS: Hey there, Willis.

GERARD: Hello, Willis. Remember me?

WILLIS: Sure. How are you?

GLADYS: Have you started the divorce proceedings?

WILLIS: Well, I've talked to the lawyer and gotten a price.

GERARD: Is my boy inside?

KATIE BELL: Yes. I think he is.

GERARD: Would you call him for me, please.

KATIE BELL: (*Calling.*) Pete. Your daddy is here.

MYRA: We'd better rest from our lesson. It's hard to concentrate with all this confusion, Vesta.

VESTA: Oh, foot.

MYRA: We'll start early in the morning.

VESTA: Oh, grand. (*PETE comes out of his room and goes outside.*)

GERARD: Hi, Son.

PETE: Hi.

GERARD: I have some news for you. Jackie Kate and I have decided to split up. And I've fallen in love with this lady here. You remember her, don't you?

PETE: Yessir.

GERARD: We're on our way to Mexico to get our divorces so we can marry.

GLADYS: And it won't cost you a cent, Willis. Gerard's paying for the whole thing. The minute I laid eyes on him in this yard I knew we were made for each other. He said he felt the same way.

GERARD: Tell your Mama to come out.

PETE: (*Calling.*) Mama, daddy is here. He wants to see you.

GLADYS: I called him the minute I got into Houston and he was all alone because his wife had gone off and left him.

GERARD: Took the boys, too. Said she was going to her Mama's in Louisiana and was never coming back.

GLADYS: And she meant it, too, When he called her and told her about wanting a divorce, she said go ahead and get it and see if she cared—so—(*MYRA comes outside.*)

GERARD: Myra, I took Gladys to see that picture show you told me and Jackie Kate to go see and she didn't like it any more than we did.

GLADYS: Oh, no I couldn't stand it.

GERARD: Gladys says she doesn't think talking pictures will last, but I think she's wrong about that.

GLADYS: You do?

GERARD: Yes, I do.

GLADYS: Well, I just bet I am then, if you say so—Miss Myra, did you hear our news? We are going to Mexico so Gerard can divorce Jackie Kate and I can divorce Willis. Then we're going to Mexico City to be married. Isn't that just thrilling?

GERARD: Of course I'm having to give Jackie Kate everything I've got except my truck to get her consent. She gets the house, the car, the swimming pool. (*MRS. JACKSON and VESTA come out.*) Well, folks, we're going to have to be on our way. (*He goes to PETE.*) So long, Son. I'll send you a postcard from Mexico. (*He and GLADYS start out.*) So long, everybody.

GLADYS: So long— (*They leave.*)

MRS. JACKSON: Now, who are they? I know I've seen them before but I can't place them.

WILLIS: That's my wife and Myra's ex-husband and they're going to Mexico to get a divorce so they can get married.

MRS. JACKSON: Why are they going to Mexico?

WILLIS: Because you can get a divorce there right away.

MRS. JACKSON: Oh. (*ESTAQUIO comes in.*) Why, Vesta, there's that little Mexican preacher boy. Good afternoon, Son.

ESTAQUIO: Good afternoon.

MRS. JACKSON: How's the church coming along?

ESTAQUIO: Not too well—thank you Ma'am. Nobody came. So my Papa says we have to go back to Mexico. We're taking the bus to the border tonight.

MRS. JACKSON: Oh, I'm sorry to hear that.

KATIE BELL: I learned "Rock of Ages" in Spanish. Do you want to hear me sing it?

ESTAQUIO: I don't have time. Our bus is leaving. If you ever get to Mexico, please look me up.

KATIE BELL: I sure will—(*He leaves.*)

MRS. JACKSON: Goodbye, Son.

ESTAQUIO: Goodbye—(*He disappears.*)

KATIE BELL: Everybody's going to Mexico, I wish I could go.

VESTA: You'll never get to Mexico, so you can just put that out of your head—

MRS. JACKSON: Did you ever hear that young man sing "Rock of Ages" in Spanish?

WILLIS: No.

MRS. JACKSON: It was something. Wasn't it girls?

KATIE BELL: I can sing it, Mama!

MRS. JACKSON: Not now. (*She goes into the house humming "Rock of Ages."*)

WILLIS: Want to play catch, Pete?

PETE: After I finish studying—(*He starts for the house. MYRA goes to him.*)

MYRA: Pete—

PETE: I'm all right. (*A pause.*) I guess I'm going to have a new step Mama.

MYRA: I guess so.

PETE: Maybe I'll try to find me a job here after school. (*He goes into the house.*)

KATIE BELL: Are you all still going to the picture show tonight?

WILLIS: I think so—

KATIE BELL: Will you tell me the story tomorrow, Myra?

MYRA: Yes, I will.

KATIE BELL: I went by the picture show this afternoon. They were trying out the sound inside and you could hear it as you went by. (*MR. JACKSON comes in. He seems very dejected.*)

VESTA: Papa, what is it? You look upset—

MR. JACKSON: Where's your mother?

VESTA: Inside—what is it, Papa?

MR. JACKSON: That fool engineer has changed his mind again and I'm being bumped after all.

VESTA: Oh, Papa—(*He goes in, the girls follow after him.*)

MYRA: Oh, isn't that too bad? They thought they were going to stay after all.

WILLIS: I'm sorry. (*A pause.*) Myra, it looks like I'm going to be free next week to ask you to marry me. Will you marry me?

MYRA: Yes, I will. Of course, I have to talk it over with Pete first. (*PETE comes out with his glove and a baseball.*)

WILLIS: I'll go get my glove. (*He leaves.*)

MYRA: The Jackson's are going to have to leave after all. The man changed his mind again.

PETE: I'm sorry.

MYRA: That means we'll have to find another place to live.

PETE: Mama, I've been thinking in there. What if I can't get a job and you can't get a job.

MYRA: Well—(*A pause.*) Pete, Gladys is divorcing Willis now.

PETE: I know.

MYRA: Now he's free to marry.

PETE: I guess he is—

MYRA: He's asked me to marry him—I said I wanted to speak to you first.

PETE: Do you want to marry him?

MYRA: Yes, but . . .

PETE: It's O.K. with me then—

MYRA: We'll have a house now, Pete. He's a kind man and he is fond of you.

PETE: I know. (*A pause.*) I used to think you and Daddy would get married again, but then he married Jackie Kate—and now—

MYRA: We'll never marry again, Pete.

PETE: I know. So you go ahead and marry Willis if you want to. (*He goes to his room. He's on the bed. MYRA sits on the steps. KATIE BELL comes out of the house.*)

MYRA: How did your Mother take the news?

KATIE BELL: She was upset at first, but she's all right. (*A pause.*) Myra, one of my friends said she saw *Peter Pan* with an actress named Betty Bronson. Did you see that?

MYRA: Yes.

KATIE BELL: And she said she has never heard of Betty Bronson since. And she wondered what ever became of her. And I told her I would ask you as you know all about the movies and movie stars.

MYRA: Well, I'm sorry. I don't know. (*WILLIS comes in. He has his glove.*) I spoke to Pete.

WILLIS: What did he say?

MYRA: He said it was all right with him.

WILLIS: Where is he?

MYRA: In our room. I'd leave him alone for awhile.

WILLIS: O.K. (*He sits beside MYRA. KATIE BELL begins singing half to herself in Spanish "Rock of Ages."*) Is that Spanish?

KATIE BELL: Yes. "*Rock of Ages*." (*She continues singing half to herself, then pauses.*) Would you ever like to go to Mexico?

WILLIS: Oh, I don't know. (*PETE comes out.*)

MYRA: Come sit with us, Son. It's cooler out here. (*He sits on the steps.*)

KATIE BELL: How far is it to Mexico?

WILLIS: Depending on where you're going. (*KATIE BELL begins to sing "Rock of Ages" half to herself then, she pauses.*)

KATIE BELL: I bet I get to Mexico one day. (*She again continues singing "Rock of Ages," as MYRA and WILLIS listen lost in their own thoughts as the lights fade.*)